DATE DUE

D1219116

RESCUE BY RAIL

ROGER PICKENPAUGH

RESCUE
BY RAIL

*Troop Transfer
and the Civil War
in the West
1863*

University of Nebraska Press

Lincoln & London

Portions of the prologue and chapter 5 appeared in "Rescue
by Rail," *Timeline* 14, no. 6 (November–December 1997):
20–35. Reprinted with permission. © 1998 by the University
of Nebraska Press. All rights reserved. Manufactured in
the United States of America. ⊗ The paper in this book
meets the minimum requirements of American National
Standard for Information Sciences – Permanence of Paper
for Printed Library Materials, ANSI Z39.48-1984.

LIBRARY OF CONGRESS CATALOGING IN PUBLICATION DATA
Pickenpaugh, Roger.
Rescue by rail : troop transfer and the Civil War in the West,
1863 / Roger Pickenpaugh. p. cm. Includes bibliographical
references and index. ISBN 0-8032-3720-0 (alkaline paper)
1. Southwest, Old – History – Civil War, 1861-1865 – Transportation 2. Railroads – Southwest, Old – History – 19th
century. 3. United States – History – Civil War, 1861-1865 –
Transportation. 1. Title.
E470.4.P53 1998 939.7–DC21 97-32444 CIP

In memory of
Thomas Olland Racey
Marion Oscar Yerkey and
David J. "Jack" Ferrell
all of the B&O
Railroad

CONTENTS

FIGURES

MAPS

ACKNOWLEDGMENTS

Nobody produces a book alone, and in the course of my research for this project I incurred numerous debts. Staff members at every institution listed below eagerly assisted me, and most showed admirable patience and perseverance. The list of archivists that follows is far from complete because I often neglected to write down every name. To those who are omitted I offer my sincere apology.

Stuart Butler (National Archives); Jeff Flannery (Library of Congress); Richard J. Sommers, Louise Arnold Friend, Michael Winey, and Randy Hackenburg (U.S. Army Military History Institute); Henry Inicki, Kathleen Lawson, Fred Bassett, and Ed McGuire (New York State Library); Elsa Meyers (New Jersey Historical Society); Rob Schoeberlein (Maryland Historical Society); Rob Cox (Clements Library, University of Michigan); James B. Kennedy (Wisconsin Historical Society); Teresa Roane (Valentine Museum); Laura Costello (University of South Carolina); Gary J. Arnold, David Simmons, and Christopher Duckworth (Ohio Historical Society); Liz Garner (Pennsylvania Historical and Museum Commission); Susan Ravdin (Bowdoin College); Margaret Merrick (University of Louisville Library); and Eric Mundell (Indiana Historical Society).

Special thanks also go to the staff of the Caldwell, Ohio, Public Library, my hometown library. Becky Milligan was especially helpful in tracking down items through interlibrary loan.

Professor Mark Grimsley of the Ohio State University, Professor Steven Woodworth of Texas Christian University, and Professor Richard McCaslin of High Point University each read the entire manuscript and made useful suggestions. Professor Grimsley also guided me through many of the vagaries of the publishing business.

Many colleagues at the Shenandoah Elementary School provided assistance and support. Deserving special mention are David Arbenz, whose thorough critique of the finished manuscript was

Acknowledgments

extremely helpful, and James Parks, who offered unwavering encouragement when it was most needed. Thanks also go to Sandra Carpenter and William Rogers, both of whom are so skilled as computer instructors that they were able to teach me at least a little.

I am further indebted to my colleagues at the *Zanesville Times Recorder*. After a couple of false starts, I am proud to be associated with a newspaper whose editorial staff upholds the highest standards of journalistic integrity. I am particularly grateful for the support and counsel of City Editor Pam Swingle, former Managing Editor Richard Stubbe, and Historian Chuck Martin.

Early in my research I had the good fortune to meet Douglas Cubbison of Madison, Alabama, president of White Star Consulting. As a result, this is a much better book. Doug tracked down several invaluable sources, particularly for the last three chapters. He also read the entire manuscript, correcting many errors of both style and content. I value his counsel and his friendship.

My final, yet most heartfelt, thanks go to my family. Whatever I have attempted, my parents, Lester and Fern Pickenpaugh, have always been in my corner. This project was no exception, and my gratitude to them goes beyond words.

My sister and brother-in-law, Jill and Eugene Stuckey, also supported me from the start. More important, they had the decency to locate in suburban Atlanta, giving me a place to stay when my research took me south. (Gene even swallowed his pride and forgave me when he learned that this book ends with a Union victory.)

Stepdaughters Anya and Jocelyn Crum have been constant sources of support—and of pride. Although they are neither Civil War nor railroad buffs, they have been very tolerant of my obsessions.

I would also like to offer a special thanks to the members of my second family, the Perkins family of Guernsey County, Ohio. Since adopting me into their fold some ten years ago, they have been a special source of support and caring.

Acknowledgments

At the top of the list is my "second mom," Carol, the family history buff. I am also proud to have on my side sisters Kim, Kay, and Jill and brothers Chuck and Ed. To brother Tom, who provided invaluable assistance with the index, goes a special thanks.

As for the next generation, Morgan and Tara Logan, Dakota and Miranda Perkins, and Layne Gress have been wonderful dividends in this special relationship. That leaves only Zachary Kent Gress, who appears to have inherited his grandmother's love of history and his "Uncle" Roger's love of writing. I look confidently forward to reading *his* first book on the Civil War in about the year 2020.

Finally, to Marion Pickenpaugh, my thanks for a few hundred valued contributions. Whether as tenacious researcher, careful proofreader, or respected adviser, Mrs. Pickenpaugh was with this project every step of the way. For this and so much more I say simply but sincerely, "Thanks, Kid."

RESCUE BY RAIL

Mr. Stanton's Proposal

A bright moon hung over Washington DC on the night of 23 September 1863, as the president of the United States nervously raced his horse toward the War Department. John Hay, one of Abraham Lincoln's two personal secretaries, had wakened him at the Soldiers' Home, where he often sought refuge on Washington's hot summer nights, and told the commander in chief that Secretary of War Edwin M. Stanton wished him to attend a council that evening. Although Hay tried to calm his boss, the message left Lincoln "considerably disturbed." Never before, the president explained, had Stanton ever sent for him.[1]

Although he did not yet know the particulars, Lincoln had to guess that the subject of the conference would be Tennessee. There Maj. Gen. William Starke Rosecrans, who had led his Army of the Cumberland on a successful if often ponderous campaign across the Volunteer State, was under siege in Chattanooga after meeting a serious setback three days before.

Almost one year earlier, on 27 October 1862, Rosecrans had succeeded Don Carlos Buell as commander of the Army of the Ohio, which was rechristened the Army of the Cumberland. At the time the army was located at Nashville, with Chattanooga its goal. In between lay Gen. Braxton Bragg and his Confederate Army of Tennessee. The new commander spent nearly two months addressing shortages of supplies and lack of morale, then moved southwest.

By 30 December, less than a week after setting out, Rosecrans was in close contact with Bragg, along Stones River, a few miles northwest of Murfreesboro. The next day he planned to hit hard on Bragg's right. He had no way of knowing that Bragg had devised an identical plan of attack—and the Confederates moved more quickly. Very early on the morning of 31 December, as the Union army was preparing to enjoy its breakfast, the Army of Tennessee assailed its right. The Army of the Cumberland took a severe pounding; its line was bent out of shape but never broken, and after the initial surprise it managed to give as good as it got. The result, as night fell, was that both armies still held their ground, the only significant change being horrendous casualty figures.

The situation remained the same throughout New Year's Day as the two exhausted forces clung to their positions but did no fighting. On 2 January Bragg ordered an attack on Rosecrans's left. When it failed, so had Bragg's campaign. The third was another day of inactivity at close range, and on the fourth the Army of Tennessee withdrew. This retreat allowed the Union to claim victory, but the Army of the Cumberland would spend the next six months in Murfreesboro recovering from its triumph.

This was a little more time than President Lincoln and the War Department felt they needed, and as spring approached summer they made clear their impatience for Rosecrans to move. Finally he did move, and with relish. Starting 24 June 1863, he led his army on a series of well-planned, well-executed flanking movements that chased Bragg all the way across Tennessee to Chattanooga. Then, halfway between Murfreesboro and Chattanooga, Rosecrans paused for six weeks, and the prodding messages from Washington resumed.

Once again Rosecrans ended a lengthy respite by launching a brilliant campaign of maneuver. This one chased Bragg out of Chattanooga, and Rosecrans entered the city on 9 September. This time success led to confidence, and confidence led to the desire to pursue what the commander felt was a retreating, disorganized foe.

It wasn't. Bragg had stopped some twenty miles below Chattanooga and was preparing for a counterattack. On 18 September twelve thousand reinforcements from Robert E. Lee's Army of Northern Virginia, led by Lee's redoubtable lieutenant James Longstreet, began to arrive. The next day Bragg launched his attack. The Battle of Chickamauga raged for two days. When it was over Rosecrans was back in Chattanooga, lucky, all things considered, that his army was still intact. Its position, however, was precarious. The Confederates had artillery well posted on Lookout Mountain, commanding the Union supply line. Rosecrans and his army were under siege, forced to rely on a circuitous sixty-mile mountain road for food, forage, ammunition, and all other supplies.[2] If something was not done soon, their situation would become desperate. All of this weighed on the president's mind as he rode toward the War Department.

Since 11 September Stanton had been receiving firsthand information about the Army of the Cumberland and its commander from Charles Dana. A journalist by trade, Dana these days was bearing the title assistant secretary of war and the position of "field observer." To the men and officers of the army, this translated into "spy," and the gossipy flavor of many of Dana's dispatches to the War Department lent credence to that interpretation.

On 20 September Dana wired Stanton: "My report today is of deplorable importance. Chickamauga is as fatal a name in our history as Bull Run." Later that day he revised his earlier "too dark . . . view of our disaster," but he still left no doubt that Rosecrans and his army had suffered a major reversal. Two days later Dana reported that Rosecrans was considering a retreat from Chattanooga. "I judge," Dana observed, "that he thinks that unless he can have assurance of ample reinforcements within one week, the attempt to hold this place will be more disastrous than retreat." Three hours later Dana again changed his message, saying Rosecrans "has determined to fight at all hazards." Still, there were only ten days of full rations on hand and ammunition enough for two days of hard fighting.

On the morning of the twenty-third Dana offered Stanton his opinion that Chattanooga and the Tennessee River could easily be held for fifteen or twenty days. He added: "No time should be lost in rushing twenty to twenty five thousand efficient troops to Bridgeport [Alabama]. If such reinforcements can be got there in season everything is safe, and this place indispensable alike to the defense of Tennessee and as a base of future operations in Georgia will remain ours."

That evening Stanton informed Dana, "Every nerve is being strained to strengthen Rosecrans and his gallant army." If Rosecrans could hold his position for half the time Dana indicated, there could "be no doubt that ample reinforcements must reach him within that period."[3]

With this assurance already given, the secretary of war dispatched Hay to fetch the commander in chief. In addition to the president, Stanton had also summoned Secretary of State William Henry Seward, Treasury Secretary Salmon P. Chase, and Maj. Gen. Henry W. Halleck, general in chief of the Union armies. Assistant Secretary of War Peter H. Watson and James A. Hardie, also of the War Department, were present as well.[4]

Stanton opened the proceedings, asking General Halleck how many men Gen. Ambrose Burnside, then occupying Knoxville, could send to Rosecrans and how quickly. Halleck thought Burnside could get twenty thousand men to Chattanooga in ten days "if uninterrupted." He could send twelve thousand in eight days. Lincoln felt this offered a sufficient solution, remarking, "After Burnside begins to arrive the pinch will be over." Stanton, however, was not persuaded. Gen. William Tecumseh Sherman was already moving east from Vicksburg with four divisions, ordered to do so by Halleck even before Chickamauga. When, Stanton wanted to know, would he reach Rosecrans? In about ten days, Halleck believed. Asked by the secretary if any other men were available in the West, Halleck replied that there were a few in Kentucky, but he was not sure how many. All of them had been ordered to Burnside.

At this point Stanton put his cards on the table. "I propose," he said, "to send 30,000 from the Army of the Potomac." These men would be detached from an army that had not been especially busy since stopping Robert E. Lee's Army of Northern Virginia at Gettysburg two and a half months earlier. At best, George Gordon Meade's army had done some light sparring with Lee's forces as the Confederates withdrew into Virginia. Stanton offered the opinion that Meade was not likely to attack Lee, although his army greatly outnumbered that of the Confederate warrior. "[Meade's] great numbers where they are, are useless," Stanton asserted. "In five days 30,000 could be sent to Rosecrans."

The proposal astounded Lincoln. Showing a cynicism born of two and a half years of military disappointments, the president responded, "I will bet that if the order is given tonight, the troops could not be got to Washington in five days."

Stanton replied, "On such a subject I don't feel inclined to bet," but the secretary had done his homework. "It is certain," he explained, "that 30,000 bales of cotton could be sent in that time by taking possession of the railroads and excluding all other business, and I do not see why 30,000 men cannot be sent as well." If not thirty thousand, Stanton urged, at least let twenty thousand go.

A lengthy conversation ensued. Like Lincoln, Halleck was skeptical of the plan to send the soldiers over so great a distance. If the move could be made at all, he felt it would take a minimum of forty days. Chase, who had received bleak reports about the situation at Chattanooga from James Garfield, his fellow Ohioan and Rosecrans's chief of staff, sided with Stanton. Seward went along with his cabinet colleagues. Still, it was Stanton who had to carry the argument, and the war secretary, a veteran trial lawyer, argued as eloquently and forcefully for his plan as he would have for a client trying to escape a hangman's noose.[5]

Another seasoned attorney, however, was jury foreman on this evening, and Lincoln was proving difficult to persuade. Finally, Stanton called in an expert witness. Daniel C. McCallum, respected superintendent of military railroads, was summoned to the meeting. The president immediately put him on the spot. "Colonel

McCallum," Lincoln began, "we are discussing a very serious proposition, and have sent for you who are at the head of the railway department, to learn your views as to the time it will take to complete such a movement." He then laid out the particulars of Stanton's proposal and asked McCallum for his views.

The colonel was prepared. Maj. Thomas T. Eckert, chief of the military telegraph department, had informed McCallum and his assistant, W. H. Whiton, of the topic of the meeting soon after it began. Eckert was certain that one of the two railroad men would be called into the council, and he suggested that they be ready. Whiton immediately dug into his timetables, made a few calculations, and came up with an estimate of eight or nine days. McCallum studied Whiton's figures and said the movement could be completed within seven days. As he did, McCallum received an order to report to the secretary.

Since all of this was supposed to be new to him, McCallum did not want to give his answer too quickly. He asked for a few minutes to sit down at a desk and "make a few figures." The room grew silent as McCallum scribbled down some notes. Then he arose, announcing, "The transfer can be begun and fully completed within seven days."

"Good! I told you so," Stanton shouted. Then, scowling at Halleck, he added: "Forty days! Forty days indeed, when the life of the nation is at stake!" The triumphant secretary turned to McCallum and said, "Go ahead; begin now."

But the president still had not given his approval to the scheme, and he reminded Stanton of that fact. Lincoln then asked McCallum if he was sure of his figures. McCallum replied, "With the whole power of the government brought to bear in the movement, I will pledge my life to accomplish it inside of seven days." This statement, along with some more impassioned oratory from Stanton, finally won over the commander in chief. He looked at Stanton and said, "Mr. Secretary, you are the captain. Give the necessary orders and I will approve them."[6]

With those words, the most ambitious transfer of soldiers by rail that would occur during the Civil War was set in motion. The XI and XII Corps of the Army of the Potomac would soon be heading westward under the command of Maj. Gen. Joseph Hooker. Stanton had won his case and was confident of his plan; but would that plan really be sufficient to move two corps of men, their horses, artillery, and equipment nearly twelve hundred miles in seven days? The railroads had proved their military value on several occasions during the war, but this proposal far exceeded the scope of anything before attempted. Hay recalled that the group "finished the evening with a supper by Stanton at one o'clock, where few ate."[7]

1

Network of Iron

Had the Civil War begun ten years earlier, had compromise failed in 1850, for instance, what Secretary Stanton had proposed would have been an impossibility. For one thing, many of the railroads over which the men were to travel in 1863, most notably the Louisville & Nashville (L&N), were far from completion in 1853. Yet even if every spike had been in place, the journey by rail from Virginia to Tennessee would have been slower, costlier, and much more hazardous for the passengers. Over ten years the railroads developed the management and operating techniques necessary to address a variety of growing pains. The railroads had begun to adopt such diverse technological innovations as coal-burning locomotives and the telegraph. In short, during that decade, America's railroads grew up.

The 1850s were a time of tremendous expansion for the American railroad system. According to one leading railroad historian, "What was little more than a scattering of short lines stretching from Maine to Georgia at mid-century became by 1860 an iron network serving all the states east of the Mississippi." Statistics bear out that observation. In 1850 there were about 8,900 miles of railroad track in operation in the United States. Ten years later that figure had grown to 30,600 miles. During the same decade the number of locomotives in use increased from around three thousand to over eight thousand. More canals were abandoned during the 1850s than were built.[1]

Although impressive today, these construction figures did not convince all contemporary observers that American railroads were progressing. Indeed, some looked upon them as a hindrance to progress. Among these critics was Henry Varnum Poor, editor of the influential *American Railroad Journal*. According to Poor, the

9

main result of all this activity was "rival roads from city to city, all running in competition, few paying any dividends at all."[2]

A series of short lines, however, first linked the East Coast with the Great Lakes. Since the early 1840s ten roads running from Albany to Buffalo had provided a 290-mile connection from the Hudson River to Lake Erie. In 1853 they merged into the New York Central. Meanwhile, the opening of the New York & Erie from Piedmont to Dunkirk in May 1851 had provided the first single-line connection of those waterways. On Christmas Eve 1852 the Baltimore & Ohio (B&O), conquering the Alleghenies, officially opened, linking Baltimore with the Ohio River. The driving of the final spike represented the culmination of a twenty-five-year effort and a daunting engineering task. On 1 January 1853 regular train service began from Baltimore to Benwood, Virginia, just south of Wheeling. The Pennsylvania Railroad had opened its line from Philadelphia to Pittsburgh a few weeks earlier, but it was still using the inclined planes of the Portage Railroad to cross the highest summits between Holidaysburg and Johnstown. It would be two more years before the Summit Tunnel would be completed, allowing locomotives to make the entire trip.[3]

The New York Central, the Erie, the Pennsylvania, and the B&O would become the dominant eastern railroads, the four great trunk lines connecting the industrial East with the growing Midwest. North and west of the Ohio River, they would spur a burst of railroad building impressive even by the standards of the busy 1850s. In that decade Ohio's railroad mileage would go from six hundred to twenty-nine hundred, Indiana's from seven hundred to fourteen hundred, and Illinois's from one hundred to twenty-eight hundred.[4] Commercially, they would link the interests of these two sections. Psychologically, they would do so as well. When war came they would provide an outlet for the crops of the Old Northwest, supplanting the Confederate-controlled Mississippi River. In short, the trunk lines, by their very presence, would help hold the North together.

Overcoming physical obstacles and linking great distances did not mark the end of the railroads' problems. These achievements only created new challenges such as American businesses had never before faced. The reason was simple: no other business had ever grown as big as the railroads. As Alfred D. Chandler, the path-breaking business historian, observed, "No other business enterprises in the 1850s had as large initial costs, operating expenses, payrolls, and required so many, so varied, and so technically difficult decisions as did the new large railroads." The sheer size of their operations forced the managers of these railroads to experiment and to devise managerial techniques for which there was no precedent.[5]

The financial challenges became apparent at the outset. Initial costs of textile mills, America's largest manufacturing concerns in the 1850s, rarely reached one-half million dollars. Railroads, in contrast, commonly cost tens of millions to construct, the price tag for the four trunk lines ranging from $17 to $35 million. The Pennsylvania would spend about $400 million before its system was complete in 1873. Although most of these funds came from private investors, state and local governments, realizing the importance of railroads to their economic futures, were often generous in subsidizing railroad construction.[6]

Once the roads were completed and in operation, expenses continued to mount. Roadbed and track had to be constantly maintained, as did locomotives, freight and passenger cars, and a variety of buildings along the line. Payrolls for the trunk lines came to exceed four thousand employees by the middle of the decade, double those of the largest manufacturers. For the Erie, these expenses produced operating costs of $2,861,875 in 1855; for the Pennsylvania, $2,049,918 — six times greater than the yearly cost of running the country's biggest textile mill.[7]

It was the scope of these activities, not just their expense, that offered the greatest managerial challenges to the large railroads that emerged in the 1850s. Even the shorter lines that had preceded them could offer few precedents. As Daniel C. McCallum, general superintendent of the Erie, explained in 1856:

A superintendent of a road fifty miles in length can give its business his personal attention and may be constantly on the line engaged in the direction of its details; each person is personally known to him, and all questions in relation to its business are at once presented and acted upon; and any system however imperfect may under such circumstances prove comparatively successful.

In the government of a road five hundred miles in length a very different state exists. Any system which might be applicable to the business and extent of a short road would be inadequate to the wants of a long one; and I am fully convinced that in the want of a system perfect in its details, properly adapted and vigilantly enforced, lies the true secret of their failure; and that [the] disparity of cost per mile in operating long and short roads, is not produced by a difference in length, *but is in proportion to the system adopted.*[8]

As Alfred Chandler has pointed out, these systems had been devised to guide employees whom the top managers never saw. Furthermore, their design had to take into account the speed with which operational decisions needed to be made on large railroads. Finally, managers had to be aware that not only the condition of valuable freight but the lives of passengers depended on their ability to make the correct decisions. On a daily basis railroad managers determined how many cars would be sent on scheduled runs to meet fluctuating demands. At a somewhat longer range, they set and adjusted rates based on demand, costs, and competition. At an even longer range yet, they had to calculate the advantages and dangers of expansion through either construction or acquisition. "The men who managed these enterprises," Chandler concludes, "became the first group of modern business administrators in the United States."[9]

These administrators first emerged on America's first common carrier, the Baltimore & Ohio. In 1847, five years before the line linked its two termini, President Louis McLane and Chief Engineer Benjamin H. Latrobe devised a new system of management for the B&O. Under this system, the operation of the railroad was divided into two categories, "The Working of the Road" and "The Collection and Disbursement of Revenue." In the former, a general superintendent would oversee the work of three officers, each of whom would work under his "immediate supervision."

One of these officers, the master of the road, was "specifically charged with the maintenance of the road, bridges, depot structures, and fixtures of every kind, water stations, and all other appurtenances of the road of a fixed character." Working under him, local supervisors of the road would oversee local maintenance and repair work. The master of machinery was responsible for "the care of all Locomotives and Cars, and the shops and buildings in which they are sheltered." The master of transportation was considered the most important member of the upper management trio. He was in charge of "the forwarding of passengers and tonnage over the road." Specifically, the person holding this position would "receive and deliver passengers, goods, and the mails at the several stations, and regulate . . . all movements of trains." With the approval of the general superintendent, the master of transportation was responsible for hiring all engineers, conductors, and depot agents. He was expected to inspect the entire line weekly and report to the general superintendent.

The collection and disbursement of revenue involved numerous ticket agents, freight agents, conductors, stationmasters, and purchasing officers, each of whom handled large sums of money daily. Also included were operating executives with responsibilities for payrolls. All told, the business of the B&O involved more financial transactions each day than any other business, including large banks. Handling these transactions were many more individuals, spread over a much greater distance.

To check and compile this flood of receipts and reports, the plan called for the establishment of the position of chief clerk. This officer was required to issue "daily comparisons of the work done by the road and its earnings with the monies received therefore." These daily figures, in turn, composed monthly reports on the company's earnings. Supervising the work of the chief clerk was the secretary, who was responsible for all internal financial transactions. It was his job to keep the president and the board of directors informed of the financial affairs of the company and to prepare reports as directed. At the top of this hierarchy was the treasurer. In addition to supervising the work of both the chief clerk and the secretary, the treasurer handled external financing, including stock and bond transactions.[10]

The first railroad to elaborate on the B&O's pioneering management plan was the New York & Erie. This line was much longer than the B&O, and it employed more men and equipment. Realizing that one master of transportation could not supervise all the traffic along the line, the board of directors established five divisions of about one hundred miles each and put a division superintendent in charge of each one. This system solved one problem but created another. While each superintendent could easily control the operations of his portion of the line, the scheme further complicated overall coordination. The Erie's directors were forced to search for a plan to increase the efficiency of the entire railroad.[11]

The responsibility for devising such a plan fell to Daniel Craig McCallum. The inventor of an inflexible truss bridge, McCallum was a respected civil engineer. He was also widely regarded as a poet (his poem *The Water Mill* was very popular at one time) and as an architect. While serving as superintendent of the Erie's Susquehanna Division, McCallum devised a detailed code for train operation. It impressed the directors, and in 1854 they made McCallum general superintendent.[12]

McCallum approached his task with enthusiasm. Realizing that he did not have "any precedent or experience on which we can fully rely," he started with six general principles of administration:

1. A proper division of responsibilities.

2. Sufficient power conferred to enable the same to be fully carried out, that such responsibilities may be real in character.

3. The means of knowing whether such responsibilities are faithfully executed.

4. Great promptness in the report of all derelictions of duty, that evils may at once be corrected.

5. Such information, to be obtained through a system of daily reports and checks that will not embarrass principal officers, nor lessen their influence with their subordinates.

6. The adoption of a system, as a whole, which will not only enable the General Superintendent to detect errors immediately, but will also point out the delinquent.[13]

To put these general principles into effect, McCallum first defined precisely the duties of such officers as master of engine repairs, general freight agent, general ticket agent, general wood agent, superintendent of telegraph, and foreman of bridge repairs. Division and branch superintendents were given broad authority in carrying out their duties except in matters pertaining to the duties of the officers already listed. McCallum felt the "enforcement of a rigid system of discipline in the government of works of great magnitude is indispensable to success." Therefore, subordinates were "accountable to [and] *directed by their immediate superiors only.*" Each officer had the authority, with the approval of the president and the general superintendent, "to appoint all persons for whose acts he is held responsible [and to] dismiss any subordinate when in his judgment the interests of the Company will be promoted thereby."

McCallum then turned to "the economical management of a freight traffic." To achieve this goal, he devised an intricate reporting system. Through it he hoped to acquire "a fund of information, the judicious use of which materially assists in directing the business of the road to the best advantage." It started with hourly reports, sent by telegraph, giving the positions of all passenger trains and "the principal freight trains" along the line. In all cases when passenger trains ran more than ten minutes behind schedule or freight trains more than half an hour, conductors were expected to give the reason for the delay when they reached the station. This information was immediately forwarded by telegraph to the general superintendent. It was important to know the cause for such delays, McCallum pointed out, because they were "frequently the result of mismanagement [and] often the primary cause of accidents."

Both passenger and freight train conductors provided daily reports, including the names of persons assigned to their trains, times of arrival and departure at each station, and "the particulars in regard to delays." Freight conductors also described the load in each car and told where those loads were picked up and let off. These could be matched with the daily reports of station agents, which were to include detailed information on every train arriving and departing that day. The division superintendents reported each month on the work of their respective divisions. The number of miles run and the costs involved made up the bulk of those reports. Officers of the railroad's various departments also reported monthly. The result was a wealth of statistical data that assisted the general superintendent in spotting areas of inefficiency and in setting rates. McCallum concluded, "*All that is required to render the efforts of railroad companies in every respect equal to that of individuals, is a rigid system of personal accountability through every grade of service.*"[14]

McCallum's efforts caught the attention of observers of the railroad industry. Among his admirers was Poor, editor of the *American Railroad Journal*. In September 1854 Poor said of McCallum, "His moral character commands respect, and we believe he is serving the company with a single eye." The editor praised McCallum's cost-cutting measures, including the dismissal of forty engineers, forty firemen, and several administrative personnel. He also approved of the reporting system McCallum had instituted, noting that "the superintendent can tell at any hour in the day, the precise location of every car and engine on the line of the road, and the duty it is performing. Formerly," Poor observed, "the utmost confusion prevailed in this department, so much so, that . . . cars in perfect order have stood for months upon switches without being put to the least service, and without its being known where they were."[15]

Praise for McCallum was not universal, however. Declaring that "the road must run safe first and fast afterward," the general superintendent instituted a rule that engineers were responsible for making sure switches at stations were properly set. They could take no one else's word for it, and if an engineer ran off the track because a switch was improperly set, he could be dismissed. It did not matter if a switchman or anyone else had signaled him to go forward. Engineers objected, claiming the rule held them responsible for another man's mistake. In 1854 and again in 1856 they struck over the issue. On the latter occasion Poor strongly endorsed McCallum's policy. "The freedom from accidents on the Erie Railroad," the editor asserted, "is another proof of the value of the discipline which Mr. McCallum is seeking to enforce."[16]

McCallum resigned from the Erie on 25 February 1857. In his letter to President Homer Ramsdell he said, "Business of a private and important character, which cannot be neglected without great pecuniary sacrifice, has induced me to make this the occasion of tendering my resignation." McCallum also remarked that he had learned that "some differences of opinion exist in the Board of Directors, in regard to the discipline that has been pursued in the superintendence of the operations of the road." It was his understanding that "a respectable number of them entertain views . . . somewhat at variance with my own."[17]

Whatever the cause, McCallum's resignation marked the beginning of a period of economic decline for the Erie. The loss of business caused by the engineers' strike was one factor. The general economic turndown prompted by the Panic of 1857 was a larger one. Perhaps larger yet was the inefficiency of the men who succeeded McCallum. Whether McCallum could have successfully met the challenges the Erie faced after his resignation cannot be known. One thing is definite—McCallum's departure meant other railroads would have the responsibility for testing and building upon his management concepts.[18]

Several lines did. Among those that adopted McCallum's principles on a limited basis were the Michigan Southern and the Illinois Central (whose chief engineer was George B. McClellan). They were put to their most thorough test on the Pennsylvania. J. Edgar Thomson, the line's president from 1852 to 1874, structured his operating department much as McCallum had that of the Erie. At the top was a general superintendent, who stayed in close communication with subordinate officers, including division superintendents. Thomson went even further, however, putting division superintendents in charge of motive power department personnel along their sections of track. As time went on, division superintendents also gained increased authority over maintenance and repair forces.[19]

The telegraph was vital to the new management systems of the 1850s. Like other railroad developments of the day, the metamorphosis came quickly. In 1850, John F. Stover noted, "No one had yet thought of using the telegraph to dispatch or control train movement." A decade later, the *American Railroad Journal* would report that "a railroad of any length without a telegraph is indeed behind the age."[20]

In this area, too, McCallum was among the pioneers. In his 1855 report to Erie stockholders, the general superintendent asserted, "*A single track railroad may be rendered more safe and efficient by a proper use of telegraph than a double track railroad without its aid.*" This was true because double tracking prevented collisions only between trains moving in opposite directions. Effective employment of the telegraph, McCallum pointed out, would also prevent accidents between trains running in the same direction. While safety was a prime consideration, McCallum was not alone in recognizing this obvious benefit of the wires. What separated him from his contemporaries was his realization that the telegraph could also be a valuable tool for coordinating operations. Without it, his system of hourly reports would have been impossible.[21]

The plans devised and the lessons learned by railroaders in the 1850s would prove valuable when war came the following decade. Here the advantages lay with the North, in part because the four trunk lines were all in Union territory, although the B&O was perilously close to the Confederacy. No such east-west road existed in the South, although a series of seven lines did provide a continuous connection between Richmond and Corinth. Track gauges varied in both sections, but the variations were greater in the South, complicating the problem posed by the lack of through lines. "Everywhere in Dixie," historian Robert C. Black noted, "railroads were stretching iron fingers toward one another, but not yet everywhere had they joined hands."[22] In addition, southern lines were generally more poorly constructed. Many had joined the North in adopting wrought-iron T-rail, but a significant number still ran trains over U-rail or even strap rail, wooden rails with thin strips of iron fastened on top. Few had siding mileage equal to 10 percent of their main line trackage; in the North this figure often exceeded 20 percent.

A further inconvenience was that railroads entering important river and seaport cities such as Petersburg, Wilmington, Charleston, Savannah, and Montgomery did not connect. In 1861 five railroads served Richmond, but none joined with any other. The noise, smoke, and fire hazard from sparks had first prompted municipal governments to halt the construction of tracks at the outskirts of their towns. Later local merchants, tavern keepers, shipping agents, and teamsters, none of whom wanted to see passengers and freight passing through without stopping, put pressure on local politicians to maintain the policy.[23]

The North also enjoyed a decided advantage in motive power and rolling stock. On the eve of the war, the four trunk lines reported a total of 876 locomotives on their rosters, a figure very close to the total for all southern railroads. In freight and passenger cars the northern advantage was nearly two to one. Moreover, the South did not possess the necessary facilities to catch up. Census figures for 1860 show that the North had nineteen factories manufacturing "wholly or chiefly" locomotives. Virginia, representing the entire South, had one. The state of Pennsylvania produced twice as many railroad cars as all the future Confederate states. Northern production of railroad iron was listed at 222,577 tons, while the South turned out 26,252 tons of "bar and railroad iron."[24]

The telegraph was also rarely used in Dixie. In 1857 the *American Railroad Journal* reported that there were 1,467 telegraph stations in the United States. Of those, only 107 could be found in the states that were destined to form the Confederacy. New York led the nation with 170 stations, while Ohio, Pennsylvania, and Illinois all had 100 or more. Virginia's 26 stations placed it eleventh in the country but first among the future Confederate states. Mississippi had 24 stations, Tennessee 18, Georgia 13, Alabama 11, Louisiana 10, and North Carolina 5.[25]

Early in the war, military and government officials in the North recognized the value of their iron infrastructure. On 4 August 1861, eight days after assuming command of the Army of the Potomac, Maj. Gen. George B. McClellan sent a lengthy memorandum to the president, advising Lincoln: "It cannot be ignored that the construction of railroads has introduced a new and very important element into the war, by the great facilities thus given for concentrating at particular positions large masses of troops from remote sections, and by creating new strategic points and lines of operation. . . . By seizing and repairing the railroads well in advance, the difficulties of transportation will be materially diminished."[26]

McClellan's advice was soon federal policy. On 31 January 1862, Congress passed a measure giving the president, "when in his judgment the public safety may require it," the authority "to take possession of any or all the telegraph lines in the United States [and] any or all the railroad lines in the United States, their rolling stock, their offices, shops, buildings, and all their appendages." The act further empowered the president to make all rules for the use, maintenance, and extension of any roads that came under government control. Officers and employees of the affected companies were to be placed

under military authority, and anyone interfering was subject to execution. The transportation of troops and all military equipment
was "under the immediate control of the Secretary of War and such
agents as he may appoint."[27]

Although the act could have been applied to any railroad in the
country, it was not invoked in the North. Soon after the law was
passed, Stanton, McClellan, and Q.M. Gen. Montgomery Meigs
met in Washington with a group of northern railroad executives.
With the hammer of a presidential takeover hanging over their
heads, the railroad men agreed to a rate schedule of two cents per
mile for transporting soldiers. Eighty pounds of baggage would
be allowed for each man. The company officials also granted the
government a 10 percent discount for carrying freight. Nine months
later Meigs reported that the railroads had "performed so zealously
and satisfactorily" that the law had not been put "into exercise over
any road not within the limits of an insurgent state." That would
remain the case for the duration of the war.[28]

The measure was, of course, put into effect in "insurgent states."
To direct the captured lines, Stanton, on 11 February 1862, appointed
Daniel C. McCallum "military director and superintendent of railroads of the United States." The former Erie chief assumed the rank
of colonel and "authority to enter upon, take possession of, hold,
and use all railroads, engines, cars, locomotives, equipments, appendages, and appurtenances that may be required for the transport
of troops, arms, ammunition, and military supplies of the United
States, and to do and perform all acts and things that may be
necessary and proper to be done for the safe and speedy transport
aforesaid."[29]

The United States Military Railroads would eventually operate
2,105 miles of trackage. Upon assuming his duties, however, Mc-
Callum discovered that he was "director and superintendent" of
only the seven-mile Washington & Alexandria Railroad (W&A).
(One month earlier the War Department had laid a track across
the Long Bridge over the Potomac River and relaid the entire line

with т-rails.) The short line would remain in Union hands for the remainder of the war. It would also be kept quite busy, carrying 51,156 cars between 9 February 1862 and 7 August 1865.[30]

The first extension of McCallum's military line came in March, when the Orange & Alexandria (O&A) went into government service between Alexandria and Manassas, a distance of twenty-six miles. A month later it was extended another thirteen miles to Warrenton Junction. In August, after extensive repairs of track and bridges destroyed by the Confederates, McCallum opened the O&A to Culpeper. Much of this work was undone a few weeks later in the wake of the retreat of John Pope and his Army of Virginia following their defeat at Second Manassas. The road would be ripped up and rebuilt again dependent on the ever-changing fortunes of the Army of the Potomac, but by the late summer of 1863 it was again open to Culpeper.[31]

On 30 September 1863, McCallum reported that in addition to the W&A and the O&A, the United States Military Railroads had operated the following Virginia lines: Alexandria, Loudoun, & Hampshire; Manassas Gap; Warrenton Branch; Richmond & York River; Richmond, Fredericksburg, & Potomac; Norfolk & Petersburg; and Seaboard & Roanoke. The superintendent noted that the success of his department was owing in part to "the stringent orders of Major-General Halleck, General-in-Chief, preventing interference of the military authorities with the running of trains."[32]

As the lines were repaired, McCallum had the gauge changed from five feet, which prevailed in Virginia, to four feet, eight and one-half inches. By converting the lines to the northern "standard gauge," McCallum was able to borrow locomotives and cars from other railroads until the government could purchase what it needed. Those purchases proved to be substantial. In May 1862 the *American Railroad Journal* reported that "several heavy orders for locomotives have been received by the builders in New England and New Jersey." One manufacturer in Paterson, New Jersey, had been called upon to supply thirty. The demand was expected to "tax the capacity of our existing shops to their utmost capacity." The trade journal quickly added, "If the general government undertake[s] to foot the bill, all the better for our manufacturing interests."[33]

The construction—and *re*construction—work on the roads was handled by Herman Haupt. A West Point graduate and former general superintendent and chief engineer for the Pennsylvania Railroad, Haupt did yeoman work supervising the building of bridges and track in Virginia. After viewing one of his unusual-looking projects, President Lincoln was reported to have remarked: "I have seen the most remarkable structure human eyes ever rested upon. That man Haupt has built a bridge across Potomac Creek 400 feet long and nearly 100 feet high, over which loaded trains are running every hour and, upon my word, gentlemen, there is nothing in it but beanpoles and cornstalks."

On 1 January 1863, Haupt's construction corps was formally separated from the operating department, but Haupt did not remain long as its head. On 14 September 1863, he resigned his position. Haupt left behind, however, a well-trained corps, which was placed under McCallum's control. Thanks to the efforts of both men, the military railroads would continue to serve the Union cause efficiently.[34]

Such was not the case in the South. Dixie's lack of manufacturing was an obvious problem. Iron rail was scarce from the start of the war, and with supplies no longer available from northern mills, it quickly became much scarcer. The same was true of locomotives and rolling stock. Trucks, wheels, and springs were also not to be had, making it difficult to maintain such cars as were on hand.

The real problem, though, went well beyond materials. If the South was to take advantage of its interior lines of transportation, it would have to make the most of its infant rail network. Thus coordination at the national level was vital. To achieve this goal, local government and railroad officials had to cooperate, but they did not. The Confederacy, after all, was a government founded on the principle of state sovereignty, and its railroads were viewed as representatives of state and local interests. This philosophy left no room for regulation from Richmond, no matter how necessary it may have been in winning the war. As a result, according to Black, "the Confederacy was never to exert an effective supervision over its railways."[35]

Three men tried to coordinate the southern railroads. On 17 July 1861, President Jefferson Davis gave William S. Ashe a major's commission, named him assistant quartermaster, and placed him in charge of rail transportation for Confederate armies in Virginia. A North Carolina native, Ashe was a former member of the U.S. House of Representatives and a former president of the Wilmington & Weldon Railroad. He went about his task energetically, working to break military commanders of the habit of using freight cars as storehouses and trying to get the lines to cooperate in lending each other sorely needed rolling stock. He had no real authority, however, and found scant support from a Confederate government fearful of alienating the states and their railroads. In April 1862 he gave up, choosing instead to raise an artillery battalion for field service.[36]

It is perhaps telling that the position went unfilled until November 1862, when William M. Wadley was "assigned to take supervision and control of the transportation for the Government on all railroads in the Confederate States." This job description sounded impressive, but the general orders announcing his appointment revealed that he would not have the powers necessary to fulfill such a bold objective. "Supervision and control" did not mean that the southern railroads would actually be placed under his direction. Rather, Wadley was "empowered to make contracts for transportation with said railroads . . . and such negotiations and arrangements with them as may be requisite or proper to secure efficiency, harmony, and cooperation on the part of said railroads."

Born in New Hampshire in 1815, Wadley had moved to Georgia in 1834. When the railroad boom reached the South in the 1850s, he worked for no fewer than five lines, becoming "a recognized railroad expert." Possessing expertise was one thing; applying it from a position of no real authority proved more troublesome. Wadley found this out one month after assuming his post, when a convention of representatives from forty-one railroads met at Augusta. Wadley had called the convention, and he asked those present to consider a plan for through train schedules and a system of interchange for freight cars. He got nothing he asked for, although the delegates did acknowledge their approval of his appointment and "cheerfully pledge[d] to the government their assistance and co-operation." Disappointed but undeterred, Wadley continued to call for government control of the railroads. Meanwhile, he traveled to the Carolinas and as far as Vicksburg, attempting to remedy individual ills that could be cured only by coordination at the national level.

Finally, in April 1863, the Confederate Congress acted. The result was a strong railroad bill empowering the government to set schedules and require carriers to give military traffic top priority. Lines that refused to cooperate could be seized. It was exactly what Wadley had been calling for, but there was one catch—Wadley himself was not to be involved. It is not at all clear what the Confederate Congress had against him—perhaps his Yankee background—but the Senate flatly refused to confirm him for the post in which he had ably served for five months.[37]

His successor was his chief assistant, Capt. Frederick W. Sims, a Georgia native, whose views were very similar to Wadley's. Although he had gained railroad experience with the Central of Georgia in the 1840s, Sims had pursued a variety of business and civic activities. On 4 June 1863, he was given the duties of "inspector and agent for the supervision of railroad transportation on the railroads of the Confederacy." Like Wadley before him, Sims spent much of his time in the field and approached his duties enthusiastically. During his first month on the job, he organized the transfer of locomotives and freight cars from northern and western Mississippi, where they were in great danger of capture or destruction, to the East. The circuitous route took the rolling stock over dilapidated rails, across twenty-five miles of Mobile Bay via steamers, and past the eyes of greedy railroad officials who coveted the engines and cars. The project was not completed until late fall. Although the exact numbers are not known, Sims's effort preserved precious equipment that would otherwise have been lost to the Confederacy.[38]

The southern rail chief's next major operation occurred in September. Along with Q.M. Gen. Alexander R. Lawton, Sims helped organize what would prove to be the largest Confederate rail transfer of the war. The move preceded by two weeks the shipment west of the Union's XI and XII Corps, offering the Confederate soldiers who took the trains adventures similar to those their blue-clad opponents would soon experience. It also played a major part in making the northern movement necessary. For those reasons, the transfer of the I Corps, Army of Northern Virginia, deserves examination.

2

Rebels Ride the Rails

No records remain of who first proposed the transfer of two divisions of Lt. Gen. James Longstreet's I Corps from the Army of Northern Virginia to reinforce Bragg's forces near Chattanooga. In his memoirs, Longstreet claimed credit for the idea. According to Longstreet, in August 1863 he wrote to Secretary of War James A. Seddon and proposed a "remedy" for the Confederacy's problems in the West. His suggested solution was "to order the Army of Northern Virginia to defensive work, and send detachments to reinforce the army in Tennessee; to call detachments of other commands to the same service, and strike a crushing blow against Rosecrans before he could receive reinforcing help."[1]

The subject came up again later that month when Lee went to Richmond for a series of meetings with President Davis. The president suggested that Lee take command in Tennessee, but the Virginian declined, expressing the view that "the duty could be better performed by officers already in that department." Meanwhile, Longstreet wrote twice to his commander offering the view that "our best opportunity for great results is in Tennessee." On the second occasion, Longstreet suggested that "we might accomplish something by . . . putting me in Gen. Bragg's place and giving him my corps."[2]

Bragg would remain where he was, but, with Lee's assent, the decision was made in Richmond to send Longstreet west. On 6 September Lee informed Davis, "I have arranged with the Quartermaster-General for the transportation of Longstreet's Corps, and have given the necessary orders for the movement of the troops and their subsistence on the road."[3]

It seems doubtful that even Lee appreciated the logistical challenge these "necessary orders" would represent for the fragile Confederate rail network, a challenge made manifestly worse by recent military reversals in the West. In his original plan, Longstreet had intended for the men to go directly from Richmond to Chattanooga, via Bristol and Knoxville, on the Virginia & Tennessee Railroad. The route covered 540 miles, and it was believed the move could be made in four days. This plan was rendered impossible on 2 September, when Burnside occupied Knoxville. Seven days later Rosecrans captured Chattanooga, and the two thousand Confederate soldiers guarding Cumberland Gap surrendered to Union troops. The direct rail link had been effectively cut.[4]

Sims was forced to map out a roundabout route, some three hundred miles longer, through the Carolinas and Georgia. He was aided by the apparently high level of cooperation he received from the fourteen railroads that he would have to depend on to carry the men to their destination. Indeed, one company official complained during the movement when troops scheduled to be carried over his line were diverted to another railroad in an attempt to relieve traffic. He explained that he had "immediately stopped all our [regular] trains except the mail [and] passenger," and he termed the change in plans "an embarrassment [rather] than relief."[5]

Although Sims's responsibilities began at Richmond, the evidence strongly indicates that virtually every regiment was transported to the capital by rail. Most of Longstreet's corps was in camp at Orange Court House, some sixty miles northwest of Richmond. Surviving letters, diaries, and unit histories indicate that portions of at least five brigades marched to Hanover, where they began their journey by freight car. (One exception was the Forty-eighth Alabama Infantry. Sent to protect foraging trains, it marched from Fredericksburg to Richmond on 8 September.)[6]

Sims's plan called for the Richmond & Petersburg and the Petersburg Railroad to carry the men from the capital to Hicksford Junction, Virginia, or Weldon, North Carolina. Units in the former group would then veer southwest through Raleigh, Charlotte, and Columbia, a total distance of 775 miles. The rest would continue south to Wilmington, then head west through Florence, South Carolina, saving about 70 miles. The two routes converged at Kingsville, South Carolina. From there two connecting single-track lines, the South Carolina and the Georgia, would take the troops to Atlanta. The last leg of the journey, delivering the reinforcements to Bragg, was to be over the Western & Atlantic. All along the way varying track gauges and a lack of direct connections would conspire to slow the movement.[7]

As the troops entered Richmond, Longstreet and Lee did some shuffling of brigades. At the time, Longstreet's corps comprised the divisions of Lafayette McLaws, John Bell Hood, and George Pickett. Decimated in the wake of its 3 July action at Gettysburg, Pickett's division was far from recovered. It was assigned to the defenses of Richmond and replaced by the brigades of Micah Jenkins and Henry Wise. In the end, only Jenkins's brigade accompanied Longstreet. Wise's brigade and G. T. "Tige" Anderson's brigade went to Charleston, South Carolina, to assist in that city's defense.

Jenkins and his command were assigned to Hood's division, joining the brigades of Evander Law, Jerome Robertson, and Henry Benning. McLaws had the brigades of William Wofford, Joseph Kershaw, Benjamin Humphreys, and Goode Bryan in his division. Col. Edward Porter Alexander's twenty-six-gun artillery battalion rounded out the contingent that would accompany Longstreet to northern Georgia.[8]

According to diarist John B. Jones, a clerk in the Confederate War Department, troops from Hood's division began arriving in Richmond during the night of 8 September and continued in a steady stream the next day. They came into town on the Virginia Central, then marched through the capital because that line did not connect with the Richmond & Petersburg. Phillips's Georgia Legion, arriving on 11 September, had only an eight-hour layover at Richmond, but other units had a lengthier wait. For some it was overnight; for the Second South Carolina it was nearly twenty-four hours. At least one brigade, Robertson's Texans, "took advantage of the local saloons with the inevitable results."⁹

As the trains rolled south, agents and other officials at key stops along the way kept Sims apprised as to the progress of the movement. On the thirteenth he learned from H. M. Drane, railroad superintendent at Wilmington, that Anderson's brigade, nineteen hundred strong, had passed through Wilmington. Kershaw's brigade left the same point the next morning, followed by Wofford's. The last telegram from Wilmington came on the fifteenth. Drane reported that Longstreet and his staff had gone through, adding that there were "no troops here to go and only a few horses."¹⁰

Meanwhile, apparently at their own behest, Drane and S. S. Soloman, his counterpart at Charleston, were diverting units through Charleston, Savannah, and Macon. This route added miles but relieved some of the traffic between Wilmington and Kingsville. It also lightened the load on the single-track South Carolina and Georgia lines. At least three regiments of Wofford's brigade (the Sixteenth and Twenty-fourth Georgia and Phillips's Georgia Legion) traveled this route, as did the Second South Carolina from Kershaw's brigade.¹¹

At Kingsville, junction point for the two original routes, trains began arriving during the night of 11–12 September, including elements of Benning's and Robertson's brigades. These units were part of Hood's division, which had departed Richmond first. The earliest reported arrival from McLaws's division, one regiment of Kershaw's brigade, departed Kingsville at 4:15 A.M. on the fourteenth. Longstreet and his staff left the busy South Carolina depot at 5:25 P.M. on the sixteenth, one day after passing through Wilmington.¹²

No telegrams sent to Sims detailing the movement beyond Kingsville survive, but itineraries recorded in the diaries of the soldiers involved shed some light on the course of events along the various routes. Lt. Robert A. Moore of the Seventeenth Mississippi traveled the inland route via Raleigh and Columbia. On 7 September his command was located in camp along the North Anna River when marching orders came for early the next morning. "Many are the conjectures," he recorded, "as to where we will go." Early the next morning Moore and his comrades began the twenty-mile march to Hanover Junction. By the time they arrived, it had "become well settled . . . that we go to Chattanooga." The ninth was spent at Hanover, waiting for Hood's division to take the trains ahead of them. Meanwhile, wagons and teams from the regiment were "turned over to the Government."

Moore's regiment left Hanover just after noon on 10 September and arrived in Richmond five hours later. They marched through the capital, crossed the James, and bivouacked at Manchester, on the opposite shore. From there they took the cars south the next morning at about nine, reaching Petersburg shortly after noon. Moore enjoyed a nine-hour layover in that "very nice and pleasant old city" before continuing on to Weldon, North Carolina. That community, "nothing more than a few houses and a grocery or two," was reached just after sunrise on the twelfth. In the approximately twenty-one hours since leaving Richmond, the Seventeenth had covered about eighty-six miles.

The regiment passed through Raleigh on the thirteenth and continued on to Greensboro. They arrived at Charlotte early the next morning and left before noon. As the trains continued to roll through the night, the last community Moore recorded in his diary was Winnsboro, South Carolina.

At 9:00 A.M. on the fifteenth, the Mississippians entered Columbia. Moore and several friends ventured from the depot to visit the city, only to discover that they had missed their train. The lieutenant was not overly concerned. After seeing the sights, including the state capitol building, then under construction, Moore concluded, "Have spent the day quite agreeably."

The next morning at 6:00, Moore caught a mail train for Augusta, reaching the Georgia community just before sunset. The train continued all night, delivering Moore to Atlanta at sunrise on the seventeenth. He caught a train to Marietta, some thirty miles north of Atlanta, at 11:00 A.M. There he waited several hours for the train that took him to Dalton. He reached Dalton "sometime during the night" and remained until 10:00 A.M. on the eighteenth, when he caught the train to Ringgold, the end of the line for Longstreet's men.

It is not clear when Moore rejoined his command. It is very clear that he was with them on 20 September, when the Seventeenth Mississippi was in the thick of the fight at Chickamauga. That day the regiment lost twelve men killed and seventy-five wounded. Among the dead was Lt. Robert A. Moore.[13]

Among the units taking the coastal route through Wilmington to Kingsville was the Third Georgia Battalion, Sharpshooters, whose members included W. R. Montgomery. Like the Seventeenth Mississippi, Montgomery's unit began its journey on 8 September, marching some twenty-five miles from its camp along the East Anna River to Hanover Junction. Also like the Mississippians, the Third spent the next day waiting for a train that never arrived. Early the following morning, Montgomery took a train with the Sixteenth and Nineteenth Georgia regiments and spent the night of 10 September at the Soldiers' Home in Richmond.

The rest of the battalion reached Richmond the next afternoon. They remained until 8:00 P.M., when they departed for Petersburg, where they arrived at 2:00 the next morning. After a nineteen-hour layover, Montgomery's unit headed further south toward the North Carolina border. Upon reaching Weldon "about daylight" on the thirteenth, the Georgians departed immediately for Wilmington, arriving "about dark." It was not until the next evening that the outfit left Wilmington. Traveling all night, they arrived at Florence at about 10:00 A.M. on the fifteenth and found themselves in Kingsville twelve hours later.

Once again there was no layover as the trains departed for Augusta, reaching that destination at 1:00 P.M. on the sixteenth. At dark the Third Battalion was rolling again. They entered Atlanta the next evening, and Montgomery met his mother and sister at the depot. He spent the next day, 18 September, in Atlanta, visiting relatives and friends, and did not leave until 8:00 the next morning. Passing through Marietta, he saw "Miss Lou," apparently a close friend or relative, but was unable to visit. "Would have given a small negro to have stopped," Montgomery recorded, "but could not." He arrived at Ringgold that night. Montgomery's unit did not participate in the next day's fighting, although he noted in his diary on behalf of those who did, "Drove the Yankies back."[14]

Following the same route was the last outfit to arrive in Georgia, Alexander's artillery battalion. After all the infantry had departed, his command left Petersburg at 4:00 P.M. on the seventeenth. They reached Wilmington at 2:00 A.M. on the twentieth, Kingsville on the evening of the twenty-first, and Augusta at 2:00 the next afternoon. Twenty-four hours later they were in Atlanta, and early on the twenty-fifth the last element of Longstreet's command arrived at Ringgold. "Our journey by rail," Alexander later reported, "had been 843 miles and had consumed seven days and 10 hours or 178 hours. It could scarcely be considered rapid transit, yet under the circumstances it was a very creditable feat for our railroad service."[15]

Among the few units to take the route through Charleston was the Sixteenth Georgia Infantry, whose surgeon, J. B. Clifton, recorded many details of the journey. Although it is not clear where they began, the men of the Sixteenth arrived in Richmond at 4:00 P.M. on 10 September. They left from Manchester twenty-four hours later. Cars were apparently scarce because, as the men rode south toward Petersburg, their horses were "sent through the country to Petersburg."

The regiment reached Petersburg at dusk on the eleventh but did not leave until the next afternoon or evening. At "about day-light" on the thirteenth they pulled into Weldon, leaving for Wilmington at 6:00 A.M. After stopping at Goldsboro long enough to eat, they arrived in Wilmington that evening. There the wait was nearly

33

twenty-four hours. At 7:30 on the evening of the fourteenth the men received orders to report to the wharf to take a boat across the Cape Fear River. No boat arrived, so at daylight the men marched back to their barracks, only to return at noon, cross the river, and depart by rail for Charleston. They reached Charleston at 1:00 P.M. on the sixteenth and had a brief layover before moving on toward Savannah.

The Georgians entered their home state during the night, finding themselves in Savannah at 1:00 A.M. Later on the seventeenth they headed for Macon, arriving at 3:00 in the afternoon. There they remained until 6:30 the next morning. At 4:00 P.M. Clifton's regiment reached Atlanta, where it spent the night. The next day, 19 September, the unit rode from Atlanta to Ringgold. They received orders the next morning to "march immediately in the direction of Chattanooga" but stopped after one mile to await rations. The rations did not reach the regiment that day, and the regiment did not reach the scene of the battle until the fighting was over.[16]

Regardless of the route, the railroads traveled were far from ideal. "Never before," remarked Moxley Sorrel of Longstreet's staff, "were so many troops moved over such worn out railways, none first-class from the beginning. Never before," he went on, "were such crazy cars—passenger, baggage, mail, coal, box, platform, all and every sort wabbling [*sic*] on the jumping strap iron—used for hauling good soldiers." At least one regiment experienced mechanical problems at the outset. Col. Asbury Coward of the Fifth South Carolina remembered that the train that was to start his regiment from Richmond was several hours late because of "hot-boxes and engine trouble." John Coxe, a soldier from Kershaw's brigade, later recalled that the engine pulling his train through the Carolinas "was in bad order, and slow progress and many stops to allow the engineer to 'tinker' with his machine greatly delayed us." Later, traveling through Georgia on the Western & Atlantic, Coxe's train paused for two hours in Cartersville so the engineer could work on the cylinders of his locomotive.[17]

As for the rolling stock, Sorrel's assessment of the "crazy cars" was verified by observers in the ranks. Cars were in short supply, so companies were often loaded one at a time—the first going in the car, the second on the roof. Even at that, the cars were crowded, one officer claiming that his men were "packed in so tightly that there was no room to sit down and many stood from Virginia to Georgia." By the time the gunners of Alexander's battalion departed, there were only enough boxcars left for the officers and their few horses. As a result, the battery horses were left behind, and the men rode on flatcars with their guns. "It was easy enough to travel during the day by sitting on the sides of the flat cars, with legs hanging over the sides," one later noted, "but at night we had to crawl between the wheels of the guns and caissons to keep from being shaken off the train."[18]

Despite all the hardships, the men found ways to persevere. As the First South Carolina entered Atlanta, the weather turned cold. Continuing north, the men found some sand (used to keep fires from burning through the wooden freight cars) at one of their stops and put it on the floors and the roofs of the cars. That evening they passed through Marietta with fires inside and on top, cooking their suppers and keeping warm.

For most units, lack of warmth was not a problem during the transfer. Indeed, it was hot enough to be uncomfortable inside a crowded boxcar. The men solved their problem, as their Union counterparts would a few weeks later, by cutting away all but the framework with their knives and axes. By the time they were done, according to D. Augustus Dickert of Kershaw's brigade, the rolling stock was "little more than skeleton cars." Beyond their desire for ventilation, Dickert observed, the men "wished to see outside and witness the fine country and delightful scenery that lay along the route; nor could those inside bear the idea of being shut up in a box car while their comrades on top were cheering and yelling themselves hoarse at the waving of handkerchiefs and flags in the hands of the pretty women and the hats thrown in the air by old men and boys along the roadside."[19]

As Dickert noted, the trip was "one grand ovation" for these veterans of the Army of Northern Virginia. In scenes that were soon to be repeated along the railroads of Ohio and Indiana, the citizens of the Carolinas and Georgia spared no effort to show their enthusiastic support for Longstreet's men. At Sumter, South Carolina, they turned out and fed the members of the Bedford Light Artillery at one long table. According to the regimental historian, it was there that a Corporal Bondurant "saw more sweet potatoes, than he had ever seen in all the days of his life. They fed him sweet potatoes, put them in his haversack, and handed them to him on the train." The First South Carolina long remembered the town of Bamberg, South Carolina. According to Pvt. Frank Mixon, when his unit arrived, the community was "all lit up with bonfires and tables spread . . . with baskets of cold chicken, rice pilau, biscuits, hams, boiled eggs, fried ham, salads and everything else that women can get up in a country of plenty." The residents greeted the soldiers "as if we were all their brothers." So impressive was the reception that the colonel in charge of the train held it for an hour so all could partake.[20]

John C. West of the Fourth Texas recalled that his outfit was welcomed at every depot in South Carolina by women of all ages who "flocked in loaded with baskets of provisions, fruits and delicacies of every character. . . . Rags and dirt seemed to be a recommendation where gilt and brass failed to excite attention." According to West, "The old brigade [Robertson's] fell in love with South Carolina's hospitality." According to Richard Lewis of South Carolina's Palmetto Sharpshooters, however, the welcome accorded the men in Georgia was even greater than that in his home state. There, too, every station included "some of Georgia's fair ones, with baskets of refreshments on their arms, to greet the hungry soldiers." Not content simply to feed the soldiers, the young women also "shower[ed] bouquets of flowers on us."[21]

Even the high brass was impressed with the reception. McLaws wrote to his wife that it had been "enthusiastic in the extreme," with "dinner and supper for all comers . . . provided with the greatest liberality. I was called upon several times to 'Show myself' to the assembled multitude," the division commander added, "as the ladies wanted to see a Georgia general." McLaws did not say how often he relented. Sorrel agreed about the hospitality, calling the journey "a continuous ovation to the troops." Many companies, he noted, "were carried through their own towns and villages and surrounded by the eager faces of kinsfolk and neighbors." Nevertheless, Sorrel went on, "there were no desertions or stops."[22]

Desertions, indeed, do seem to have been rare. Stops, however, were not. Many men passed directly through their hometowns, forgoing visits with family members they had not seen for two years; but as would be the case with the Union XI and XII Corps, for many the temptation was too great. Even Longstreet conceded that, with two brigades from South Carolina and four from Georgia, the commanders had "some little trouble in keeping the men on the cars [when] passing by their homes."[23]

On 18 September Col. Axalla John Hoole of the Eighth South Carolina wrote his wife lamenting that about forty men from his regiment stopped when the trains passed through Florence, South Carolina. "I know with *some*," he conceded, "it was too hard a trial to pass," but others had seen their families when on leave a few weeks earlier. Virtually all the men of Company A, he reported, were left behind when the trains pulled out. Hoole remained aboard. "Oh my dear wife," he wrote, "what a trial it was to me to pass so near you and not see you, but it had to be." Two days after writing that letter, Colonel Hoole was killed at Chickamauga.[24]

William Isom of the Fifth South Carolina enjoyed a night at home because of the forceful courtesy of a comrade. In his recollections of the war, Lt. John Daniel McDonnell recalled that when they passed through "Smith's Turnout," Isom's wife was at the station with a baby the father had never seen. "He kissed her and the baby and got back on the train," McDonnell remembered. "I shoved him off with my foot and told him to spend the night and come on the next day." Isom complied and some time later "got up with us all right."[25]

When the trains entered Georgia, members of the Columbus Guards, "a crack company in the days of peace," received permission —or claimed to have—to take a side trip to Columbus. Of course, they were on their own, and one man with two dollars in his pockets later figured he had been "the largest capitalist in the company." Soon the conductor arrived to collect the fares. He was greeted by a group of men armed with Enfield rifles, one of whom announced, "I paid my fare at Gettysburg."

As word spread that the popular outfit was passing through, "at every station the people shoved good things through the windows of the cars to us, without money and without price. Figs, watermelons, cakes, pies, apples, everything one could desire, were thrust on us in profusion." At Macon, the men were invited to supper at Brown's Hotel, but many were too full to accept. The real treat, of course, came at Columbus—twenty-four hours with "no drums, no orders, no bullets," just "kind words, feasting, peace and pleasure" with family members and friends.[26]

Not only were desertions rare, but so were other serious difficulties. Here, too, the Confederate experience paralleled the Union movement that was to follow. Yet the southerners learned, as the Yankees soon would, that it is impossible to move so many men so many miles without a few incidents. One occurred at an idle turpentine distillery somewhere in the Carolinas. Hundreds of barrels of resin were stacked, turpentine covered the ground in many places, and some men from Kershaw's brigade decided a good way to battle the cool of the evening would be to set fire to a few of the barrels. Soon the fire was out of control. Soon after that, the distillery and the buildings were gone. And soon after that, Kershaw "delivered a lecture in which he enjoined the men in [the] future to be more careful of the preservation of private property."[27]

Another incident involved Robertson's Texans, who paid a visit to Paddy's Hollow, a notorious section of Wilmington's waterfront. After indulging their thirsts, many of the men became, as one historian has noted, "boisterous, obnoxious, and abusive." When uniformed lawmen arrived on the scene, the Texans apparently mistook them for Yankees. A battle line of sorts formed, the Rebel Yell pierced the air, and the men charged the constables. The police yielded the field, but only after one suffered two knife wounds and others were badly beaten.[28]

Even more serious was an episode that allegedly involved some of Benning's Georgians. On 10 September Governor Zebulon Vance of North Carolina informed President Davis that members of a Georgia regiment had "destroyed the office of the [Raleigh] Standard newspaper the previous evening." Later that day, Vance, prickly under the best of circumstances, said soldiers passing through Weldon had "indulged in threats of further violence" when they reached Raleigh. "For God's sake," the governor implored, "save us from this state of things." If Davis failed to act, Vance threatened to recall all North Carolina troops "from the field to the defense of their own homes."[29]

The *Raleigh Standard*'s support of the southern cause was considered lukewarm at best. Its editor, William W. Holden, had been a late convert to secession and a frequent critic of the Confederate government. Three weeks after the incident, in a lengthy editorial, Holden said he had heard threats made against him, but "I entertained no serious apprehension that they would be executed." He changed his mind when he and a friend, looking out the window of Holden's house, saw a group of soldiers gather in front of the *Standard* office, located on the same lot as his home. "I immediately retired from my house," Holden recalled, "feeling that I was not safe on the premises."

Meanwhile, some of Holden's friends summoned the governor, who hurried to the scene with a member of his staff and the mayor of Raleigh. "When they arrived," Holden claimed, "the men were engaged . . . in pouring the type in the street, and some of them were trying to pull down the power press. A Maj. Shepherd was called for," Holden continued, who informed the men that the governor was present and ordered them out of the office and into line. They complied, and Vance "reproved them in the strongest and most pointed terms." The men cheered him, and one officer replied, "Governor, we have done what we came to do, and will now retire."

Neither the building nor the presses were seriously damaged, Holden reported. Type, however, was strewn everywhere and pens and other office supplies "mysteriously disappeared." The editor also learned that "some of the mob were engaged [the] next day in showing some old federal postage stamps which I had before the war, as evidence that I was a traitor and in correspondence with the enemy!"

Holden also condemned an attack launched the next day on the *Raleigh State Journal* and an attempted attack on the *Register*, both staunchly Confederate in their leanings, apparently made in retaliation for the incident at the *Standard* office. He did not hesitate, however, to "trace this mob spirit to the course pursued" by the two rival papers, along with the *Richmond Enquirer* and the *Charlotte Bulletin*. All four, he claimed, had "repeatedly called for mob law against the *Standard*."[30]

Two days after the incident, Vance again wired Davis. He reported that orders issued by the president forbidding any troops to enter Raleigh were preserving the peace. Still, he was not entirely satisfied. The governor charged that the attack had been executed "with the knowledge and consent of General Benning, as he remarked to a gentleman an hour or two previous that his men had threatened it." Vance felt it was his duty to "demand that punishment . . . be inflicted on the officers who assisted or countenanced" the mob activity.[31]

Davis turned the matter over to Adj. and Insp. Gen. Samuel Cooper, who dispatched a wire to Benning asking for "a full report of all facts." He added that the request "is not designed to elicit from yourself or the officers of your command any statement which may tend to your personal crimination." Cooper concluded, "It is earnestly hoped that such explanations may be given by the officers concerned as will entirely exonerate them."

Benning replied, supplying the response for which Cooper had "earnestly hoped." After busily arranging transportation details on the evening of the ninth, the brigade commander began, he had gotten some sleep in the railroad yard, his head on a cross-tie. It was only while putting the men aboard the cars for the next leg of the journey that he learned of "the outrage on the printing office." As for Vance's charge, Benning added, "Nothing came to my notice on the way to Raleigh or after we arrived there to excite suspicion that any plot was brewing against the Standard newspaper." If it had, "I should have taken the most rigorous measures to suppress it."

Benning blamed the whole affair on "a party of North Carolinian troops," who were on their way to Salisbury to arrest some deserters. These troops had hitched a ride at Weldon, and Benning had granted permission for them to travel with his brigade. After leaving Raleigh, "this party freely avowed themselves the authors of the deed." Benning conceded that they had "led some of my men into it with them," adding that it had been but a few "unorganized individuals, each acting for and by himself."[32]

Benning's explanation apparently satisfied the authorities in Richmond because no further action was taken. Vance expressed doubts about North Carolinians being present but concluded that Benning's denial of his personal involvement was "satisfactory." Benning's account was later corroborated by yet another Raleigh paper. On 26 September the *Spirit of the Age* reported that four soldiers from the Forty-eighth North Carolina had appeared at its office to confess. "*We* concocted, originated and executed the attack," one of the men reportedly said. The Georgians who went along, the man added, "were on the same train, and heard us arranging our plan and said they would back us in case we met with resistance likely to prove too strong for our forty men."[33]

If Raleigh proved to be an interesting stopping point for at least a few of Longstreet's men, Atlanta was often a lengthy one. The delay was caused in part by the arrival of the eastern troops at the same time that reinforcements from Joseph E. Johnston's forces reached the city from Mississippi. On 12 September, the day that Benning's brigade pulled into Atlanta, Evander McNair and John Gregg's brigades arrived from the West. A traffic jam resulted, which was compounded by a lack of rolling stock. Complicating the situation further, Col. Moses H. Wright, the Confederate officer in command at the Georgia capital, was not certain "if the re-enforcements arriving are to be forwarded on arrival here."[34]

William C. Oates of the Fifteenth Alabama recalled that his regiment was delayed in Atlanta for one day. Capt. Joab Goodson of the Forty-fourth Alabama told his niece that his outfit remained there for two days. The Fiftieth Georgia camped in the public square while awaiting a train north. For some units the wait was a profitable one, allowing them the opportunity to secure badly needed supplies. Sgt. John Dykes Taylor of the Forty-eighth Alabama later wrote that all the men in Law's brigade who needed clothing, shoes, and hats got them. Thanks to the "indefatigable energies" of Col. James Sheffield of the Forty-eighth, Taylor's unit was among those that were well provided. Wright reported that Benning's brigade also stopped "to ration and get shoes for barefooted men."[35]

Early in the afternoon of 16 September, the men of Hood's division began to arrive at their destination. Hood's renowned Texas Brigade, now led by Robertson, was the first to reach Catoosa Platform, near Ringgold, followed shortly by Benning and his Georgians. Law's brigade reached the scene the next day. All three brigades participated as the Battle of Chickamauga got under way on the nineteenth. Hood, arriving "shortly after noon," found a waiting courier with orders from Bragg to report immediately to the front and take charge of the right column. In Longstreet's absence,

Hood assumed command of the corps. Law became division commander, and Sheffield took command of Law's brigade.[36]

Longstreet, along with members of his staff, reached Catoosa that afternoon at about two. Surprised—and a bit peeved—that Bragg had sent no staff officers to greet them, the officers bided their time at the platform for two hours until their horses arrived. Then they started off for their new commander's headquarters, guided by the sounds of the battle. Darkness overtook them, and they took a wrong road, ran into a group of Union pickets, rode quickly away as a volley was fired in their direction, and finally reached Bragg at about 11:00 P.M.

If his first day with the Army of Tennessee had been inauspicious for Longstreet, the next was not. Kershaw and Humphreys arrived that night with their brigades, and on 20 September they joined Robertson, Sheffield, and Benning on the battlefield. All participated in a late morning attack that inadvertently but decisively exploited a gap Rosecrans had created when he ordered an entire division out of line to support his left. The decision, invariably described as "fateful," cost Rosecrans the battle and eventually his career.[37]

It also led to the frantic telegrams that Dana sent to Stanton and to Stanton's midnight council with Lincoln and his cabinet. There is no way of discerning to what extent the Confederate transfer influenced Stanton's thinking as he offered his proposal. Perhaps the irascible war secretary wanted to demonstrate that the Union's rail network was capable of meeting—and exceeding—the Confederate feat. Perhaps he simply desired to get the greatest number of reinforcements he could to Tennessee the fastest way he could. Whatever the motivation, Stanton had assumed a tremendous challenge. As his skeptical late night visitors left the War Department, he went to work to prove that both he and the northern railroads were up to that challenge.

43

3

Plans and Personalities

Stanton did not get any sleep that night; nor, if contemporary reports can be believed, did he get much for the next several nights. He was, as Lincoln had said, "the captain," and the urgency of the situation and the force of his personality caused him to drive himself, and all others associated with the project, relentlessly. At 3:30 A.M. on 24 September he informed Dana, "We have made arrangements to send fifteen thousand infantry under General Hooker from here and will have them in Nashville in five or six days from today with orders to push on immediately whenever General Rosecrans wants them."[1]

About seven hours later the men who would help Stanton fulfill this bold promise started to arrive at the War Department. The secretary of war had summoned some of the nation's most respected railroad officials the previous evening shortly after 11:00, before Lincoln even approved the plan. Telegrams saying simply, "Please come to Washington as quickly as you can," went out to John Work Garrett, president of the Baltimore & Ohio Railroad, Thomas A. Scott, vice-president of the Pennsylvania, and S. M. Felton, president of the Philadelphia, Wilmington & Baltimore line. Garrett was asked to bring with him master of transportation William P. Smith. Colonel McCallum of the Military Railroads would also be on hand for the conference.[2]

Garrett arrived first, reaching the capital at about 10:00 A.M. Forty-three years old, Garrett had been president of the B&O for five years. He would remain at the post for twenty-one more.

The 1850s had been a tumultuous time for America's first common carrier. Four presidents served during a decade that witnessed both triumphs and reverses. In 1852, the B&O had completed

45

construction of its track to the Ohio River, realizing the goal for which it had been chartered in 1827. Net receipts rose accordingly, from $615,000 in 1852 to just over $2 million in 1856. Then the picture suddenly changed. Competition from rival roads and the Panic of 1857 combined to drive receipts down to $1.3 million in 1858.

Dividends decreased accordingly—and some years disappeared altogether. Stockholders were understandably upset. Among them were Garrett and Johns Hopkins, who soon emerged as leaders of the disenchanted. In 1858 their group succeeded in electing Garrett president of the road. "Of huge size," in the words of B&O historian Edward Hungerford, Garrett "usually dominated the men round-about him, both physically and mentally." He immediately set out to increase his line's profits by cutting both wages and personnel and by adjusting rates. The strategy paid off. With the panic still hanging on, the B&O's gross receipts fell by nearly $240,000 in 1859. Garrett's cuts, however, reduced expenses by almost $900,000, and net profits showed an increase of over $600,000.[3]

The positive trend continued, and by the time the guns fired at Fort Sumter, Garrett's efficiency and ability as a railroad executive were beyond doubt. His patriotism, however, was not. Running through Maryland and northern and western Virginia, the B&O main stem lay entirely within slave territory. Garrett himself was a prominent Democrat, and in 1860 he asserted in a Baltimore speech, "It [the B&O] is a Southern line. And if ever necessity should require—which heaven forbid!—it will prove the great bulwark of the border, and a sure agency for home defense." He further urged that "Baltimore should declare her position in the 'irrepressible conflict' threatened and urged by Northern fanaticism."[4]

When that "irrepressible conflict" finally came, it brought with it realities that led Garrett to moderate his views. For one, the main stem, despite passing entirely through slave territory, also passed entirely through Union territory. Although some Marylanders pressed for secession, the state remained loyal, and the portion of Virginia through which the railroad ran was completely within the border of the soon to be created state of West Virginia. Beyond the Ohio River, the B&O's principal connecting lines continued westward through the Union states of Ohio, Indiana, and Illinois. Despite Garrett's emotional claim that his was a "Southern line," his keen business head quickly overcame his heart when war threatened the prosperity of that line. Doubts would persist in some minds for some time, but by 24 September 1863 no one any longer seriously questioned Garrett's devotion to the Union cause.[5]

The secretary of war, who had known Garrett for several years, had served as general counsel for the Central Ohio Railroad, a connecting line that the B&O would eventually acquire, when he was an attorney in Steubenville, Ohio. In that position he came to know Garrett, and the two became friends. Washington's rumor mill held that the railroad president was among the very few men who could "handle" the often obdurate cabinet minister. Stanton evidently had already provided Garrett with some idea of the plan he had in mind. As he boarded the eight o'clock train at Baltimore, Garrett wired the secretary, "Have arranged full information regarding Engines and cars."[6]

Thomas Scott arrived about noon, accompanied by Felton. Like Garrett, Scott had risen quickly in the railroad ranks. Joining the Pennsylvania Railroad in 1850 as the line's representative at Holidaysburg, Pennsylvania, he earned successive promotions to Pittsburgh agent, superintendent of the Western Division, and general superintendent of the entire line. In 1860, at the age of thirty-six, he became vice-president.[7]

When the war broke out, Governor Andrew Curtin of Pennsylvania assigned Scott the task of supervising troop transportation in and out of Harrisburg. His talents soon took him to Washington, where Scott worked for an old friend, Secretary of War Simon Cameron. In August 1861 Scott's role became formal when he assumed the newly created post of assistant secretary of war. Although he mainly worked on railroad matters, Scott's tasks also included ferreting out Confederate spies, organizing and equipping diverse state regiments, and supervising the purchase of arms and supplies.

Scott stayed on when Stanton succeeded Cameron in January 1862. His first assignment under Stanton was the preparation of a detailed report on military transportation that anticipated the creation of the United States Military Railroads. Stanton next dispatched Scott on a two-month western tour. The new war secretary shared President Lincoln's desire for a major offensive in the West. Scott was to determine the number of soldiers available, their location, and what equipment they had. In addition, Stanton wanted Scott to discern what facilities were available in case it became necessary to transport eastern soldiers west and to estimate the time that would be involved. The assistant secretary reported that seventeen hundred men could be transferred from Washington to Pittsburgh each twenty-four hours; Washington to Cincinnati would take seventy-eight hours. "It is an immense undertaking," Scott wrote, "*but it can be done.*"

Scott resigned his government post on 1 June 1862. Pennsylvania Railroad president J. Edgar Thomson was sailing to Europe, and he wanted his vice-president back on the job to oversee things during his absence. There was another factor involved in Scott's decision, however. His tenure under Stanton, who had a tendency to rebuke him over relatively small matters, had not been as pleasant as his service with fellow Pennsylvanian Cameron. The resignation seems to have come as a relief to both Scott and Stanton. Nevertheless, Scott continued to work closely with the secretary of war, and when he again reported to the War Department the relationship between the two men was friendly.[8]

If Scott's relations with Stanton had occasionally been strained, those with Garrett had at times bordered on hostility. These hard feelings, mutually held, began with the rivalry between the two men's railroads, and they were intensified by events during the early months of the war.

Their difficulties grew out of Scott's association with Cameron. The two had met in the 1850s during Scott's corporate ascension. At the time Cameron was serving as a U.S. senator from Pennsylvania. The businessman and the politician soon discovered that their abilities and their connections complemented each other. Throughout the decade the pair bought control of several railroads connecting with the Pennsylvania. Cameron willingly used his political clout to counter their competitors whenever possible.[9]

At the 1860 Republican Convention, Cameron delivered the Pennsylvania delegation to Abraham Lincoln. His reward was the War Department. It was an appointment the new president was reluctant to make, Cameron's reputation for corrupt practices being well known, but the senator's friends lobbied hard, reminding Lincoln's men of the great debt owed by the president-elect.

It soon appeared that Cameron's policies as war secretary were being tempered by personal financial concerns. This seemed particularly obvious in the case of the Northern Central Railroad, a line that ran from Baltimore to Harrisburg, where it connected with the Pennsylvania. Cameron was a director of the line and a large stockholder, his son was also a large stockholder and vice-president as well, his brother-in-law was president, and the Northern Central was commonly known as "Cameron's Road." Moreover, the Camerons had gained control of the road in cooperation with friends Thomson and Scott of the Pennsylvania. When events gave the secretary of war the opportunity to increase the line's traffic at the expense of the rival B&O, he was not long in exploiting it.

On 15 April 1861, President Lincoln declared that a state of rebellion existed and called upon northern governors to supply troops from their states. They were to be sent by rail to Washington, a decision that proved to be fateful. Three major routes into Baltimore were available: the B&O main stem, the Pennsylvania and Northern Central connection, and the Philadelphia, Wilmington, & Baltimore. From there only the B&O's Washington branch continued on into the nation's capital. Thus Baltimore, whose loyalty was hotly in question, became a crucial point. On 19 April, as large numbers of soldiers began to arrive, Baltimore residents with southern leanings rioted. They refused to let the men pass and attempted to ensure that no more would be forwarded by threatening the B&O with destruction and by tearing up as much track as they could.

Cameron responded by ordering out soldiers to guard, not the B&O, but the Northern Central. Railroad and military officials meanwhile devised a detour around Baltimore. Troops would take the Philadelphia, Wilmington, & Baltimore (PW&B) to Perryville, where the Susquehanna River empties into Chesapeake Bay. They would then be ferried to Annapolis. From there the Annapolis & Elk Ridge Railroad would deliver them to Annapolis Junction, where they would board trains for Washington on the B&O's Washington branch. Ignoring B&O officials, Cameron called upon Scott to take charge of the line into Washington.

Despite this treatment, when Scott asked Garrett to supply engines and cars for the transportation of troops, the B&O president offered him all he might need. Hoping to capitalize on his gesture of cooperation, Garrett then sought permission to reopen his line from Baltimore to Washington. Cameron, however, was not in a grateful mood, and he informed Garrett that his request would not be approved until unimpeded transportation of men and supplies through Baltimore was guaranteed.

Meanwhile, Confederate raids on the B&O main stem had shut the line down. With the Mississippi River closed and the Pennsylvania Railroad largely occupied with military traffic, the lack of transportation became an acute problem for farmers and businessmen west of the Ohio. As summer led into fall the clamor to reopen the line grew appreciably. Garrett made political capital of the complaints by offering to bear the entire cost of repairs if only his road could have military protection. He also worked with loyal government officials in Maryland and western Virginia to keep up the pressure. At the same time, Cameron's political enemies were publicizing his interests in the Northern Central. Still, it was late autumn before the secretary of war yielded. By then Garrett's antipathy toward Cameron and his friends with the Pennsylvania Railroad was intense.[10]

Although Samuel Felton accompanied Scott to the War Department, he too had not always enjoyed cordial relations with the vice-president and other officers of the Pennsylvania. President of the Philadelphia, Wilmington, & Baltimore since the early 1850s, Felton had assisted Thomson in coordinating the initial troop movements at the outset of the war. His line prospered as all New York troops passed over the PW&B en route to Washington. This situation changed in May 1861 when Cameron divided this traffic between Felton's road and (to no one's great surprise) the Northern Central. Felton was already upset at having to repair Confederate damage to his railroad at company expense while the War Department footed the bill to fix the Northern Central. This latest development reinforced his opinion that a conspiracy was afoot to benefit Cameron's line at the expense of his own, views he made public in a series of newspaper articles. Felton's writings embarrassed Cameron, and he dispatched Scott to smooth things over. This was no easy task, largely because there was no sound justification for the change of route. Felton was unimpressed with Scott's claim that Cameron wanted the troops sent through Harrisburg so Pennsylvanians could see how well the New England soldiers had been equipped.[11]

Whatever their differences in the past had been, the veteran railroad men put them aside as they gathered at the War Department. Garrett, Smith, Scott, Felton, and McCallum, united by their common cause, spent much of the day studying railroad maps in an attempt to determine the most efficient route. To guide them the group had Scott's 1862 report about the possibility of sending troops westward. His conclusion of its feasibility suggested that the timetable McCallum had promised Lincoln for the movement could be met.[12]

Modifications were necessary, however. The group appears to have determined upon a route to Zanesville, Ohio, rather quickly. From there the most direct line would have been to Cincinnati via the Cincinnati, Wilmington, & Zanesville Railroad. There the troops would have crossed the Ohio and traveled on to Louisville on the Covington & Lexington and the Lexington & Louisville Railroads. The Louisville & Nashville and the Nashville & Chattanooga would have delivered them the remainder of the way.

At 11:20 A.M. Stanton telegraphed R. P. Bowler, president of the Covington & Lexington, to determine the feasibility of this route. Bowler's response was discouraging. His road was five-foot gauge, the same as the L&N, but the Lexington & Louisville was six-foot gauge. This meant neither his line's cars nor those of the L&N could be used over the Lexington & Louisville, and time-consuming unloading and reloading procedures would slow the movement. Smith suggested transporting the men to Cincinnati by rail, then putting them on riverboats for Louisville. It was the dry season, however, and there was no guarantee that the Ohio would remain at a sufficient depth to complete the movement.[13]

The route upon which the group finally decided was circuitous, but it was also reliable, leaving little chance for unwelcome surprises from either nature or the enemy. McCallum's United States Military Railroads would move the two corps from their positions in Virginia to Washington. From there they would take the Baltimore & Ohio through Maryland and West Virginia to Benwood, just south of Wheeling on the Ohio River. A collection of local lines would transport the troops west across Ohio and on to Indianapolis. There they would turn south on the Jeffersonville Railroad, which would take them to Jeffersonville, Indiana. Once again they would cross the Ohio, this time to Louisville, Kentucky. The Louisville & Nashville would transport the men from one terminus to the other, and the Nashville & Chattanooga would deliver them to their destination, Bridgeport, Alabama, about thirty miles from Chattanooga and Rosecrans's besieged army.

McCallum would be in charge of the first part of the movement, along the military line, and would have official responsibility for the entire operation. Garrett, assisted by Smith, was to take control at Washington and supervise operations not only along the B&O but all the way to Jeffersonville. Scott would head immediately for Louisville and superintend the movement from there to Bridgeport. Felton's part was limited to helping supply rolling stock for the movement. Maj. Gen. Joseph Hooker, former commander of the Army of the Potomac, would be in command of the two corps selected to make the transfer.

The meeting broke up late that afternoon, and the telegraph wires began to hum with orders and instructions. General Halleck had already put his part of the operation in motion, wiring Meade at 2:30 A.M. to ask if he had "positively determined to make any immediate movement." If not, he was to prepare the XI and XII Corps to be sent to Washington by the morning of the twenty-fifth with five days' cooked rations. Meade replied that he contemplated no immediate movement, adding disingenuously that "though until your telegram [arrived] the decision was not positive." He noted that the XII Corps was on picket duty at the front and could probably not reach Washington as quickly as Halleck had ordered.

At 9:30, after consultation with the president, Halleck directed Meade to prepare the two corps for the transfer "as conditionally ordered before." Fifteen minutes later, Halleck made the message clearer. "It is intended by my last dispatch," the general in chief explained, "that the Eleventh and Twelfth Corps are positively to be sent here with the least possible delay. Every effort must be made to have them ready to-morrow morning." General Meade replied that he would do all in his power to comply.[14]

Meade was true to his word. Orders immediately went out to Maj. Gen. Oliver Otis Howard, commanding the XI Corps, and to XII Corps commander Maj. Gen. Henry Warner Slocum. Howard was to notify officials of the United States Military Railroads at Alexandria where the trains should be to pick up his troops. The

XI Corps would have little traveling to do because it was already assigned to guard the line of the Orange & Alexandria. Meade informed Slocum that the I Corps would relieve his command. Once it was relieved, the XII Corps should fall back to Brandy Station, where it would take the trains to Alexandria to begin the journey.[15]

Halleck followed up his morning messages to Meade with an early afternoon dispatch informing him that the artillery of the two corps was to be transferred with them. No cavalry would go. Halleck then wired Brig. Gen. Benjamin Franklin Kelley, commander of the Department of West Virginia, that "detachments of troops" would soon be sent west over the B&O. Kelley was to "take all possible precautions to protect the road from rebel raids." He also received orders to close the saloons at all principal stations along the way. Finally, the general in chief sent word to Rosecrans that help was on the way. "The government deems it very important," he admonished, "that Chattanooga be held till re-enforcements arrive."[16]

The secretary of war, meanwhile, was dispatching wires, assisted by his able assistant, Peter H. Watson. Stanton informed Brig. Gen. J. T. Boyle at Louisville that Scott was on his way and asked Boyle to have the managers of the Louisville & Nashville, the Kentucky Central, and the Nashville & Chattanooga Railroads there to consult with him. Q.M. Gen. Montgomery Meigs, who went west after Rosecrans's defeat to inspect supply lines, was at Nashville. Stanton directed this capable officer to report the per diem capacity of the Louisville & Nashville and to do whatever he could "to organize and augment it [the L&N] within the next five days to the utmost extent." The war secretary was indefatigable. On the evening of the twenty-fourth, Meade wired Halleck to ask if the departing men should take any more than the forty rounds of ammunition in their cartridge boxes. Halleck was home for the evening, but Stanton, still on duty, replied that forty rounds would be sufficient.[17]

Garrett, too, was busy, making sure that no one connected with the B&O missed a single detail. On the twenty-fifth, a flood of telegrams poured from his Baltimore office, demonstrating that the management techniques his line had developed during the previous decade could be marshaled for military use. Virtually every officer of the company had a part to play. To Thatcher Perkins, master of machinery, he sent instructions "to carefully examine locomotives and cars" and "see that the most reliable engines and careful engineer men are selected for this service." Master of the road J. L. Wilson received orders to "let all bridges & other structures, as well as parts of the road dangerous from slips, etc. be most carefully guarded." Even his veteran master of transportation was the recipient of some last-minute advice from Garrett. All trains should be equipped, the president reminded Smith, with signals, lamps, bell ropes, and other "necessary details." Brakes must be carefully checked. Finally, Garrett urged, "Let no engine be overheated. Moderate loads and regular running will accomplish the best results. Especially avoid fast speed at any point upon the line."

The B&O president let nothing escape his vigilance. Later in the day he again wired Perkins. Five damaged passenger cars from a wreck along the line had "attract[ed] considerable remark from passengers." Considering the large number of military passengers the road would be carrying in the next few days, Garrett wondered, "Can you not clear up this wreck at once?"[18]

Garrett also detailed trusted subordinates to supervise various portions of the movement. Alexander Diffey, general supervisor of trains, would oversee the operation from Washington to Piedmont, West Virginia. J. P. Willard would take over at Piedmont and see things through to Benwood. Wheeling agent J. B. Ford would be responsible for the transfer of the troops across the Ohio and for reloading them at Bellaire. Lewis M. Cole, general ticket agent, would then be in charge all the way to Jeffersonville. Cole also received the title of aide to General Hooker.

As master of transportation, Smith was the officer most familiar with the entire line of the B&O. He therefore would supervise the portion of the operation for which the company was responsible, keeping Garrett informed of the progress. It was also up to Smith to see that sufficient cars were secured and delivered to McCallum for the military lines. Diffey, Willard, Ford, and Cole all received captaincies from the War Department. Smith was offered one but declined, feeling his responsibilities entitled him to a higher grade.[19]

As if handling the details along his own line was not enough, Garrett also had to make arrangements with the railroads that would carry the men beyond the Ohio and with connecting roads that would be called upon to supply cars. Hugh J. Jewett, president of the Central Ohio Railroad, was told to concentrate 125 passenger cars and 50 baggage cars at Bellaire by 10:00 P.M. on 26 September and to repeat that performance the next two days. "This is a vitally important movement," Garrett wired, "and I am directed to inform you that all business must be suspended that will in any way interfere with the prompt transportation of these troops and equipment." A similar message went to Dillard Ricketts, president of the Jeffersonville Railroad. He was to have cars waiting at Indianapolis on 27, 28, and 29 September. Presidents L. M. Hubby of the Cleveland & Columbus, J. M. McCullough of the Cleveland & Pittsburgh, S. L. L'Hommedieu of the Cincinnati, Hamilton, & Dayton, W. H. Clement of the Little Miami, and John Newman of the Indiana Central all received requests for rolling stock from Garrett.[20]

The man who had to make the most immediate plans was Colonel McCallum. Stanton had placed the former Erie president in charge of "all matters of transportation of the Eleventh and Twelfth Corps," adding that "all officers of whatsoever grade will obey your instructions." In addition to his overall duties, McCallum would be specifically responsible for getting the two corps loaded and started toward Washington and the B&O.

Assisting him was John Henry Devereux, whose official title was "superintendent of the military railroads which terminate at Alexandria, with their connecting roads." A native of Massachusetts, born in 1832, Devereux had been associated with various Ohio railroads before becoming resident engineer for the Tennessee &

Alabama in 1852. He held that position until the war began and assumed his duties with the United States Military Railroads in 1862. Devereux's main responsibility had been with the Orange & Alexandria, and his familiarity with that line made him a valuable assistant to McCallum.[21]

With the railroad men employing their specialized talents to arrange the details of the transfer and with Stanton overseeing things, the military leaders had few responsibilities. President Lincoln issued an order authorizing Hooker to "take military possession of all railroads, with their cars, locomotives, plants, and equipments, that may be necessary for the execution of the military operation committed to his charge." In reality, Hooker could do little more from his headquarters in Washington than relay information from the War Department and railroad officials and give orders to his corps commanders on matters so basic that Howard and Slocum had undoubtedly figured them out for themselves. No more equipment should be taken than was necessary. Officers should reduce their number of horses to the smallest limit. Men were to be placed on the cars "uniformly and comfortably." Guards must be posted on the cars. Care and cleanliness of arms and equipment should not be neglected, and horses should be regularly watered and fed.[22]

Concern for the comfort of his men and an energetic attention to detail so extreme as to annoy subordinates were two traits indicating that Maj. Gen. Joseph Hooker had changed little during his two and one-half years in the Union army. Born in 1814 in Hadley, Massachusetts, Hooker had graduated with the United States Military Academy's Class of 1837. His grades were high, but a large number of demerits dropped Hooker to twenty-ninth in the fifty-member class that included William H. French, John Sedgwick, Braxton Bragg, Jubal Early, and John Pemberton.

The young second lieutenant was assigned to the First U.S. Artillery and sent to Florida to fight the Seminoles, then on to Tennessee to help drive out the Cherokees. In July 1838 Hooker's outfit moved north to Vermont. They soon found themselves in Maine, where a border dispute with New Brunswick threatened for a time to escalate into war. Hooker became adjutant of his regiment in October 1841. For the next four years he traveled between First Artillery headquarters in Portsmouth, New Hampshire, and posts scattered throughout New England, performing a variety of administrative chores.

On 13 May 1846, prodded by an eager President James Polk, Congress, with some reluctance, declared war on Mexico. By then Hooker and the First Artillery were stationed at Pensacola, Florida, where the ambitious lieutenant waited for an assignment that would give him the opportunity to achieve glory in combat. It came in the form of an appointment to the post of chief of staff for brigade commander Thomas Lyon Hamer. Hooker headed from the Gulf Coast to the Rio Grande.

He saw action almost immediately. Hamer's brigade was among those serving under Gen. Zachary Taylor in the fierce Battle of Monterrey. They were in the thick of the battle, fighting hard but gaining little ground in the face of withering artillery fire from the Mexican forces. Hooker received high praise from his brigade commander for his gallantry as well as favorable mention in Taylor's report. He also earned a brevet promotion to captain.

On 25 April 1847, Hooker became chief of staff for Brig. Gen. George Cadwallader, whose brigade was about to head for Vera Cruz to accompany Gen. Winfield Scott in his march to Mexico City. Cadwallader's command caught up with Scott on 8 July at Puebla. Along the way Hooker led an attack that captured a Mexican fortification and some heights adjacent to the vital National Bridge over the Antiqua River. In the process he also captured another brevet promotion and was now Major Hooker.

A new assignment came as well, assistant adjutant general to Maj. Gen. Gideon Pillow. A "political general" and former law partner of President Polk, Pillow wisely deferred to Hooker on many military matters, much to the relief of General Scott.

When the American forces successfully stormed the heights at Chapultepec on 13 September 1847, Mexican general Antonio López de Santa Anna withdrew from Mexico City, and the fighting was over. Hooker was actively involved in this battle as well, leading two regiments that captured outlying breastworks early in the fight. His third brevet promotion of the war followed, making Hooker a lieutenant colonel. For the ambitious soldier the Mexican War had been an exciting and successful experience.[23]

Hooker found that the peacetime army did not hold his attention the way wartime service had. Late in 1848 he went to California to assume the post of adjutant general of the Pacific Division. Boredom and pay much lower than the inflated civilian wages in booming California led him to resign his commission in 1853. He spent the next eight years engaged in ranching and the timber business, dabbling from time to time in Democratic politics and gambling. It was an adequate existence but hardly sufficient to challenge Hooker's talents or satisfy his dreams. Looming on the horizon was an opportunity that would. Soon after Fort Sumter fell, he headed back east.

Hooker encountered a serious roadblock to his ambition in the person of his former commanding general. At the close of the Mexican War, Hooker had testified in behalf of General Pillow when Scott accused Hooker's immediate superior of disloyalty. Scott, now the commander of U.S. forces, had not forgotten, and Hooker arrived in Washington to find no positions available for him.

According to one account, Hooker eventually went over Scott's head and secured an interview with President Lincoln. The California officer had witnessed the Battle of First Manassas, a debacle for the Union cause. Frustrated by his many rebuffs, Hooker reportedly informed the president that "I am a damned sight better general than you, sir, had on that field." The story may be apocryphal, but the confidence it revealed, as well the willingness to criticize superior officers, would become Hooker trademarks. Apparently his spirit and candor impressed the president. On 31 July 1861, Lincoln sent Hooker's nomination for the position of brigadier general of United States Volunteers to the Senate, and it was approved. The boastful officer now had but to prove himself.[24]

He did. After spending an uneventful fall and winter of 1861–62 on the lower Potomac, Hooker's command joined McClellan in his Peninsular Campaign. At Williamsburg they endured heavy fire, and their general earned a reputation for aggressive tactics and calmness under fire. He earned a nickname as well. The commonly accepted story is that a newspaper account of the Battle of Williamsburg bore the headline "Fighting-Joe Hooker," and in the retelling, the hyphen disappeared. Whether true or not, the name stuck, often to Hooker's chagrin.

Hooker's star rose as he performed capably in the Seven Days' Battles and at Second Manassas. Following the latter battle, Hooker assumed command of the III Corps, Army of Virginia, which soon became the I Corps, Army of the Potomac. After fighting hard at South Mountain, the I Corps was ordered to make the initial morning attack at the Battle of Antietam. It was Hooker's corps, on the Union right, against that of Thomas J. "Stonewall" Jackson, and it was a horrible spectacle as the blue- and gray-coated soldiers engaged in a gigantic slugging match. The battle swayed back and forth most of the morning, and when it was over Hooker concluded, "It was never my fortune to witness a more bloody, dismal battle field." Hooker remained in the thick of the fight until a bullet wound to the foot put him out of commission.

Hooker took nearly two months recovering from his wound, rejoining the army on 11 November. Four days earlier Gen. Ambrose Burnside had succeeded McClellan as commander of the Army of the Potomac. Burnside reorganized the army into three "grand divisions" of two corps each. Hooker became commander of the Center Grand Division, which consisted of the III and V Corps.

What followed was a disaster. On 13 December 1863, Burnside directed his army against the well-entrenched Army of Northern

Maj. Gen. Joseph Hooker, commander, XI and XII Army Corps. (Courtesy
Military Order of the Loyal Legion, Massachusetts Commandery, the U.S.
Army Military History Institute.)

Virginia at the Battle of Fredericksburg. The battle was little more than a slaughter, and Hooker's two corps were in the thick of it. Hooker was extremely critical of his commanding officer after the battle, but it was not simply hindsight. He had attempted to persuade Burnside to abandon the effort before sending the Center Grand Division into the fray. Still, his words were harsh beyond the bounds of professionalism, adding greatly to a reputation for indiscretion which Hooker had already earned.

In the weeks following the battle, Hooker visited Washington and engaged in still more loose talk. He spoke of the terrible job Burnside was doing, of how much better he could do, and even of the desirability of a dictator to run the government. When word of all this reached Burnside, he attempted to have Hooker dismissed from the service. Burnside delivered an order to that effect, along with his resignation, to Lincoln. The president's choice was simple: approve the order or accept the resignation. Lincoln opted for the latter.[25]

On 26 January 1863, Hooker realized the goal for which he had worked so hard and schemed so ruthlessly. In giving him command of the Army of the Potomac, Lincoln also presented the general with a now famous letter. The president acknowledged that his new commander was "a brave and skillful soldier." His self-confidence was a "valuable" quality, and so, "within reasonable limits," was his ambition. In his treatment of Burnside, however, Hooker had done "a great wrong to the country, and to a most meritorious and honorable brother officer."

As for his talk about the desirability of a dictator, "of course it was not for this, but in spite of it, that I have given you the command." Only successful generals could set up dictators, Lincoln reminded him. "What I now ask you," the commander in chief implored, "is military success, and I will risk the dictatorship." The president promised his support and that of the government and concluded, "Beware of rashness, but with energy, and sleepless vigilance, go forward, and give us victories."[26]

Energy and sleepless vigilance characterized Hooker's actions during the next four months. The commanding general worked hard and quite successfully to improve his army's sagging morale. Drills, reviews, and other duties kept the men busy. Better food and improved sanitary conditions reduced the rate of sickness dramatically. Administrative changes included forming the cavalry, which had been scattered among various units, into a single corps. All army corps received distinctive badges, a move designed to enhance unit pride and loyalty. Finally, Hooker increased security to make it more difficult for the enemy to gain information about the army's plans, and he formed a Bureau of Military Information to help him find out more about the Confederates' plans.[27]

After accomplishing all these feats, Hooker fashioned a strategy to bring Robert E. Lee and his Army of Northern Virginia to their doom. Even Hooker's severest critics among historians concede that the plan was excellent, and even his staunchest supporters have been forced to admit that Hooker's failure to execute it was a grave and unconscionable error. Civil War students are familiar with the story of how, by near flawless planning and execution, Hooker placed some seventy-five thousand soldiers on Lee's rear by the evening of 30 April 1863. They are equally familiar with the way Hooker then froze the army in its tracks, throwing away all the advantages he had gained, and how Lee and Jackson ruthlessly exploited Hooker's malaise with Jackson's daring flank attack on 2 May.[28]

After his failure at Chancellorsville, Hooker's days as army commander were clearly numbered. He resigned on 28 June following a series of disputes with Halleck. His future did not appear bright, as precedent indicated that Hooker would follow the other former commanders of the eastern armies into virtual oblivion. He spent most of the next three months in Washington. There he impatiently awaited an assignment, talking to reporters, politicians, and anyone else who would listen.[29]

The appointment to the command of the XI and XII Corps was a step down for a general who had recently headed the country's most famous (though not most successful) army. Nevertheless, it was an opportunity for command and one that Hooker grabbed enthusiastically. He quickly realized, however, how drastically his status had fallen. When Hooker sent a telegram on 25 September to the quartermaster at St. Louis to arrange for transportation at Nashville, Stanton promptly suspended the message. Hooker might command the two corps, but the secretary of war was in control of the operation.[30]

The general was left to vent his energy by issuing the innocuous orders that went out to his corps commanders. It is doubtful that Howard and Slocum were any more enthusiastic about their commander's messages than Stanton had been. Both men were less than eager to serve under Hooker again. Each had been present at Chancellorsville, and each had come away with unpleasant memories.

Chancellorsville had been particularly horrible for Howard, whose XI Corps bore the brunt of Jackson's sledgehammer flank attack. Born in Maine in 1830, Oliver Otis Howard was an 1850 graduate of Bowdoin College in Brunswick and an 1854 graduate of West Point, where he ranked fourth in his class. Peacetime service in New York, Florida, and Maine followed. Howard returned to West Point in 1857 and was teaching mathematics there when the war broke out. A devout Christian, the young lieutenant had considered leaving the army for the ministry. The attack on Fort Sumter changed his mind, and on 29 May 1861, Colonel Howard assumed command of the Third Maine Volunteers.

His West Point background helped Howard earn command of a brigade under Gen. Irvin McDowell before the Battle of First Manassas. At the battle his command failed in an afternoon attack on Henry House Hill but performed well in its baptism of fire.

In early September Howard received a brigadier's commission and a new brigade in McClellan's Army of the Potomac. The following 1 June, at the Battle of Fair Oaks, Howard was in front of two advancing regiments when Confederate bullets struck his right elbow and forearm. Doctors amputated the arm between the

Maj. Gen. Oliver Otis Howard, commander, XI Army Corps. (Courtesy Military Order of the Loyal Legion, Massachusetts Commandery, the U.S. Army Military History Institute.)

shoulder and the elbow, and the general returned home to Maine, where he convalesced until late August.

Howard next saw action at Antietam, leading a brigade in John Sedgwick's division of Edwin Sumner's II Corps. When Sedgwick was seriously wounded in the fierce fight for the West Wood, Howard assumed command of the division. He retained it after the battle, leading the division at Fredericksburg. There, serving in Sumner's grand division, his performance won praise from his superiors.[31]

In January 1863, Howard was rewarded for his efforts with promotion to major general. Two months later he replaced Franz Sigel as commander of the XI Corps. The thirty-two-year-old general had reached another cherished goal, but the appointment did not sit well with his new command. The XI Corps, containing a large contingent of German American soldiers, had adored Sigel, and the men felt Howard's elevation had come at the expense of their popular commander. In addition, Howard's pious style contrasted sharply with that of the liberal-minded Germans under his command. Under the best of circumstances it was a questionable mix. Coming at the start of a major campaign, the joining of Howard and the XI Corps was a risky move.

The XI Corps was posted at the extreme right of Hooker's army at Chancellorsville. There, at dusk on 2 May, Jackson struck. It was the crowning achievement of Stonewall's military career, and the final one, as fire from his own men in the dark wilderness left him mortally wounded. The effect on Howard's corps was devastating. Only two regiments had been posted to refuse the right flank. The Confederates quickly rolled them up and sent virtually the entire corps fleeing in panic. Howard courageously rode forward to stem the tide, but the situation was beyond anyone's control.

After the battle, Hooker was quick to cite the performance of the XI Corps as a major factor in his defeat. The commanding general had sent word to Howard the morning of the attack to see to the defense of his right flank. Howard claimed he had never received the message. This point has been debated since, but historians have found enough evidence in the actions (and inactions) of both generals to make Hooker and Howard equally culpable for the debacle that followed. Most have added, however, that Jackson's flank attack, although devastating to one corps, was not enough to let Hooker explain away the final outcome of the battle. Whatever the facts may have been, the events of early May weighed heavily upon both generals as they started west some five months later.[32]

The commander of the XII Corps was also thinking about Chancellorsville—and about General Hooker—as he received orders to report to his former commanding general. Henry Warner Slocum was born in 1827 at Delphi, New York. An 1852 graduate of West Point, where he ranked seventh in his class, he battled the Seminoles in Florida before resigning from the service in 1856. Slocum spent the remainder of the decade in Syracuse, where he engaged in the practice of law and politics.

When the war began, Slocum resumed his military career, assuming command of the Twenty-seventh New York Infantry in May 1861. The colonel and his regiment were in the thick of the fighting at First Manassas, and Slocum received a wound to his left thigh. He was home recovering when, on 9 August 1861, he received a brigadier's commission.

Returning to duty the following month, Slocum was given command of the Second Brigade of William B. Franklin's division, which was soon assigned to Irvin McDowell's corps of the Army of the Potomac. The following May, during the Peninsular Campaign, Franklin became the commander of the VI Corps, and Slocum assumed command of one of his divisions. He saw a great deal of action during the Seven Days' Battles that followed. On 4 July, Slocum was promoted to major general.

The division saw its next serious action in the Antietam Campaign. Although only slightly involved in the battle, Slocum's men helped set the stage for the showdown when, on 14 September,

Maj. Gen. Henry Warner Slocum, commander, XII Army Corps. (Courtesy Military Order of the Loyal Legion, Massachusetts Commandery, the U.S. Army Military History Institute.)

they made a heroic bayonet charge that cleared Crampton's Gap of Confederates.

On 15 October 1862, Slocum became commanding general of the XII Corps, formerly the II Corps of the Army of Virginia. He succeeded Gen. Joseph K. F. Mansfield, who had commanded the corps for only a week before being mortally wounded at Antietam. Slocum's corps spent the remainder of autumn at Harpers Ferry, moving to Fairfax Court House in mid-December to assist in the defense of Washington. It joined the Army of the Potomac after the Battle of Fredericksburg.[33]

At the Battle of Chancellorsville, Slocum had command of Hooker's right wing. (In addition to his own corps, this included Howard's XI and George G. Meade's V.) Slocum's corps made a bold stand against Jackson's men after the Confederates had demolished Howard's command. Throughout the evening Slocum sent messengers to headquarters requesting ammunition and reinforcements for his desperate force. Instead, when Slocum ordered John W. Geary, commander of the Second Division, to retire from his dangerously exposed position, Hooker soon appeared and ordered Geary back into the breach.[34]

Like Howard, therefore, Slocum found service under Hooker a disagreeable assignment; but while Howard held his tongue, Slocum made his feelings quite clear. On 25 September the unhappy general sent his resignation to Lincoln. "My opinion of General Hooker both as an officer and a gentleman," Slocum informed the president, "is too well known to make it necessary for me to refer to it in this communication." Slocum nevertheless made it clear that his opinion of "Fighting Joe" was so low that "it would be degrading in me to accept any position under him."[35]

The harried commander in chief refused to accept the resignation. Instead he sent a wire to Rosecrans, informing him of the poor relations between the two generals. "Therefore let me beg, almost enjoin upon you," the president wrote, "that on their reaching you, you will make a transposition by which General Slocum with his corps may pass from under the command of Gen. Hooker and Gen. Hooker, in turn, receive some other equal force." It was a request that would not be honored until well after Rosecrans had departed the scene.[36]

The message to Rosecrans came after a visit to the White House by Slocum, who received a promise from the president that he would be separated from Hooker. Lincoln's personal secretary, John Hay, had been present. In his diary he described the general as "peevish, irritable, [and] fretful." Hay wrote, "Slocum's hostility is very regrettable," adding, "Hooker does not speak unkindly of him while [Slocum] never mentions Hooker but to attack him." According to Hay, Hooker attributed Slocum's attitude to "his digestive apparatus being out of repair."[37]

Howard also paid a call at the White House. His visit was more pleasant than Slocum's, but he did receive some military advice from the president. Pulling down a map and pointing to the Cumberland Gap, Lincoln asked, "General, can't you go through here and seize Knoxville?" He spoke of the mountaineers of eastern Tennessee and asserted, "They are loyal there, they are loyal!"[38]

Hooker's last visit with Lincoln came on 27 September, the day before he left his Washington headquarters to catch up with his new command. Hay accompanied the departing general to the Soldiers' Home. "I hope they give him a fair show," Hay wrote, quoting Lincoln as saying, "Whenever trouble arises I can always rely on Hooker's magnanimity." The president asked Hooker to write to him and, according to some accounts, urged the general, who had a reputation for hard drinking, to avoid "Bourbon" County Kentucky.[39]

West to the Ohio

The month of September 1863 had not been a particularly active one for the men of the XI and XII Corps, Army of the Potomac. While the former outfit remained well behind the rest of the army, guarding the line of communications, the latter was primarily engaged in picket duty along the banks of the Rappahannock. There was some sparring between Lee's and Meade's armies, but mainly there was just the monotony of camp life.

From time to time a division was required to witness the execution of a deserter. On those occasions the offender would be marched to his freshly dug grave, stood behind a new pine coffin, and blindfolded. The firing squad would then take aim and fire as the men looked on. To some these affairs "looked too much like murder." To others they were a sad necessity. In at least one case the sentence followed a third offense, this one "in the face of the enemy." A New York soldier concluded that in this particular instance, "It was deemed necessary, therefore, to make an example." When the work of the firing squad was done, the offender's clothing would be opened to make the wounds visible and the men made to march past the body as a way of making certain that the point was not lost. "Then the bands," according to a soldier recalling one occasion, "which had played dead marches in the assembling, struck up quick step tunes and we marched away to camp by lively music."[1]

On 24 September the men got their first hint that a different sort of diversion was about to take place when orders came to draw eight days' rations. Some had heard reports of the fighting at Chickamauga, and a few made accurate guesses as to what was afoot. They were lost, however, in a sea of rumors that placed the destination all the way from the Atlantic coast to Mobile and on to Texas.

Col. Daniel Craig McCallum, superintendent, United States Military Railroads. (Courtesy Military Order of the Loyal Legion, Massachusetts Commandery, the U.S. Army Military History Institute.)

Meanwhile, one of the few men who knew for certain where the troops were headed was facing his first serious challenge in getting them there. Soon after reaching Alexandria, Colonel McCallum learned from General Howard that his corps numbered seventy-five hundred men, two thousand more than McCallum had originally understood it to have. The B&O had agreed to furnish 140 cars by 25 September. Now some 60 more would be required for the additional men, plus an extra 50 stock cars for regimental and artillery horses. The colonel urged the B&O's master of transportation to send them forward as quickly as possible. In the meantime McCallum made such arrangements as he could to speed things along. He directed Howard to march his men to Manassas Junction, where there was ample side track to load them quickly, and to send his artillery to Alexandria, which had the best facilities for loading heavy freight. A message from Smith promising 200 cars by noon on the twenty-fifth gave McCallum room for optimism.[2]

Indeed, the loading of the XI Corps went smoothly. All but seventeen hundred of the men were sent out on 25 September. The remainder started west beginning at 6:00 the next morning. By early afternoon all were on their way. Following them later would be camp and garrison equipment, artillery, and horses.[3]

The men were riding in boxcars, about forty per car, most with boards provided as seats. Officers traveled in passenger cars. Most trains were twenty to thirty cars in length, generally bearing two regiments. Artillery pieces went on flatcars, and additional boxcars transported commissary stores, forage, and other supplies. Officials intended for stock cars to be used exclusively for transporting horses, but a few soldiers ended up in them. Unfortunately for the passengers, most had not been cleaned after last being used.[4]

The men riding on the stock cars may not have agreed, but the quick departure of the XI Corps suggested that the organizational techniques the railroads had developed during the previous decade were paying off. Still, the extra cars quickly forwarded by the B&O did not cover the needs of the XII Corps, and Slocum's command was delayed. As they waited, the corps commander issued a general order designed to ensure that all would go smoothly once his command got under way. "Division[,] Brigade[,] and Independent Commanders," Slocum asserted, "[would] be held responsible for the safe conduct of their men." An officer would be placed in command of each train, with a subordinate officer posted on each car. "The most stringent measures" were to be taken "to prevent desertion and straggling."[5]

Slocum's division commanders followed his lead with supplemental orders of their own. Heading the First Division was Brig. Gen. Alpheus S. Williams. A Connecticut native, born in 1810, Williams studied law at Yale but devoted much of his early life to spending a seventy-five-thousand-dollar inheritance. In 1836, out of cash and in need of a career, he located in Detroit, where he served as probate judge and postmaster and also worked as a bank president and newspaper publisher. Meanwhile, Williams rose through the ranks of a local militia company. The outfit departed for service in the Mexican War in 1847 but arrived after the conflict had ended. They performed garrison duty during the winter of 1848, and this limited service earned Williams a reputation as an able military administrator.

In August 1861 Williams received a presidential appointment as a brigadier general of volunteers. He took command of the First Division when the XII Corps joined the Army of the Potomac in September 1862. One of the least pretentious general officers in the Union army, Williams was not much for excessive verbiage. He added little more to Slocum's orders than a directive calling for morning and evening roll calls.[6]

The Second Division commander, Brig. Gen. John White Geary, went further. Born 30 December 1819 in Westmoreland County, Pennsylvania, Geary studied engineering at Jefferson (later Washington and Jefferson) College and secured employment with the Allegheny Portage Railroad. As a lieutenant colonel he served with the Second Pennsylvania Infantry in the Mexican War. A presidential appointment as postmaster of San Fransisco followed, as did a term as mayor of the city.

Geary retired to Pennsylvania in 1850 to pursue a career in agriculture. He returned to public service in 1856 when President Franklin Pierce asked him to serve as governor of the Kansas Territory. The Kansas-Nebraska Act, calling for popular sovereignty on the slavery issue, had produced a virtual civil war in the territory. Two previous governors had been driven out before Geary arrived on the scene. The Pennsylvanian served ably and courageously and remained at the thankless post for over a year and a half.

After resigning in March 1857, Geary again retired to his farm, remaining four years before war called him back to the service of his country. Soon after Fort Sumter, he organized the Twenty-eighth Pennsylvania Infantry Regiment. The outfit was augmented when Charles Knap of Pittsburgh donated four guns. The regiment organized an artillery battery and named it in honor of the donor. Among the battery's early duties was guarding the line of the B&O.

Geary was promoted to brigadier general in April 1862. That October he assumed command of Slocum's Second Division and was wounded twice. His reputation as a soldier was unspectacular but solid. Ever the politician, he announced to his men, "The Corps of which you are a part has for veteran attributes been selected for a special and responsible trust. The high compliment belongs to each and every one of you." Geary urged them to "forget not the pride of your Organization and you will not abuse the unbounded confidence thus placed in you." Finally, Geary asked his command to "look forward and scorn retrogression."[7]

How many men in Geary's division could define "retrogression" is not known; but even those eager to scorn it could not do so as long as they were waiting for cars to start them on their way. The B&O was ahead of its quota, but the shortage of rolling stock was still so acute that most XII Corps outfits endured a lengthy wait for transportation. McCallum pressed Smith for more cars, and Smith replied on the twenty-sixth that he had sent 390 already even though

Brig. Gen. John White Geary, commander, Second Division, XII Army Corps. (Courtesy Military Order of the Loyal Legion, Massachusetts Commandery, the U.S. Army Military History Institute.)

his company had another day under the original agreement to supply 420. Stanton, meanwhile, urged his railroad superintendent to "crowd the B and O . . . every hour with a fresh telegram."[8]

Most of the men were now waiting at Bealeton Station, ten miles closer to Washington than Brandy Station. McCallum had instructed Slocum to march his corps the extra distance when he discovered that there was very little room for switching trains at Brandy. Gen. A. A. Humphreys, Meade's chief of staff, sent word that the march must be made at night because the enemy had already detected the movement to Brandy. The men were not aware of the shortage of cars or the reason for the march, and after "trudging ten miles, in sight of the railroad all the way," one was left to wonder, "If the cars could carry us 1,186 miles, why not the other ten?"[9]

The situation at Bealeton did not improve the men's dispositions. On 28 September, after a forty-eight-hour wait, Sebastian Duncan of the Thirteenth New Jersey wrote his mother and offered a comparison. "I suppose in the course of your life," Duncan began, "you have experienced some of the unpleasantness connected with waiting for cars or stage coaches. Even for a few hours or minutes in a pleasant depot[, t]his is dull business, but when the hours are stretched into days & nights, [in such] circumstances as we are it becomes tenfold worse." Trains had left at three-hour intervals for the past two days with "bands playing and troops cheering" as they started away, but entire brigades remained. Duncan and his comrades did not have to wait much longer, however. At 1:30 P.M. on the twenty-eighth Stanton received word from McCallum that all troops had left.[10]

As they began their journey, the men took time to reflect on the land and the army they were leaving. Their feelings were clearly mixed. Sgt. David Nichol of Independent Battery E, Pennsylvania Light Artillery, wrote home: "This news was hailed with delight by all. Any place but Virginia. It will just be the making of this Army, this change will put new life in the men & I think in this new field of operation everything will go on better."[11] The men harbored few regrets about leaving their old adversaries, Robert E. Lee and his Army of Northern Virginia. Nevertheless, the Army of the Potomac had become their home, and many expressed regrets about leaving it while important work still lay ahead.

This ambivalence was especially acute in the Twenty-seventh Indiana Volunteer Infantry of the XII Corps. The only Hoosier regiment involved in the transfer, the Twenty-seventh had made a good record for itself in the East. Two of its noncoms had discovered Lee's famous "lost order" that led to the Battle of Antietam, and the regiment lost two hundred men in the fight that followed. They had also fought hard at Chancellorsville, where they helped stem the rout in the wake of Jackson's flank attack, and at Gettysburg, where the outfit lost one-third of its men during a futile charge against Confederates occupying Culp's Hill.

Yet, despite its achievements and sacrifices, the Twenty-seventh never felt wholly accepted by the Army of the Potomac. "Because we were from the 'wild and wooly West,'" one later recalled, "pronounced Indiana 'Ean-dy-an-ny,' spoke of being 'raised,' made liberal use of the word 'heap' as an adjective of quantity and, in general, sharpened our a's and slurred our ing's," the men were frequent targets of taunting remarks from their eastern comrades. At the same time they received letters from friends and relatives serving with western armies dismissing the Army of the Potomac as a "review and dress parade" outfit with no desire to fight. Nevertheless, the Twenty-seventh was proud of its service with the eastern army, and "if the question had been left to a vote of the Twenty-seventh . . . whether or not we should leave the Army of the Potomac, the negative would probably have won."[12]

In the XI Corps, feelings about leaving were less mixed. Like the XII Corps, it had not joined the Army of the Potomac until late 1862, and both had come from the Army of Virginia, an organization the Potomac soldiers viewed as a hated rival. Its heavy German contingent, which actually composed only about 40 percent of the corps, was a second strike against it in the eyes of many prejudiced soldiers. Chancellorsville provided the third strike; and if three strikes were not enough, the corps had fared little better at Gettysburg, where the unit's lines had once again broken during the first hours of battle. Impartial observers have since noted that the odds against the corps were simply too overwhelming on 1 July 1863, but following Chancellorsville there were few impartial observers in the Army of the Potomac when it came to the "Dutch" corps.

Under the circumstances, it is not surprising that the XI Corps saw the transfer as a welcome opportunity to start over with a clean slate. This attitude started at the top. On 1 October General Howard wrote his wife from Louisville: "I feel that I am sent out here for some wise and good purpose. I believe my corps will be better appreciated. Already the good conduct of the soldiers excites wonder." The view of those common soldiers of the corps was expressed by George Metcalf of the 136th New York. Under Hooker's program every corps had been assigned a distinctive badge. The XI wore a half-moon. Upon spotting it, the men of other corps, harboring memories of Chancellorsville, would cry out, "There goes a flying half moon." As he started west, Metcalf looked forward to the day when he would no longer feel compelled to tear off his badge and put it in his pocket when comrades from other units approached.[13]

Two divisions composed the XI Corps as it headed west, each led by a German American commander. Brig. Gen. Adolph von Steinwehr commanded the Second Division, while Maj. Gen. Carl Schurz led the Third. (George H. Gordon's First Division had been transferred to the Carolinas one month earlier.) The former Baron Adolph Wilhelm August Friedrich von Steinwehr may have had the distinction of possessing the longest name of any Civil War general. A native of Germany, the Prussian soldier had journeyed to America during the Mexican War, serving with an Alabama regiment. His Civil War record included a brigade command under John Frémont in the Shenandoah Valley and service with the XI Corps since its inception.

Like Steinwehr, Carl Schurz was also a native of Germany, but unlike his fellow countryman, Schurz brought no formal military experience to the Union army. Born near Cologne in 1829, Schurz became part of the unsuccessful German revolutionary movement. He escaped from Prussia in 1849 and arrived in New York three years later. In 1855 he settled in Watertown, Wisconsin. Schurz soon became involved in politics, shunning the Democratic Party that attracted most immigrants in favor of the new Republican Party, whose antislavery views matched his own.

In 1860 Schurz campaigned tirelessly for Abraham Lincoln. Although historians would later disagree on the importance of the immigrant vote in Lincoln's victory, at the time Republican leaders and the president-elect felt Schurz's role in delivering it had been vital. His reward was the post of ambassador to Spain.

Schurz served ably as ambassador, but he yearned for a military position. He returned home in January 1862 and in May was given a division under Frémont, soon to be part of Franz Sigel's corps in John Pope's Army of Virginia. Schurz's division suffered heavy losses at Second Manassas, but the general won praise from both the press and his superiors for his skill and bravery. His performance went a long way toward erasing the doubts of officers and men who had considered him nothing more than a political general. In March 1863 he received promotion to major general.

Two months later, Schurz and the rest of the XI Corps saw their reputations severely damaged at Chancellorsville. For reasons that are less than clear, press accounts were particularly hard on Schurz and his division. Howard defended his subordinate, but in the wake of the debacle on the Union right, Howard's endorsement carried little value. Although he had again performed well and with courage at Gettysburg, Schurz headed west feeling that he had much to prove.[14]

Whatever their feelings about their new assignment, the men of both corps were quickly growing accustomed to their mode of transportation. "This long journey in box cars," a Pennsylvania soldier

Maj. Gen. Carl Schurz, commander, Third Division, XI Army Corps. (Courtesy Military Order of the Loyal Legion, Massachusetts Commandery, the U.S. Army Military History Institute.)

later reflected, "would have been regarded as a hardship to men in civil life, but to these hardy soldiers of the Union it was a holiday." After two years of marching and fighting, the "hard and cheerless box cars were like newly invented Pullmans in their eyes," and he recalled a comrade chuckling, "From this day [forward] I do my marchin' on wheels and my fightin' by proxy." Another wondered, "Why didn't . . . Joe [Hooker] think of it before?" An Ohio soldier later wrote that his car included "a violin and banjo [players,] good singers and story tellers," and he and his comrades "crowded more fun & amusement into that week than I ever had known before." That verdict was common but not unanimous. The men aboard the stock cars had ample cause for complaint. Many cars were crowded, and insect bites posed a problem aboard some. Nevertheless, accounts that survive indicate that a majority were more than willing to ignore the hardships and sit back and enjoy the ride.[15]

After a brief trip on the Orange & Alexandria, the soldiers crossed the Long Bridge over the Potomac and entered Washington DC. They rode directly to the B&O's New Jersey Avenue passenger station and yards, thanks to a track that had been put down only a few months earlier through the streets of the nation's capital. Here the trains changed engines from those of the military lines to those of the Baltimore & Ohio.[16]

For most trains the stop in Washington was brief. It was long enough, however, for several of the men to locate some whiskey, "and here," noted Col. Ezra Carman of the Thirteenth New Jersey, "our troubles commenced." Civilians were prohibited from selling to the soldiers, but as a New York veteran later recalled, "where there's a will there's a way and every man who desired was supplied with what he wanted to drink and a full canteen besides. Women by the scores hovered around the train and supplied the men with [whiskey,] which they concealed under their skirts." As a result, Carman recorded in his journal, the liquor soon "gave evidence of itself by throwing men from tops of cars and causing fists to meet eyes."

Although the spree resulting from the whiskey was the most severe in Washington, the problem would plague the officers during the entire movement. Orders from both military and railroad officers to close all saloons preceded the trains, but stifling private sellers proved to be an impossible task, and Carman reached Bellaire, Ohio, two days later only to discover that "whiskey had been at work . . . and many [men lay] dead drunk all around the depot." Still, there were occasional victories over the demon brew. General Howard would later report that when he and his officers caught "an eager vender, selling bottles secretly in spite of all precautions, we found it a good policy to give him a free ride for some distance, and then permit him to walk back."[17]

From Washington the trains headed north on the B&O's Washington branch to Relay House, some six miles southwest of Baltimore, where they turned onto the line's main stem. This was the track that would carry the men west through Maryland and West Virginia to the Ohio River. It was also a section of railroad that had been fought over for the entire war, and it had suffered accordingly.

The B&O's first serious Confederate nemesis was the redoubtable Thomas J. Jackson. Although the legendary warrior did the B&O much harm, the most famous story about Jackson and the railroad, first related by cavalry commander John D. Imboden, is now considered apocryphal. In May 1861, while occupying Harpers Ferry, Jackson reportedly complained to B&O officials that the chugging trains along the busy main stem were disturbing his men's rest. The general insisted that they could pass through the community only at certain times. Gradually, so the story goes, he narrowed that period to one hour per day. The wily Jackson then sprung his trap, capturing fifty-six locomotives and more than three hundred freight cars waiting on either side of town.[18]

As the war continued, the B&O's problems along the main stem grew worse. One month after his alleged train heist, Jackson received orders to abandon Harpers Ferry. Since this meant Union reoccupation of the railroad, he made sure that little of value was

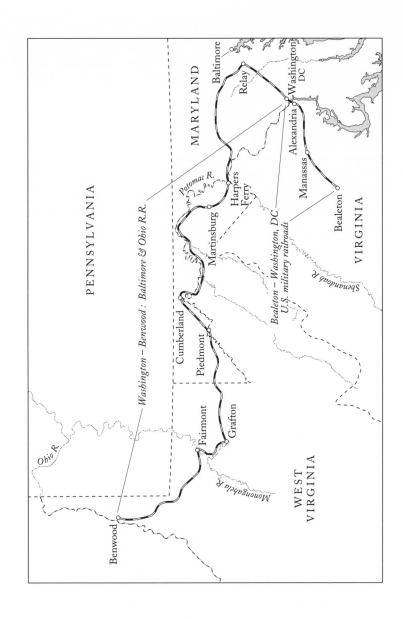

Route of the XI and XII Corps from camps in Virginia to the Ohio River.

left behind for the Federals to claim. Jackson's men burned large amounts of rolling stock, removed track and sent it south, tore down telegraph lines, and destroyed bridges, among them the eight-hundred-foot bridge at Harpers Ferry, brought down with gunpowder on 14 June.

Jackson continued to jab at the line throughout the remainder of 1861. At the same time, bridge and track crews appeared whenever possible to repair the damage. In January 1862 Jackson went into winter quarters, Stanton succeeded Cameron at the War Department, and things began to look better for the B&O. Repair crews began their work in earnest in March, when winter weather began to ease. Work on a new bridge at Harpers Ferry started on the fourth and was completed in just fifteen days. On 30 March the line reopened, and some thirty-eight hundred freight cars rolled over it that first day. Passenger service resumed the following day, and Wheeling marked the occasion with a one-hundred-gun salute.

The ecstasy was short-lived. In September Robert E. Lee invaded Maryland. Jackson, of course, came along and on his way to occupy Harpers Ferry tore up track in the vicinity of Martinsburg. More destruction occurred during Lee's retreat following the Battle of Antietam. But once again the dauntless B&O workers were up to the task, and on 6 January 1863 through traffic resumed over the main stem. The next challenge came after Confederate brigadiers William E. Jones and John D. Imboden led a colorful raid into West Virginia in April 1863. Jones's forces cut the line in several places and destroyed sixteen railroad bridges, including the three-span, six-hundred-foot iron bridge over the Monongahela River at Fairmont. This structure took several weeks to replace, but the other damage was repaired within a week after the raiders left the state. Pontoons were used at Fairmont, and the line quickly reopened.

In June the familiar pattern repeated itself when Lee began his second invasion of the North. On this occasion the occupation of the B&O lasted for five weeks, ample time for the eager Confederates to make mischief along the railroad. Jackson was dead, but his successors proved equally able. Among their accomplishments was the destruction of every bridge between Cumberland and Harpers Ferry. (The replacement bridge at Harpers Ferry was blown up on 5 July by an overly eager Union commander.) Despite this destruction, the road reopened on 11 August, less than two weeks after the last occupying Confederate left and six weeks in advance of the transfer of the XI and XII Corps.[19]

The Baltimore & Ohio's annual report for the fiscal year ending 30 September 1863 showed the results of an active twelve months. The Confederates had destroyed twenty-five bridges, some more than once. All had been burned or blown up, except for the three-span iron bridge at North Branch, which had been "battered and destroyed by cannon shot." The poles and telegraph lines between Harpers Ferry and Evatt's Creek, a distance of ninety-two miles, "were so destroyed as to require almost entire renewal," and "considerable damage" had been sustained by lines elsewhere. Ten water stations were victims of Confederate attacks, as were all the sand and tool houses between Harpers Ferry and Cumberland. At Martinsburg the Rebels destroyed the "large and valuable polygonal engine house and half round engine house," along with the company's hotel, warehouse, ticket and telegraph offices, master mechanic's house, coal bins, machine shop, and blacksmith shop.

The company's balance sheet also reflected the extent of the destruction. The B&O had spent only $42,613 for repair of bridges during the 1861 fiscal year. That figure more than tripled to $140,032 in 1862 and was $126,949 in 1863. Repair of locomotives had been slightly more than $138,000 in 1861. In 1863 the bill came to over $304,000. Total working expenses were $1,391,095 in 1861, $1,427,206 in 1862, and $1,965,847 in 1863. Perhaps the most telling statistic came from master of transportation Smith, who reported, "The entire road was in the Company's possession and use . . . only six months and six days during the year."[20]

Assuming the daunting task of guarding the B&O in West Virginia was Brig. Gen. Benjamin Franklin Kelley. A New Hampshire native, born in 1807, Kelley had come to the Wheeling area as a youth. At the outbreak of the war he was working for the B&O in Philadelphia. Returning to Wheeling, he was commissioned colonel of the first loyal regiment raised in Confederate territory. On 3 June 1861, at the Battle of Phillipi, he had the more dubious distinction of being the first Union officer to be wounded. The wound was at first believed to be mortal, but Kelley recovered, was promoted to brigadier general, and assumed command of the Department of Harpers Ferry and Cumberland. His primary duty was guarding the railroad between those two points.

In March 1862 Kelley was placed in charge of railroad defense for the Mountain District, encompassing the area between Allegheny County, Maryland, and the Ohio River. If this assignment was not difficult enough, Kelley's effectiveness was compromised by departmental commanders, who weakened his command to secure reinforcements for themselves. At one point Kelley reported to Washington that he had only two regiments with which to perform his vital task. In June 1863 the government attempted to remedy the situation by creating the Department of West Virginia, with Kelley in command. The new department covered the portions of Maryland and West Virginia west of Hancock, Maryland, over which the B&O ran, Trans-Allegheny West Virginia, and Ohio counties bordering the newly created Mountain State. This was the command situation when the transfer of the XI and XII Corps got under way, and at least for this operation, it proved to be effective. Both units passed over the main stem without any interference from the Confederates.[21]

Early on the morning of 26 September the lead elements of the XII Corps crossed the Potomac from Maryland into West Virginia, entering the state at Harpers Ferry. The historical community had suffered as the contending armies took turns occupying it. "As we passed through the town," one soldier recorded, "I could only see the ruins of tottering walls and a few shanties, lately erected for a covering for those who were left houseless by the invaders."[22]

An unidentified military movement through Harpers Ferry, West Virginia. A strategically important point along the B&O's busy main stem, Harpers Ferry witnessed numerous troop shuttles during the war. (Courtesy Special Collections, U.S. Military Academy Library, West Point, New York.)

At 8:45 A.M. the first train reached Martinsburg. Two more arrived within an hour, stopping so the men could partake of hot coffee and soft bread. "By passing around 2 or 3 times," Sgt. Rufus Mead of the Fifth Connecticut informed his family, "our craving empty stomachs were filled." Soon the citizens of the community were out in force, supplementing the rations with meat. They also "saluted from the windows with handkerchiefs, towels, the stars and stripes and aprons, which were shaken to the breeze to cheer us on to victory." It was a scene that was to be repeated in countless locations along the route, and the men "returned the compliment with hearty cheers as we passed along."[23]

The movement was off to an excellent start. On the evening of the twenty-sixth, Smith informed Stanton that the three trains that had arrived at Martinsburg that morning passed through Cumberland, Maryland, before four in the afternoon. The next morning Smith reported that they had reached Benwood, on the banks of the Ohio. By then the B&O had started west from Washington 12,600 men, thirty-three cars of artillery, and twenty-one cars of baggage and horses. Stanton was also receiving regular dispatches from George Koontz, the B&O's Washington depot agent. "Fifteen cars of baggage &c of the 11th Corps left this station at 7:35" and "A train of 30 cars of troops of 1,300 men left this station at 10 o'clock" were typical of the messages flowing from the depot to the War Department.[24]

Shortly after noon on the twenty-seventh, Stanton received a less encouraging wire from Smith. Someone had ordered the station agent at Grafton to hold all trains of the Third Division, XI Corps, until General Schurz arrived. "May I suggest," Smith asked, "that this kind of thing will cripple your entire movement?" The master of transportation had already answered his own question, informing Stanton that he told the agent to ignore the order and not hold any trains "unless his order comes from you."

"You have done right," the secretary immediately replied. He instructed Smith to have his agents "disregard every order but your own" and "report immediately to me any officer that presumes to interfere with you." He also wanted the identity of the man who sent the order to Grafton.

The guilty party turned out to be General Schurz himself. The conscientious officer had found himself at the rear of his division. Hearing reports of straggling and a lack of discipline among some elements of his command, Schurz was determined to catch up and straighten things out. His motives were honorable, but his methods threatened the smooth operation of the transfer, and this the irascible war secretary would not tolerate.

Schurz reached Grafton in a bad humor that was not improved by the fact that a lowly station agent would choose to disregard the orders of a major general. He attempted to commandeer an engine to chase after his men, an act the agent prevented with "great difficulty." Schurz did manage to get a message off to Fairmont to hold the trains there until he arrived, but the Fairmont agent had received his instructions from Smith, and he, too, disregarded Schurz's order.

In addition to having his orders subverted by the railroad men, Schurz soon received two reprimands from his military superiors. Under orders from Hooker, Chief of Staff Daniel Butterfield told Schurz that "you will under no circumstances order any trains of troops stopped or delayed for a moment. . . . Such orders are dangerous, and a serious annoyance, and in conflict with all orders."

Stanton also sent Schurz a telegram that, not surprisingly, was brief and pointed. "Major-General Hooker," the message said, "has the orders of this Department to relieve you from command and put under arrest any officer who undertakes to delay or interfere with the orders and regulations of the railroad officers in charge of the transportation of troops."

Schurz felt in some doubt about his status, and he wired the secretary, "Am I to understand from your dispatch that I am relieved from command?" Defending his actions, Schurz claimed that the columns had become so mixed up that putting them in order would have "expedite[d] matters instead of causing delay." He concluded by stating, "An answer to [the] above question is respectfully solicited."

By this time Stanton, never known for his patience, had lost any he might have held for this particular general. "General Hooker is authorized to relieve from command any officer that interferes with or hinders the transportation of troops in the present movement," he testily replied. "Whether you have done so, and whether he has relieved you from command, ought to be known to yourself." Stanton concluded by warning Schurz, "The order will certainly be enforced against any officer, whatever his rank may be, who delays or endangers transportation of troops."

One might have thought that at this point Schurz would have had the good sense to quit crossing swords with his contentious superior. Instead, three days later, he sent a lengthy message to Stanton in an attempt to explain his side of the situation and to secure the "reparation" to which he felt entitled. Schurz claimed the railroad officials had "confusedly mixed up" his regiments during the loading procedure at Alexandria and Washington. As a result, "the control of the officers over the men [was] much impaired." The general learned that several men had met with accidents, two had been killed, and others left behind. In addition, there was a "lack of system and order on board the cars."

"I endeavored," Schurz continued, "to get to the head of the column in order to establish that order which was necessary to avoid these evils." It was only after suffering the repeated frustration of reaching depots a few minutes after the preceding trains had left that Schurz sent his message to Grafton. Realizing that he had two Ohio regiments under his command, Schurz was especially eager to catch up before reaching the river so as to prevent the loss of men from straggling.

The general concluded, "If I have done any wrong, I am willing to submit to any punishment I may deserve. But if, upon a closer examination of the facts, you have arrived at the conclusion that I was innocently condemned, then I would most respectfully request you, as an act of justice, to withdraw the censure you have inflicted upon me."

Along with Schurz's message came endorsements from his two superiors in the field. Howard's was gracious. "No delay occurred through General Schurz," the corps commander wrote, "and certainly none was intended." He dismissed as "unfounded" any "suspicion of remissness on the part of the general."

Hooker's message was less helpful. "It is fortunate," he asserted, "if the repeated efforts of General Schurz to delay his train caused no delay in the general movement." The accidents mentioned in

Schurz's message were caused by men falling from the roofs of the cars, where they should not have been riding. This, Hooker contended, was "a luxury they would indulge in whether their officers were with them or not." By the time these messages reached Stanton, the secretary was occupied with the problem of transporting the remaining supplies of the two corps, and if he bothered to respond, which seems doubtful, that dispatch has not survived.[25]

As Hooker mentioned, many of the men chose to ride on the roofs of the cars. They did so to escape the crowding inside, get more fresh air, and enjoy the scenery. He had warned Howard against allowing them to ride atop the cars before the movement got under way, but as the commands became spread across the Alleghenies, it became impossible, as Schurz asserted, to maintain control over such details.[26]

In some cars half or more of the passengers headed to the roofs. Many stayed there overnight, using cartridge boxes as pillows and protecting themselves from the dew with rubber blankets. Canteen straps and gun slings hitched to the brakemen's catwalks kept the men from rolling off. On one occasion a member of the Tenth Maine, considered "a queer fellow indeed," fastened the strap around his neck. When his comrades discovered him, his legs from the knees down were dangling over the side of the car, with every jolt of the tracks inching him closer to strangulation. At other points the men were "obliged to throw ourselves flat on the car tops to avoid being swept away by a tunnel lower than common."[27]

Several men were not so alert, and reports of tragic deaths followed the movement. A Zanesville, Ohio, newspaper reported on 28 September that a drummer from the Fifty-eighth New York was knocked from the top of a car and killed almost instantly as his train crossed over an iron bridge. He was standing up when his head struck a beam. The victim's brother was a member of the same regiment, and he saw to the interment at a local cemetery. The next day the *Ohio State Journal* of Columbus told of two soldiers who had fallen from the trains at different locations near that city. Both had been discovered some time after the accidents, one dead, the other critically injured.

Three men died when they were knocked from the car upon which they were standing near Richmond, Indiana. A fourth was "badly injured, so that he will probably die," according to the *Richmond Jeffersonian*. The same issue reported a similar incident. A member of the Forty-sixth Pennsylvania was attempting to board a moving train when he slipped and had a leg "terribly crushed." The limb had to be amputated. Near Indianapolis a soldier was swept from the roof of his car and fell beneath, losing both legs and one arm. Total casualty figures for the transfer were not recorded, but the XI Corps medical director, Robert Hubbard, writing to his wife on 29 September, reported that eight men from Howard's command alone had been killed from falling from the roofs of the cars.[28]

If the decision to take to the roofs often had tragic consequences, it was also understandable considering the scenery the men encountered in the Mountain State. At Hancock, Maryland, they noticed changing leaves for the first time, and as they continued into the Alleghenies the autumn vistas grew more spectacular. "We could never tire while daylight lasted with viewing the grand, picturesque and romantic scenery," recalled a Maine soldier. "I thought some points of the Erie [Railroad] wild and romantic," wrote another, "but nothing compared to this. At one time," he continued, "we would be on the side of the mountain, on one side the rocks towering over us hundreds of feet, on the other the river roaring as many feet almost underneath us."[29]

These conditions provided magnificent views for the passengers, but they represented enormous obstacles overcome by the B&O. The completion of the main stem from Baltimore to Benwood on Christmas Eve 1852 marked the culmination of a fantastic feat of engineering requiring a twenty-four-year effort. Especially challenging had been the two-hundred-mile portion from Cumberland to the Ohio River. For the trainmen the biggest challenge began twenty-eight miles west of Cumberland at Piedmont,

West Virginia, where the line began a 16.8-mile climb to Altamont, Maryland. The grade was 116 feet to the mile much of the way before reaching the 2,628-foot summit of the Alleghenies near the latter point.

At Piedmont the B&O divided the trains into two or three sections for the trip up the grade. The trains abandoned their wood-burning engines for coal-burning "camel-backs," one in front, with a helper engine at the rear. Sergeant Mead correctly pointed out to his parents that the strange-looking engines with eight small drivers (a 0-8-0 pattern) had been built for the railroad by Ross Winans and Company. Winans was a former B&O employee, and he perfected a design that would pull heavy coal drags over the line's steep grades. A cab placed directly over the boiler gave the locomotives their distinctive look and also their name. The B&O had built a sixteen-stall engine house at Piedmont, so there was ample motive power to keep the men moving.

Continuing "slowly & surely, every mile bringing new and more beautiful scenery," the "clumsy & awkward" looking engines gamely bore their passengers up the grade to Altamont. At the summit the helpers stayed behind as the trains "thundered down the other side of [the] mountain at an awful rate."[30]

The next site of note was the famous Kingwood Tunnel, some thirty-seven miles beyond Altamont. At forty-one hundred feet it was the longest of eleven tunnels on the main stem, taking over two years to complete. As they passed through the tunnels, one man wrote his mother, the veteran soldiers "yell[ed] like demons," like boys on a marvelous adventure. To an extent they were. Occasionally the trains halted for an hour or more, usually waiting for a mail train to pass. If there was a nearby creek, "hundreds of naked forms would be seen glistening in the sunlight." The young women waving their handkerchiefs had provided the motivation, and "the men were eager now to improve on every opportunity to bathe." Only the occasional sight of "the debris of burned buildings and bridges" reminded them of the war they were briefly escaping.[31]

After Martinsburg the men were next fed at New Creek, between Cumberland and Piedmont. The next rations came at Grafton. Founded by the railroad, Grafton was the point where the main stem turned northwest after meeting the B&O-leased Northwestern Virginia Railroad, which continued westward to Parkersburg. To the men Grafton was mainly remembered for what Colonel Carman described as "very poor coffee." A chaplain with a Massachusetts regiment simply and unforgivingly dismissed it as "something which was called coffee."[32]

The quality of the coffee notwithstanding, the movement was proceeding without serious incident. The only accident on the line occurred on 30 September at a small water station called Belton. According to the report Garrett received, the train being pulled by Engine 175 was stopped when Engine 209 ran into its rear. The conductor of 175 said he was worn out and did not go back to give notice because he knew all trains were required to stop at that point for water. The engineer aboard 209, borrowed from a branch line and not familiar with the main stem, was "feeling his way cautiously," which may have averted a serious mishap.[33]

The first four trains arrived at Benwood during the morning of 27 September. They had covered the 412 miles from Washington in forty-two hours. Early the next morning McCallum reported, "All troops gone." The entire column was in motion, stretching nearly five hundred miles, with its head near Columbus.[34]

The news came as a relief to Federal authorities because a press leak had made speed more essential. Before the transfer began, Stanton had sent a War Department officer to every newspaper correspondent in Washington requesting that the reporters make no mention of the movement in their dispatches. They not only agreed to the request but also wired their papers and instructed them to hold any information they might receive about the operation. It came as a great shock, therefore, when word reached the capital that the *New York Evening Post* had printed complete details of the transfer in its edition of Saturday, 26 September. Other papers repeated the story the next day, although some castigated the *Post* for publishing it first.

According to observer Noah Brooks, Stanton "raged like a lion" when he learned of the story. Even Lincoln, Brooks noted, "was exceedingly angry." Their anger must have been mixed with confusion because the editor of the *Post* was William Cullen Bryant, a strong supporter of the administration. The Washington papers maintained their restraint, mentioning neither the transfer nor the controversy in their Monday editions, and the papers that had reported it apparently did not fall into Confederate hands until well after the fact.[35]

The Confederates had other sources, however, and they soon became aware that something was afoot. On 28 September, Richmond officials learned for the first time just what it might be. From his camp at Orange Court House, Lee informed President Davis: "A report was sent to me yesterday from the Shenandoah Valley which, if true, furnishes additional reason for prompt action on the part of General Bragg. It is stated that Generals Slocum and Howard's corps, under General Hooker, are to re-enforce General Rosecrans. They were to move over the Baltimore and Ohio Railroad, and to commence on the night of the 25th."

Lee's source would prove to be correct, but the general was not yet certain. He had read in the *Washington Chronicle* that Slocum's corps had been reviewed on the twenty-fourth by Sir Henry Holland and Asst. Adj. Gen. Edward D. Townsend. Lookouts had reported the review of a corps that day "and the disappearance of a large encampment east of Culpeper Court-House and some changes in those west of that place." He noted that Howard's corps had been guarding the Orange & Alexandria. "I have not heard of its withdrawal," Lee reported, "though it may have been replaced by other troops from the rear." Even if his information was accurate, Lee could not be sure of the troops' destination. Perhaps, he speculated, they were heading for the Virginia Peninsula "as a diversion to Meade's advance." This possibility seemed likely enough that Lee asked Gen. Arnold Elzey, commander at Richmond, to send "bold and reliable scouts" south of the James River to learn if any Union forces had arrived there.[36]

The next day Lee still was not sure. "The report has been repeated from the valley," he informed Davis, "without giving the circumstances on which it was based." Yet scouts north of the Rappahannock were stating that reinforcements were on their way to Meade. On the thirtieth Lee told Davis that two scouts had informed him of the transfer, but one was a man "in whom I have not entire confidence." The general was still skeptical. "None of the scouts have yet seen troops in motion," he cautioned, "nor can any material change be observed in their camps in our front."

William Norris, chief of the Signal Corps, was more certain, though little more timely. On 30 September he relayed to Secretary of War James A. Seddon a dispatch from a "reliable" spy in Washington. The report said that the "Eleventh Army Corps, 30,000 strong, is at Alexandria; is to be forwarded at once to the relief of Rosecrans." The source added that Hooker was to command the force and that several railroad presidents had arrived in Washington to help with the arrangements. Lee became convinced the next day, informing Davis that one of his scouts had observed Howard boarding the train. By then the entire movement had crossed the Ohio.[37]

At Benwood the river crossing had not gone as B&O officials had originally planned. They had first intended to employ ferryboats, but by the time the movement started the river stage had fallen to less than a foot. Garrett informed Stanton on the twenty-fifth that he had ordered the construction of a pontoon bridge, assuring the secretary that it would be completed before the first trains arrived. It was, and on the twenty-seventh Stanton received word that "a substantial and superior bridge of scows and barges, strongly connected, is in full readiness to make the transfer across the Ohio."[38]

The bridge proved to be a bargain. The transfer of all XI and XII Corps equipment was completed on 12 October, but the War

Department had the bridge maintained in place through the end of the month in case it decided to send more men westward. As a result, it was up for thirty-six days at a cost of $1,510.52. The largest single expense was "use of the Steam Tug Buck," which cost $340. The smallest was $6 for a laborer who provided four days' work.[39]

The crossing took approximately thirty minutes per trainload, according to the records of J. B. Ford, B&O agent at Benwood. Across the river at Bellaire there were occasional delays, the longest coming on 1 October, when a railroad bridge just west of the city had to be repaired. Even then the delay was only a few hours and proved to be a partial blessing. The horses arriving at Benwood were "much wearied. A few hours rest will be worth much to them," Ford reported.[40]

By then all the soldiers were across the river. The last of them had crossed on the afternoon of 30 September. In seven days the B&O had completed the portion of the movement along its own line, using thirty trains and approximately six hundred cars, and had transferred the men safely across the Ohio. Smith was justified in boasting to Stanton, "We only wonder that under such circumstances such results have been secured." The column now reached from Jeffersonville to Bellaire, bracketed on each flank by the Ohio River; in between the soldiers were meeting friends (and occasional foes) whose enthusiastic greetings provided memories that would cling for decades to come.[41]

5

"Like an Oasis"

As they crossed the shallow Ohio River and entered the Buckeye State the soldiers felt they were finally, if only temporarily, "home." For eight infantry regiments and two artillery batteries raised in Ohio this was literally true. But even for the men from other states the Ohio River marked a significant border, a border between civilian and soldier life, between slave and free territory, between idyllic boyhood memories and the harsh realities of the past three years. In short, the pontoons that the B&O had installed bridged that geographically indefinite but emotionally distinct boundary between the North and the South. Never mind that West Virginia had just been born a free and loyal state. The boys had to get across that river to feel really at home.

Yet even here the tensions of war had intruded. It was a gubernatorial election year in Ohio, and the choice of candidates made the canvass one of the most critical of the war for the Lincoln administration. On the Republican side was John Brough, loyal supporter of the president and his war policies. His Democratic opponent was Clement Vallandigham, who, depending on one's point of view, was the courageous leader of the Peace Democrats or the most notorious of the treasonable Copperheads. Vallandigham was not even present in the state he desired to lead. In May, General Burnside, then commanding the Department of the Ohio, had ordered the former congressman arrested for allegedly treasonable utterances made at a Democratic mass meeting. Although he meant well, Burnside had created a political martyr. The Ohio Democracy, which until then had largely been a voice of moderation, quickly rallied behind the persecuted leader.

99

President Lincoln tried to undo some of the damage. He commuted a military tribunal's sentence of confinement in prison for the duration of the war. Instead he ordered Vallandigham exiled to the Confederacy. Not quite sure what to do with their prominent guest, Confederate authorities allowed him to "escape" on a blockade runner, and in mid-July he wound up in Niagara Falls, Ontario. By then Ohio Democrats had tendered him their nomination, and from the Canadian border Vallandigham conducted his campaign.

Lincoln knew the election of Vallandigham would be a disaster for the Union cause. Support for the war was shaky at best in the Northwest, and the elevation of a Copperhead governor in such a crucial state would suggest that it was virtually nonexistent. Victories at Vicksburg and Gettysburg that summer provided reasons for Republican optimism, but in certain portions of Ohio opposition to the war was intense. In March some one hundred armed Noble Countians had prevented a deputy United States marshal from arresting an alleged deserter. Three months later, a draft riot in Holmes County produced a few injuries and was not broken up until 420 soldiers arrived on the scene. All things considered, the situation in Ohio was uncertain enough that the election was being watched hopefully in the South, anxiously in the North, and apprehensively at the White House. In Ohio the campaign had created a tense atmosphere that was certain to be enhanced by the appearance of twenty thousand soldiers clad in blue.[1]

One group of Unionists, from an Ohio regiment no less, quickly learned how strained the situation was after arriving in Bellaire. Some officers of the Seventh Ohio Infantry went to a hotel to secure some food. The proprietor, who was reportedly sheltering some of the paroled officers of Confederate cavalry raider John Hunt Morgan, informed the Union officers that he would not feed "any of Lincoln's hirelings." Upon hearing that, Col. William R. Creighton, commander of the regiment, gave him ten minutes to get breakfast on the table or "have his house ripped up from top to bottom." The owner complied.[2]

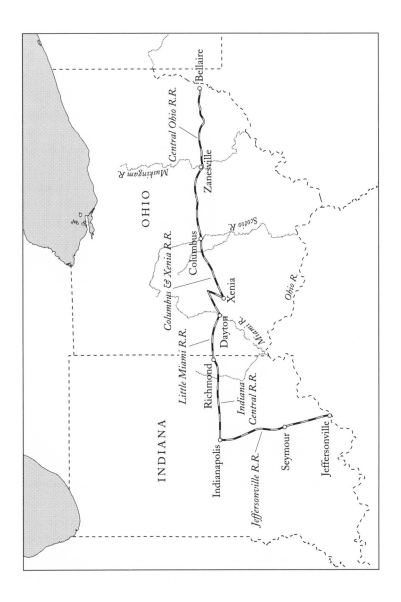

Route of the XI and XII Corps through Ohio and Indiana.

From Bellaire the two corps traveled westward to Columbus over the Central Ohio Railroad. Chartered on 8 February 1847, the Central Ohio was designed to operate as an extension of the Baltimore & Ohio west of the Ohio River. John H. Sullivan, the first president of the line, was a Baltimore native, and he emphasized the potential benefits to the B&O when soliciting stock subscriptions from the citizens of Baltimore as construction of the road got under way.

When the line opened from Columbus to Zanesville on 19 January 1853, it was already a quarter of a million dollars over cost estimates. Expenses continued to mount as construction crews advanced over the seventy-nine miles eastward toward the Ohio River. Originally projected to cost $2,644,000, the total had risen to $4,661,557 by the time the road's first train ran from Columbus to Bellaire on 1 November 1854.

Although the Central Ohio enjoyed a brief period of initial success, its heavy debt and the Panic of 1857 soon combined to throw it into receivership. In March 1863 the B&O gained a measure of control over its connecting line when it assumed $1,223,933 of the Central Ohio's mortgage bonds. In return the company agreed that passengers and freight passing over its line would "be directed exclusively over the Baltimore and Ohio" to the extent possible. The B&O also extracted favorable freight rates and a promise that the Central Ohio would not enter into any agreements with competing lines "to the detriment of the Baltimore and Ohio Railroad Company."[3]

Since 1857 Hugh J. Jewett had been president of the Central Ohio. A prominent Zanesville attorney (and future president of the Erie Railroad), Jewett had been the Democratic candidate for governor in 1861. He associated himself with the Stephen Douglas wing of his party and remained a staunch War Democrat. In 1863 Jewett was again the leading contender for the gubernatorial nomination until Vallandigham's arrest turned the political tide among Ohio Democrats. Disgusted by Vallandigham's extreme positions,

Jewett refused to participate in the campaign. He had no qualms about aiding the Union cause and willingly assisted Garrett in the transfer, seeing promptly to arrangements between Bellaire and Columbus.[4]

Leaving Bellaire, the soldiers discovered a problem with their new railroad. On the B&O, holes had been cut into the sides of the cars so the military passengers could get air and light and enjoy the scenery. No such luxury existed on the Central Ohio rolling stock, so the men took matters into their own hands and quickly corrected the oversight. Company axes were pressed into service and splinters sent flying, in some cases before the trains were even out of sight of Bellaire. Outfits lacking tools converted musket stocks into battering rams. By the time they were through, in the words of one participant, "The cars presented the appearance of having run through a gauntlet of artillery fire."[5]

As they traveled over and around the rolling hills of Belmont, Noble, and Guernsey Counties, the troops encountered more Copperheads. They would rush down to the tracks, shouting cheers for Vallandigham and "Jeff" Davis as the trains passed by. Traveling at twenty-five miles per hour, the men were unable to jump off, deal with their taunters, and catch back up with the trains. "We had our guns," a member of the Twenty-seventh Indiana recalled, "but shooting under the circumstances was a more radical measure than seemed advisable." They solved their dilemma at the next stop by loading their haversacks with rocks from a nearby creek. "It was most amusing to watch the result," the Hoosier recounted, "when the next group of men, thinking to take advantage of the fact that we were on a moving train, began to shout their taunting hurrah's. How they did dodge and scamper, when it began to rain good-sized stones in their midst!"

As the trains continued to roll across Ohio, surprised southern sympathizers received like treatment. Not far from Bellaire some men from the Sixtieth New York employed the same ammunition as their Indiana comrades to silence a lone rider on horseback who shouted a cheer for Vallandigham just as the cars were stopping. As they began pelting him with stones, General Geary appeared. The division commander did nothing to halt the proceedings but instead "looked on with much satisfaction," shouting, "That's right, boys, give it to him, damn him!"[6]

Although the Copperheads often provided the provocation, they were not always to blame. The soldiers decorated many a railroad car with slogans such as "Death for Vallandighamers" and "No Peace Makers Among Us." Other cars bore caricatures of Copperheads being hanged from lampposts or prodded with bayonets. Occasionally when the trains stopped for wood or water, one of the men would rush out to the platform and call for three cheers for Vallandigham. Anyone who responded was immediately treated to a volley of rocks or coal. At Cambridge a group of citizens on horseback was returning from a Vallandigham rally and cheering for the candidate. One of the troop trains had stopped there for an hour, and the soldiers overheard the cheers. A dozen or more immediately grabbed their weapons, loaded them with blank cartridges, and fired them in the direction of the riders. "They thought that they were to be massacred sure," one soldier later recalled, "and they urged their horses to their greatest speed, and were soon out of sight."[7]

Cambridge was also the scene of one of the most serious incidents involving civilians to occur during the entire movement. Although contemporary newspapers and subsequently published unit histories vary greatly as to the details, a few facts can be sifted from the conflicting accounts. One of the trains stopped briefly in the community, and a few men jumped off and entered a grocery store with a saloon attached. A member of Battery I of the First Ohio Light Artillery ordered some refreshment, lifted his mug, and said, "Here's to Brough." The store owner objected to the salute, which prompted the soldier and some of his comrades to send up a louder "Hurrah for Brough!" Harsh words followed, and then the proprietor picked up a cheese knife and stabbed the original Republican enthusiast in the back.

One of the men yelled out, "Battery 'I,' where are you?" the signal for a general rush on the store. The owner fled out a back door, and the soldiers pursued, rifles blazing. They brought their man down with a bullet in his thigh. Meanwhile, the soldiers ransacked the store, helping themselves to brushes, handkerchiefs, and other notions, which they later distributed to young female admirers along the route of their journey.[8]

The men had ample opportunities to meet admirers as the trains continued across Ohio. Most Ohioans were not Vallandigham supporters, as they would soon demonstrate conclusively at the polls, and the soldiers' letters and diaries are well garnished with accounts of hospitality along the way. "Our trip through the Buckeye state was a perfect ovation," wrote one Pennsylvania officer. "All along the route of travel men cheered—and women waved their handkerchiefs and bade us God speed in the good cause."[9]

Better yet, they brought food, homegrown and home-cooked, a most welcome respite from army fare. Even a regimental historian who wrote gleefully of showering a Vallandigham supporter with stones conceded that the people of Ohio "supplied the soldiers with all the delicacies of the land, refusing all compensation." Most of the territory through which they passed was farm country, and at remote crossings farmers would appear on wagons laden with apples, which they tossed to the soldiers as the trains rolled by. At towns too small for the trains to stop, the citizens turned out to throw food and other gifts to the passing soldiers.

There were young women in these crowds, and one officer of the 149th New York recalled, "Many dainty little notes were attached to apples and thrown into the cars when the train was passing, and about every man in the regiment received one and some as many as a dozen. Many romantic incidents and much correspondence grew out of these little favors," he added. Among the soldiers receiving such missives was David Mouat of the Twenty-ninth Pennsylvania. At Cambridge, Mouat later recalled, a young woman gave him some cakes and apples with the following note: "Soldier may God bless and protect you is the wish of a truly loyal girl."[10]

Individual acts of kindness took many forms and sprang from a variety of motivations. Three and a half decades after the war a New York soldier still remembered a small gesture offered by a mysteriously compelling woman he encountered at Zanesville. Charles Benton of the 150th New York had run to a market to find something to eat while the train made a brief stop. Some watermelons caught his eye, and he picked out two of them. As he approached the counter, the woman, who had been standing nearby, pressed forward to pay for the purchase. Benton assured her that he had plenty of money, but she insisted and "would not be refused." The soldier had no choice but to acquiesce. "She was pleasant and lady-like in her appearance," he recalled, "dressed in deepest black, and in age I judged was on that vague neutral ground called 'middle life.' But what impressed me most," Benton continued, "was that over her pale, refined face there flitted never the ghost of a smile." The grateful soldier realized there had to be a story behind the act of kindness, the dress of mourning, and the sad face, but he never knew what it was.[11]

Zanesville was only one of many larger communities where the trains stopped for wood or water or to provision the men. Often their arrival was cause for a municipal celebration. The first trains "advertised" the movement, and soon wires were meeting commanding officers as they arrived, informing them that refreshments were waiting. "Steaming caldrons of coffee" and a variety of food, served by young women invariably described as "charming" by the grateful boys in blue, welcomed them at virtually every stop. At Columbus, Governor David Tod's daughter was among those waiting on the soldiers.[12]

Often the trains arrived as political rallies were getting under way, and bands and speakers frequently gravitated to the depots. The Odd Fellows greeted many of the trains at Dayton, forming a procession and marching past, "headed by a fine brass band." A quartet of singers was also present, offering one of the popular songs of the campaign:

We will not vote for Val and Pugh,
Oh no, Oh no.
You'll vote for Traitors if you do,
Rally once again.

Dayton, however, was Vallandigham's hometown, and some soldiers observed that the reception was not always so friendly there. It all seemed to depend on which group was closer to the depot when the troop trains arrived.[13]

By contrast, the welcome was always warm at Xenia, a small community that was the first stop for most trains west of Columbus. Although small in numbers, Xenia was large in patriotism and hospitality, and its citizens provided the soldiers with memories that still lingered decades later. Among the fondest, at least to General Howard, was that of little girls flocking to the cars with bouquets of flowers. Of course, the people also offered food: "huge quantities of meat, potatoes, eggs, pies, cakes, fruit, and milk, which they proceeded to deal out to the soldiers most lavishly," remembered one recipient. One man asked the price and was instantly informed, "Nothing. We are not Vallandigham people; we take no pay of soldiers!"

Most of the benefactors were the residents of a ladies' seminary, who showed up en masse, waving flags and singing patriotic songs. As the trains continued to pass, the women acquired reading materials, needle books, and other useful items, which they passed out to the eager men, who had known no such hospitality during their time in Virginia. The enlisted men had the first priority, and a few officers who felt rank should determine place in line received a polite but firm rebuke from their hostesses. Fathers and brothers joined the women when night fell, holding lanterns as the work of provisioning the guests continued. When the trains moved out, it was to the strains of more patriotic airs.[14]

The Columbus & Xenia Railroad Depot at Xenia, Ohio, ca. 1850. The men of the XI and XII Corps long remembered the warm welcome they received in Xenia. (Courtesy Greene County Historical Society, Xenia, Ohio.)

As the men enjoyed the ride, the man responsible for sending them continued to wait upon every word of news from along the line. The reports Stanton received were positive. At 3:00 P.M. on 28 September, soon after the last of the XII Corps's trains left Bealeton, Smith informed the secretary that the first three trains had passed through Columbus twelve hours earlier. At 8:00 P.M. he reported that, according to Jewett, more than two hundred cars, containing a total of over eight thousand men, had been forwarded from Bellaire. Among them were General Howard and his staff.

The next day Smith sent word that the first train had reached Indianapolis at 3:40 P.M. on the twenty-eighth. Smith bragged, with some justification, "These trains are . . . carrying their masses of men and material from Washington to the western border of Indiana, a distance of 640 miles, with ample intervals for refreshment, in less than three days, say fifty hours, over the Alleghanies [*sic*], and upon a track three times rebuilt by private enterprise since the present war began."[15]

Garrett, too, was keeping a close watch over the operation. The B&O president had gone to Philadelphia on business, but aides in Baltimore kept him posted with a stream of telegraph messages. Shortages of stock cars and of water at some stations were among the problems his line confronted. There were also delays at Indianapolis (see chapter 6), but on the whole, Garrett had to be pleased with the way his subordinates along the route had conducted the operation. On the twenty-eighth he informed Scott, by then in Louisville, to be ready for larger numbers than originally anticipated. Eighteen thousand men would be on the move by the time the message arrived.[16]

It was also on the twenty-eighth that Garrett's thoughts returned to the regular business of his line. The president informed his master of transportation that three and a half days of exclusive service to the government had resulted in an accumulation of some two hundred carloads of westbound freight. The troop movement had also deposited a surplus of engines at the western end of the system. Garrett asked Smith to see about getting some heavy freight trains started eastward "to the greatest practicable extent that will not interfere with the remainder of the military movement."[17]

The men on the trains were of course oblivious to these corporate concerns. Their leading elements were entering the Hoosier State, where the hospitality they enjoyed equaled, and perhaps exceeded, that of Ohio. The trains entered the state at Richmond, described by a Pennsylvania soldier as "a business place of great activity." It was also a community that provided the soldiers with a very friendly welcome. The officers of the 149th New York went into town to get a bath and a meal at the hotel and discovered that everything "from bread to whisky was as free as a lunch counter." Meanwhile, the men on the train received a visit from a group of Quakers, "among whom were beautiful maidens who did not think it a sin to show their sympathy for a soldier."[18]

Just a few miles west of Richmond was the small town of Centerville. As they neared the depot, one regiment spotted a man on a two-horse wagon, "driving his horses for all they were worth" so he could share a large load of apples with the men. Like Xenia, Centerville had a ladies' seminary, and like Xenia, Centerville provided overwhelming hospitality and lasting memories for the soldiers. A "bevy of fair pupils" offered songs, words of encouragement, and, according to a Maine soldier, "even in some cases . . . much warmer testimonials of their affection." Once again the provisions offered by local citizens were measured by the wagon load.[19]

Indianapolis was the next stop for most trains. It was also the transfer point from the Indiana Central Railroad to the Jeffersonville Railroad, which would take them south to the Ohio River. The men had begun the portion of their journey from Columbus to Indianapolis on the Columbus & Xenia Railroad. This road had been chartered on 12 March 1844, its goal being to put down tracks along "the most practicable route" between the two Ohio cities. Money problems interfered, and it was February 1850 before the project was completed.

On 30 November 1853, the Columbus & Xenia merged with the Little Miami Railroad Company. The joint operation proved to be successful. For the year ending 30 November 1863, the combined lines reported net earnings of $882,868. Of that total, the Columbus & Xenia's profit was $127,521. Although the line was well north of Confederate territory, the report also noted that, "in July, four passenger cars and one baggage car in one of the line's trains were destroyed by the Rebels in the Morgan 'raid.'"[20]

Observing the movements in Indianapolis was the "special correspondent" for the *Chicago Evening Journal*. On 29 September he reported, "Indianapolis is full of troops. . . . Of course they do not remain here," he added, "but whence they come and whither they go I can't tell you; it would be 'contraband' to state it." Still, he did note, "One need not be gifted with more than ordinary shrewdness to surmise, with a great deal of accuracy, that Jef. Davis' game is about to be blocked in the Southwest."

The correspondent went on to report that, as he wrote his dispatch, a train of over twenty cars, "filled within and without with eastern troops," had just arrived at the Union Depot. "The troops are in excellent spirits," the reporter observed. "They dance upon the roofs of the passing cars, wave their hats and shout in response to the fluttering of handkerchiefs in the fingers of loyal and sympathetic women."[21]

Before changing trains, the men marched nearly a mile to the Soldiers' Home, where their next meal was waiting on "an acre or two of tables." Among those greeting them was Governor Oliver P. Morton, a staunch Republican loyalist. Also awaiting the eager soldiers were ham, smoked beef, bread, and cheese.

In addition, the 149th New York received "two mammoth cheeses," a gift of the loyal local citizens. One the men immediately divided. The second remained in its original box. It accompanied the regiment until their train reached Jeffersonville. By that point several men had become separated from their companies, and their comrades were carrying the absent men's arms and baggage from the cars to the ferries. They entrusted the cheese to "a wiry little Frenchman," who promptly disappeared. He did not show up again for two days. By then the regiment was at Murfreesboro, and the guardian was "without so much as the smell of cheese about his garments."[22]

Some of the men also took advantage of their visit to the city to do some shopping. This prompted one enterprising merchant to place the following advertisement in a local newspaper:

ROSECRANS REINFORCED — *Everybody knows when and how Old Rosy was reinforced, but it is not generally known that the battle-worn heroes, en route for Chattanooga, bought their boots of Chase, Mayo, & Dawse, Glen's Block. Their stock and prices suited them.*[23]

If boot and shoe bargains were not enough, the men also arrived while the Indiana State Fair was under way. Because of the military's monopoly of the railroads, out-of-town visitors were fewer than in previous years, but local residents crowded the grounds. One Ohio soldier observed that some of the men visited the fair "and other places where liquids were the principal product."[24]

Regardless of the attraction or the smug observation of the Ohioan, one group that was glad to be at the fair and in Indianapolis was the Twenty-seventh Indiana. They were the only Hoosier outfit making the transfer, and they were home. They even got to stay a while. Most groups of soldiers remained in Indianapolis for only a short time, but the Twenty-seventh arrived early in the morning and immediately received word that they would not be heading out until that night. The men particularly appreciated this gesture because many had been able to notify family members that they were on the way, and several reunions took place in the capital city.

Most of the men gave General Slocum credit for this courtesy. He had already endeared himself to the regiment shortly after it had crossed the Ohio. Coming around and receiving the men's cheers, the corps commander asked, "How are the Twenty-seventh boys standing the trip?" One of the less timid souls replied, "We would feel better about passing through Indiana if we had some money." Slocum expressed surprise that the regiment had not been paid and promised to look into the matter. That evening their train passed onto a siding, and a paymaster appeared with two months' pay.

While at Indianapolis an enlisted man summoned up enough courage to approach Slocum and ask for a special pass. He explained that the train would be passing through his hometown. The man had not been home, nor had he been absent from the regiment a single day since enlisting over two years earlier. Was there any way, he asked, that he could stop off and spend a day with his family? Slocum explained that he was very sorry, but no passes could be issued except under the direct authority of the secretary of war. "Still," the general continued, "if I had served in the regiment that you have, for over two years, without being at home once, or absent from duty a single day, and was passing directly through my home town, I would most certainly stop for just a little while, on my own responsibility." Slocum concluded that if the man did so and found himself in trouble, "I will do all I can to help you out."[25]

Several men from the Twenty-seventh took advantage of this understanding attitude to enjoy brief visits at home. Regimental organization had to be maintained, however, and many men remained on the trains as they passed within sight of their homes. Those whose parents were elderly or in poor health were encouraged to stop off, while the men who stayed behind on the cars willingly performed double duty. Many of those who spent a few hours with their families would never return home again, and many who self-lessly remained would never again have the opportunity. Men who left the trains, lacking passes or furloughs, found guards waiting for them at Louisville. These officers sent them immediately to their regiments, and nothing more was said. Once again, Slocum received credit for his courtesy.[26]

Indiana soldiers were not the only ones who took advantage of the movement to enjoy a brief but unauthorized furlough. An Ohioan took "French leave" as soon as he reached Bellaire, venturing all the way to Cincinnati for some time with his parents and "best girl." From there he took a mail boat to Louisville to rejoin his outfit. One group of men from Battery E of the Pennsylvania Light Artillery slipped away to visit family in the Pittsburgh area. They got to Bellaire only twenty minutes after their battery had left and caught a train carrying the unit's horses. Several men who had been left behind when the troop train pulled out were also aboard. They spent a cold night on the stock cars and caught up with the battery late the next day at Indianapolis. One soldier wrote that he immediately encountered his captain, whose only question was how the man's family had been.[27]

An Ohio soldier was met in Columbus by his wife. There was a delay of a half day there, but he felt "the hours alotted was to short to suit my ideas of a visit." As a result, he explained, "When the train pulled out I was not there to go, because I was not ready, and I did not get ready untill noon of the following day." He and some other men who had likewise tarried took a shortcut by passenger train and caught up with their regiment at Seymour, Indiana.[28]

Although several men were temporarily absent from their outfits, desertion was not a major problem. Bounty jumpers proved an exception. When the 111th Pennsylvania reached Louisville, one hundred of its substitute recruits were missing. Most had jumped off during the night as the trains passed through the mountains of West Virginia, despite the presence of guards in the cars.[29]

The first trains reached Jeffersonville just before midnight on the twenty-eighth, only about eight hours after they had arrived in Indianapolis. Their route between those two points was over the Jeffersonville Railroad. The state legislature had chartered this line as the Ohio & Indianapolis in February 1832, but nothing came of the project. The lawmakers tried again in 1846 and this time gained results. Construction began in 1848. It became the Jeffersonville Railroad in 1849, and in the fall of 1852, the line went into operation from Jeffersonville to Columbus, Indiana.

The directors hoped to continue from Columbus to Indianapolis via the Madison & Indianapolis Railroad (M&I), but they were unable to strike a deal with officials of that line. Instead they began building their own track northward. It got as far as Edinburg before, in late 1853, the M&I agreed to let them run trains from that point into Indianapolis. By the end of the war the Jeffersonville Railroad Company would gain control of the M&I.[30]

The line carried the men in the direction of the Confederacy once again but provided a bit of compensation by offering views of some of Indiana's most scenic farm country. Dr. Robert Hubbard, medical director of the XI Corps, complained that the region was "monotonously flat," its people "coarse and vulgar in appearance," and the dwellings "entirely destitute in the majority of cases of evidence of taste." Yet even this harsh critic conceded that the Hoosier State's forests were "heavy[,] indicating a good soil and beautiful decked as they are now in the varieties of their autumnal colors." More representative was the view offered by a Connecticut soldier that both Ohio and Indiana had been "like an Oasis in the Desert of our Soldier experience. All honor," he proclaimed, "to the Buckeye and Hoosier States. To their green fields, fertile country, [and] thriving villages."[31]

All too soon the trains reached Jeffersonville, and the interlude through the free and prosperous North was over. Across the Ohio lay Louisville and the South. True, Kentucky had remained loyal to the Union, but the decision had been very much in doubt, it was still a slave state, and in many sections it presented stark evidence of the ravages of war. There would be no more warm welcomes at virtually every station, no more bountiful rations provided by charming young women. The men had indeed enjoyed an "oasis" for some forty-eight hours. Now they would recross the river that had delivered them there. It would return them to the South and start them on the last leg of a journey that would soon return them to the war.

6

Return to the Confederacy

For the second time in forty-eight hours, soldiers at the head of the column were crossing the Ohio River. The channel was deeper at Jeffersonville than it had been at Benwood, and the men crossed to Louisville by ferryboat. On 29 September Thomas Scott informed Stanton that the first troops reached the Louisville depot at 4:00 A.M. They received rations and continued on their way ninety minutes later. Four more trains were sent out that day, and a steady stream of men was still arriving. His plan unfolding with remarkable success, Stanton replied, "Your work is most brilliant. A thousand thanks. It is a great achievement."[1]

Scott's achievements had been many, and his work did indeed merit the secretary's praise. Arriving at Louisville at 2:00 P.M. on the twenty-sixth, he wired Stanton one-half hour later to report that arrangements for ferriage at Jeffersonville were complete. The next morning Scott visited Jeffersonville, where he discovered 43 government railroad cars. He immediately made arrangements to transport them across the Ohio. After a visit to Nashville, Scott estimated that it would require an additional 365 cars and twenty-five locomotives to get the two corps from Louisville to Bridgeport.

Scott also made suggestions to improve the general rail situation in Kentucky. One was to extend the route of the Louisville & Nashville Railroad through Louisville to the river. It would then be closer to government warehouses, saving on drayage charges and also connecting the line with the Louisville & Lexington. Another recommendation was to change the gauge of the Louisville & Lexington from four feet, four and one-half inches to five feet, the gauge of most other Kentucky roads. Scott explained that cars from nearby lines could not be used for the current movement because there was no way to get them to the L&N. Ever protective of the autonomy of the railroads, Scott felt the government should pay the Louisville & Lexington thirty-eight thousand dollars, the estimated cost for converting the rolling stock, and let the company do the job. The government, he felt, could perform the eighteen thousand dollars in track work. Stanton approved all of these plans without question.[2]

For the men, Louisville was the first important stop after Indianapolis, and there they enjoyed what one called a "rousing good supper" at the Soldiers' Home. Beef, ham, cheese, and biscuits and butter were included on the bill of fare. For most of them the layover in Louisville was not long, but Col. John Love, a surgeon with General Williams's division, decided to stay until the rest of his division had caught up with him. He secured a bath, got into clean clothes for the first time in two weeks, and "got a darkey to say he would have my dirty clothes washed and dried." On Sunday morning he went in search of a church service, deciding on the way that Louisville was a "queerly laid out city." He settled on an Episcopal church and was "very much pleased with my choice—the church was a very fine one, the congregation large, the music Magnificent and sermon about as good as you generally get from an Episcopal clergyman."[3]

Louisville was also where the general in command of the movement caught up with his men. Hooker had remained in Washington until the morning of 28 September. Accompanying him were Butterfield, about a half dozen staff officers, and servants. The group had followed the route of the troops as far as Columbus, then taken a train directly to Cincinnati, where they spent the night of the twenty-ninth. While in the Queen City, several hundred "friends and admirers" turned out to serenade Hooker at his hotel. He appeared on the balcony in full dress uniform and thanked the crowd for "this compliment and honor you have seen fit to bestow upon me." The general had little to say that night but, in typical Hooker style, told the gathering that soon "you shall hear from me through my artillery and musketry." He further promised the crowd that "when I am through [with] my duties in the field, I will talk to you until you get tired of hearing from me."[4]

At Cincinnati, Hooker ran across an old acquaintance, journalist Henry Villard, whom he invited to ride along to Nashville. Realizing that the high-ranking party would travel by special train, Villard was quick to accept. He found the general to be "in the highest of spirits, and full of confident expectation of new distinction in the field." True to character, Hooker "talked in a lively and gay manner on the way, but was very indiscreet in discussing his past disappointments."[5]

Hooker continued to evoke mixed feelings among his brother officers. To Dr. Hubbard, Fighting Joe was "looking finely and was very unceremonious and sociable." The physician found his commanding officer to be "a splendid looking man, full six feet high . . . a stout robust but not corpulent person." Hubbard concluded, "He is a good leader for the command of a force the size of the one he now has and all I think have confidence in his fitness." Another physician, Colonel Love, disagreed, telling his wife he was planning to resign his commission "especially if compelled to be under Hooker. I know he is an able man in some things," Love conceded, "but he allowed himself to be completely outgeneraled at Chancellorsville [and] I have no confidence in him."[6]

Hooker's mind was still occupied, at least in part, with his unhappy XII Corps commander. As the trains headed south, Hooker invited Col. Ezra Carman of the Thirteenth New Jersey to share his breakfast of hardtack, ham, and eggs. He spoke briefly, Carman recalled, "on ordinary topics," then addressed Slocum's displeasure at serving under him. Hooker told Carman that he had informed the president that a junior corps commander should have been sent in Slocum's place, but Lincoln refused to alter the orders. Hooker reasserted his claim that Slocum was indignant because he had not been chosen to succeed Hooker as commander of the Army of the

Potomac. He also told Carman that Slocum did not enjoy a high reputation in Washington.[7]

The Louisville & Nashville Railroad provided the transportation for the next leg of the journey, delivering the men from one terminus of its main stem to the other. Although it would eventually boast over ten thousand miles of track, the L&N was a relative infant in 1863. It had been chartered in 1850 by the state legislatures of Kentucky and Tennessee, each of which was eager to protect its terminal city's interests against those of the other. Disputes followed as several communities, equally interested in protecting their interests, competed to bring the line through their towns. Construction began in May 1853, only to stop and start several times when shortages of money shut down the work. The money crisis eased in 1857, when several Louisville citizens purchased three hundred thousand dollars worth of L&N bonds. This influx of capital allowed the line to be completed on 18 October 1859.[8]

At the same time a corporate leadership crisis eased with the emergence of James Guthrie. The son of an Irish immigrant, Guthrie was born in Bardstown, Kentucky, in 1792. An ardent Jackson Democrat in a Whig state, he nevertheless spent nine years in the state legislature and also served as president of Kentucky's 1849 state constitutional convention. The pinnacle of his political career came in 1853, when President Franklin Pierce named him secretary of the treasury. He served the entire four years of Pierce's term, gaining a reputation as a reformer and a foe of debt.

After retiring from the cabinet, Guthrie was elected vice-president of the L&N. The president of the road at that time was John L. Helm. A former governor of Kentucky, Helm had been influential in getting the L&N its charter. As construction costs mounted, however, more and more directors of the road became disenchanted with their president. On 21 February 1860, they secured Helm's resignation. Seven months later the board named Guthrie to succeed him.[9]

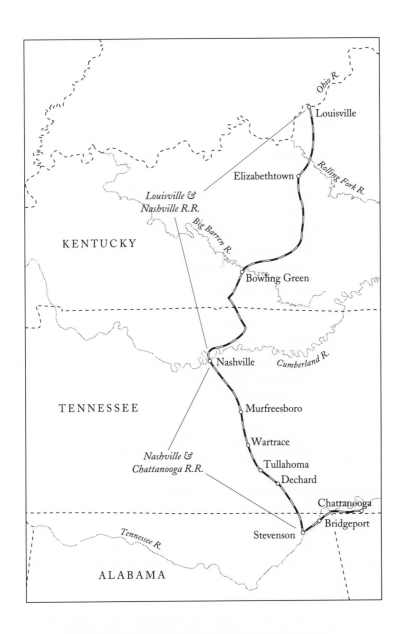

Route of the XI and XII Corps from Louisville, Kentucky,
to Bridgeport, Alabama.

Guthrie had been at the post slightly more than one month when Abraham Lincoln was elected president. Like Garrett of the B&O, Guthrie both personally and politically was prosouthern. He also shared Garrett's business acumen, but his choice was more difficult than that faced by the B&O president. With half its main stem in the Union state of Kentucky and half in Confederate Tennessee, the L&N inhabited what one historian has termed "a physical and emotional no-man's land." It had run its first train from terminus to terminus only thirteen months earlier, it had just 269 miles of track, and it was deeply in debt; now the L&N was apparently about to be in the middle of a war zone. If his young railroad were to survive, Guthrie would have to tread carefully and cleverly.

He did just that. At first Guthrie followed his state in its pathetically hopeful policy of neutrality. The L&N president was a true believer. Although he indicated that his sympathies lay with the South, he represented Kentucky at both the futile Washington peace conference of February 1861 and a conference of border states.

If neutrality was a politically naive policy, it was also, at least for a time, good for business. After Fort Sumter brought war, Guthrie's line continued to transport freight to and from both the North and the South, using the state's neutral stance to justify the activity. Crop failures the preceding summer in Georgia and Alabama produced a large demand for provisions, and because of its strategically located route, the L&N was the only railroad that could supply that demand. Indeed, the traffic was so heavy at one point that the line had to refuse any new business for ten days. Virtually all of the loads went south, accounting for 83 percent of the revenue freight between 1 October 1860 and 30 June 1861. Ninety-five of every one hundred through freight cars sent from Louisville to Nashville returned empty.

Although the traffic provided obvious aid to the South, President Lincoln was reluctant to interfere. The loss of Kentucky would have made the Ohio River the northern border of the Confederacy, which would have been disastrous to the Union cause. Lincoln reportedly once said he would like to have God on his side, but he must have Kentucky. The story may be apocryphal, but as an assessment of the strategic situation in the spring of 1861 it was not far off the mark.

Others in the administration did not share the president's lenient attitude toward the Blue Grass State. On 2 May 1861 the Treasury Department issued an order forbidding the shipment of provisions and munitions to points controlled by the Confederates. Guthrie disregarded the order, claiming it did not apply to a neutral state. On 12 June the collector for the port of Louisville ordered the L&N to comply. Guthrie responded by taking the matter to court. When a Federal circuit judge ruled against him one month later, Guthrie acquiesced.[10]

Meanwhile, southern leaders were pushing Guthrie into the Union camp. On 4 July, enforcing a similar Confederate embargo, Governor Isham Harris of Tennessee seized the entire line of the L&N within his state, along with some eighty pieces of rolling stock. Guthrie protested vociferously, but to no avail. The L&N placed its loss at $110,277.[11]

In September the situation became more serious. On the eighteenth, Gen. Simon Bolivar Buckner ("of the so-called Confederate states," as Guthrie now put it) and his small army seized the L&N from the Tennessee border north to Lebanon Junction and, for good measure, the branch to Memphis as well. Only about thirty miles of main stem remained in the company's hands. Buckner also appropriated half of the rolling stock the L&N retained following Tennessee's seizure. When Buckner offered to reopen the line on the condition that shipments to the South be resumed as well, Guthrie flatly refused. In the company's annual report Guthrie explained that to have agreed "would have been giving aid and comfort to the enemy." Clearly, the L&N president was no longer neutral.[12]

In the months that followed, the story of the Louisville & Nashville was similar to that of the Baltimore & Ohio. Raids and invasions resulted in damage and lost business amounting to many hundreds of thousands of dollars. A few days after Buckner's thrust into Kentucky, William T. Sherman led a home guard from Louisville that recaptured the road as far as Elizabethtown. This would be the only portion of the main stem the company would operate for the remainder of 1861.

Late in the fall Gen. Don Carlos Buell began his advance toward Nashville. L&N repair crews, led by the railroad's renowned superintendent, Albert Fink, followed. Their task was daunting. Among the victims of the destructive Confederate retreat was Fink's masterpiece, the 115-foot-high Green River Bridge. Two of its five iron spans had been brought down when the Rebels blew up the southern pier. Numerous other bridges also fell victim, along with buildings, water towers, and roadbed. Wrecked rolling stocked garnished the right-of-way. Buell reached Nashville in late February 1862, but the first L&N through train did not enter the Tennessee capital until 8 April. It was the first to run the entire length of the main stem since 4 July 1861.

The road's problems were still far from over. On 15 March 1862, Confederate cavalry raider John Hunt Morgan struck the L&N at Gallatin. It was the first of many attacks Morgan and his men would make against the railroad. They tore up track (and harassed crews sent out to repair it), cut telegraph wires, and set fire to piles of wood placed along the tracks for locomotive fuel. In August 1862 they pushed burning boxcars into the tunnel seven miles north of Gallatin, catching the timbers on fire. The cave-in that resulted left a twelve-foot-high pile of debris that stretched eight hundred feet.

If Morgan's antics were annoying, Braxton Bragg's invasion of Kentucky in the late summer of 1862 was much more ominous. As the Confederate general approached Louisville, Guthrie closed the company's shops, and the employees formed militia companies to help defend the city. The threat was real, but Bragg inexplicably stopped short of his goal, moving toward Lexington instead. After the 8 October Battle of Perryville, he retreated from Kentucky. As he did, his army wreaked whatever damage it could on the L&N. The danger to Louisville had passed, but Guthrie and Fink faced another extensive rebuilding project. It would not be the last—Morgan and his men would return sporadically through July 1863.[13]

The L&N's annual report for the year ending 30 June 1863 was largely a summary of the damage inflicted by the busy Confederates. Fink reported that all but five bridges on the main stem and branches had been destroyed and rebuilt at least once during the year. Some had been destroyed twice, a few three times. As a result, the company had operated the entire 185 miles of the main stem only seven months and twelve days that year. Since the beginning of the war the railroad had sustained damages totaling $543,743.[14]

For the men of the XI and XII Corps, the L&N's problems often resulted in a difficult ride. One Connecticut soldier thought the line was "the smoothest road yet traveled," but his was a minority view. More common was the opinion of an Indiana man that the trip from Louisville to Nashville was "the roughest and most disagreeable of any part of our long journey." This difficulty he largely attributed to "the reckless manner in which the trains were run." Often the equipment was the source of the problem. An officer who missed his train when it pulled out from Louisville caught up with it after a wheel broke, throwing one car from the track. At Bowling Green an Ohio soldier recorded simply in his diary, "Engine give out at this place." For him the trip from Louisville to Nashville would take nearly twelve hours.[15]

Kentucky's countryside also lowered the men's spirits, reminding them that their brief respite from the war was nearing an end. "Much of this land of superb fertility," General Howard observed, "had become waste and barren." One soldier thought the region would have been "very pretty" were it not for "the blighting effects of slavery and rebellion." Another noted, "War in one locality is much the same as in another." Like Virginia, Kentucky offered images of "the same ubiquitous blue uniforms, the same mystical and potent 'U.S.,' painted or stenciled upon almost everything movable, and some things that were not." The mood of the people along the route had also changed. "No letters, no hot coffee, and none of those thousand and one little courtesies which had been shown during the two or three preceding days," one man observed. "If there were any loud huzzas, they were from Union soldiers stationed along the route and not from the people."[16]

Nashville was the next important stop for the men. Although several days on the rails had dampened the enthusiasm of the military tourists, many were impressed with the state capitol building, still under construction. Even Dr. Hubbard, General Howard's complaint-prone medical director, who found Nashville "a corrupt city both physically and morally," appreciated the structure. The capitol, he conceded, was "one of the finest public buildings in the country." It sat atop a high knoll, and several of the men observed that it was surrounded by earthworks, barricades, and artillery. Indeed, the entire city presented a very military appearance. It was an important supply depot, and boxes, barrels, and "all kinds of army property were piled up everywhere and seemingly without limit." Nashville was also home to some Unionists, and one soldier noticed that "many flags were waved by fair maidens, old men and little girls and boys." The male residents cheered the soldiers "lustily and with a will."[17]

Tennessee's capital city was also the transfer point for the final leg of the journey. For most of the men it was not necessary to change cars at Nashville, but many complained of a lengthy wait as engines were switched. Some used the time to draw rations or simply look around. Among those that did not was a portion of the 149th New York, which discovered its cars had been switched onto a high trestle.

One group that came close to wishing it had not ventured from the cars included David Mouat and four comrades from the Twenty-ninth Pennsylvania. Before beginning their tour of the capital city, the men found an old woman who proved willing to sell them some whiskey. They soon had a number of "growls" with the

In this view from the N&C's Nashville yards, Tennessee's new state capitol building can be seen dominating the city. Although Nashville generally left Hooker's men unimpressed, many commented on the grandeur of the capitol. Courtesy of the Library of Congress, no. B811-2651.

provost guard, which grew increasingly heated as more men arrived from the XII Corps. The climax reportedly came when "some of our fellows got into a fight in the theatre and one of our corps threw a provost guard over the railing into a pit of the theatre." The next morning the provost marshal ordered all men of the XII Corps out of town. Those that remained, he warned, would be arrested, placed in a chain gang, and put to work sweeping the streets. It was not long before Mouat and friends were at the depot eagerly awaiting the first train south.[18]

That train would belong to the Nashville & Chattanooga Railroad (N&C). The last railroad over which the men would travel, the N&C was first proposed in 1837 by civic leaders in Chattanooga.

The Nashville & Chattanooga Railroad depot and yards in Nashville, Tennessee, March 1864. This was the transfer point for the XI and XII Corps from the Louisville & Nashville to the N&C. Here they began the last leg of the journey. Courtesy of the Library of Congress, no. B8184-8504.

Officials in Nashville, who were advocating turnpike construction, were less enthusiastic. Their attitude and the depression that followed the Panic of 1837 combined to sidetrack the project.

Interest revived in the mid-1840s. The depression was over, and successful railroad projects launched by South Carolina and Georgia were spreading north and west. In 1849 Georgia's Western & Atlantic (W&A) became the first to reach Chattanooga. Long under construction, the W&A had already caught the attention of A. O. P. Nicholson, editor of the *Nashville Union*. In early 1845 Nicholson penned his first editorial in support of a line connecting the Tennessee and the Cumberland Rivers.

Others joined him, and support for the project quickly spread. On 24–25 November 1845, some 150 delegates assembled at a convention in Nashville. They adopted resolutions advocating con-

struction of the line and encouraging the state legislature to grant
"a liberal charter." The next day, by large majorities, both houses of
the Tennessee legislature passed a bill to incorporate the Nashville
& Chattanooga Railroad Company.

On 19 January 1846, the board of commissioners employed J. Edgar Thomson, future president of the Pennsylvania Railroad, to
survey the route. The route he suggested took the line through
the northwestern corner of Alabama, staying away from the Cumberland Mountains and avoiding steep grades. Thomson estimated
that the total cost of construction would be $2,810,000. There was
no doubt, he added, that the line would be profitable.

Encouraged by Thomson's optimistic report, the directors dispatched Vernon K. Stevenson to solicit stock subscriptions. One of
his first stops was Nashville, where the city council pledged to purchase $500,000 in N&C stock. Stevenson addressed meetings along
the proposed route and in Georgia and South Carolina as well. By
the end of 1847, he had secured $1.2 million in subscriptions. On 24
January 1848, the board of directors met for the first time, rewarding
Stevenson's efforts by naming him president. He would hold the job
until 1865. Construction began in August 1848, and in February 1854
trains began running from Nashville to Chattanooga.[19]

When Tennessee left the Union in 1861, both Stevenson and
his railroad went with it. Whether the N&C president based his
decision more on conviction or geopolitical realities is not certain.
It is known that in September 1861 Stevenson accepted the position as head of the Confederate Quartermaster's Department for
Tennessee, Kentucky, Missouri, and Alabama. He first established
his headquarters at Nashville, but after the fall of Fort Donelson he relocated to Decherd, Tennessee. As the war continued,
the headquarters moved successively to Chattanooga, Atlanta, and
Augusta.[20]

In April 1862 advancing Union forces seized the N&C. It would
not, however, pass officially into the hands of the United States
Military Railroads until February 1864. The line would eventually

become, in the words of Colonel McCallum, "the great military thoroughfare over which passed all supplies for the armies in the Atlanta campaign," but in the fall of 1863 it was a war-weary road. When the Military Railroads assumed control, McCallum later reported, it was in "a very dilapidated condition." Some 115 miles of main track and sidings required new rails, ties, and ballast, and McCallum's crews would build or replace twenty-two thousand feet of bridges.[21]

These improvements were still in the future when the XI and XII Corps arrived. To many of the soldiers the Nashville & Chattanooga was "a curiosity." The cross-ties were about five feet apart, and much of the rail was "strap rail," wooden rail with a strip of iron nailed to the top. Often the wood was rotted, and the men observed several wrecks as they continued down the tracks. Even the officers were inconvenienced. Accustomed to riding in passenger cars, one observed ruefully that the N&C furnished "but one very small dirty caboose for [a] large number of officers. It was with much difficulty," he complained, "that we could find room to lie down for sleep."[22]

At 10:30 P.M. on 30 September, Scott reported to Stanton that the first four trains had reached Bridgeport, Alabama, the end of their journey. The next day he informed President Lincoln, "in reply to your inquiry," that fifteen trains had gone south from Louisville. All of the XI Corps and part of the XII had passed through. The same day Smith reported to Stanton that the rear of the troop column was due at Jeffersonville. All the artillery had crossed at Benwood and was on its way to Indianapolis.[23]

On 3 October, Hooker arrived at Stevenson, Alabama, where he was to make his headquarters. He had informed Stanton the previous day that the entire XI Corps had reached Bridgeport and that the XII Corps was passing through Nashville. Although Hooker did not yet know it, Confederate general Joseph Wheeler was leading a cavalry raid that would soon prevent a portion of Slocum's command from reaching its destination. That delay aside, the two corps had completed their twelve-hundred-mile journey in eight days. Most of the men had made it within the seven days McCallum had promised Lincoln.[24]

It was a remarkable feat, but there was no time for those involved to congratulate themselves. The railroads had justified Stanton's faith in them. They had not, however, completed their task. The horses, mules, wagons, and much of the baggage of the two corps remained to be shipped west, and that was a tall order. For the XI Corps it included 261 six-mule teams, 75 two-horse ambulances, and 3 spring wagons. Transportation for the XII Corps consisted of 150 four-horse teams, 156 six-mule teams, and 75 two-horse ambulances.[25]

The process started on 27 September, when McCallum began loading the horses of the XI Corps at Alexandria. The work required five days, largely because of a shortage of cars. Devereux requested cars from the B&O's Smith, who had to scrape to get a handful from other roads. The B&O, he explained, had a large number of empties ready to return east from the previous movement, but getting them back was a problem. Water was in short supply along the line, and the company had to preserve what it had for the upcoming westward shipment. Besides, Smith complained, some of the cars previously sent west with artillery horses had not been loaded to half their capacity. Devereux conceded this point, noting on 30 September, "The officer in charge to-day has promised me to put 15 horses into each car. Last night the conductor had as much as he could do to get 10 horses loaded per car." The military officers had "stood out to put 4 horses only in, and bed them."[26]

The movement would soon be back in the hands of the B&O, and on the evening of 3 October, Garrett arrived in Washington at the request of the secretary of war. Although the upcoming equipment transfer was undoubtedly the subject of the conference, Stanton sent Garrett a telegram the next day to make sure the point was not lost. "The speedy and successful movement of the transportation—teams, wagons, &c.—of the Eleventh and Twelfth Corps," he reminded his friend, "is nearly as important as the movement of the troops, and very essential to the success of the whole operation." It was therefore his desire that "the energy and skill that have thus far been manifested shall not be relaxed, but, on the contrary, that whatever experience may have improved shall be manifested now in the movement of the army transportation." Stanton concluded, "I beg you, therefore, to bend yourself to this job and make it an equal success."[27]

Once again Garrett was up to the task, and once again the wires crackled with messages from the B&O president's office. Smith, Jewett, Ford, Diffey, and Cole all received instructions for the task that lay ahead. "The government is much pleased with your energy and success," he told Jewett, "and with this notice I trust cause for continued satisfaction will be given." Garrett informed Ford, "All business on the entire line to Jeffersonville must be subordinate to this transportation." If necessary, "locomotives and cars must be seized from connecting roads to ensure rapid and successful movement." The Benwood agent was to report at least twice daily on the progress of the operation. In Indianapolis, Cole received orders to be certain that sufficient cars were on hand to forward everything south toward Jeffersonville. "If necessary," Garrett wired, "exercise the power placed in your hands in securing such cars, to the extent required, from as many roads as may be requisite to accomplish the object." He also instructed Cole to prepare platforms if necessary to complete the transfer promptly and to "confer fully with parties in charge of the roads where deficiency of water has occurred. Urge upon them," Garrett instructed, "preparations so as to prevent delays from this cause."[28]

Less than twenty-four hours after his meeting with the secretary of war, Garrett sent Stanton a full report of his progress. In addition to sending the above messages, Garrett had ordered all available cars sent to Washington for the movement. House cars, altered so they could transport horses and mules, were already arriving. Meanwhile, trains sent from Alexandria with the first shipments of the two corps' transportation were chugging toward the capital.

They reached Washington at 5:00 P.M. on 4 October, and three hours later the B&O had unloaded forty wagons and 300 mules and reloaded them onto their own cars. Sufficient cars were on hand for one hundred more wagons and 350 more mules. "We hope to accomplish large work to-morrow," Garrett assured Stanton.[29]

Once again, Garrett was true to his word. By this time Washington agent George Koontz had the loading of military cargo down to an art, and by the end of 5 October, nine hundred mules and one hundred wagons were rolling out of Washington. The loading of the XI Corps transportation was completed the next day, and on the seventh the entire job was done. Yet another convoy was moving west.[30]

At first it progressed as smoothly as the movement of the troops had. Smith reported to Stanton on the morning of 6 October that the first two trains had passed Grafton, 312 miles west of Washington. That evening Garrett sent word that thirteen trains had reached Harpers Ferry during the afternoon. He expected the head of the column to arrive at the Ohio River later that evening. The river stage at Benwood was down to one foot and falling, but the B&O's pontoons remained in place, and no one anticipated any problems getting the military freight across the river.[31]

At Benwood, however, the movement soon experienced a bottleneck. In response to an inquiry from McCallum, Smith explained that it was proving "impossible" to make transfers there at night and that this caused "nearly all" of the delay. He did not explain what the problem was, and when word of the slowdown reached Garrett, he was not satisfied with the excuse. On 9 October the B&O president informed Smith that the evidence indicated "a shocking want of capacity and energy at this important point." In a message to Jewett, Garrett advised the Central Ohio president to make arrangements for loading and unloading during the night, never mind that his master of transportation considered it impossible.[32]

Somehow Stanton never learned of this delay, or if he did he chose to disregard it, which seems even more unlikely. The war secretary definitely did not ignore the message he received from Smith on 1 October. Reporting on the progress of the troop column, the master of transportation reported, "The only place where any real impediment has been threatened is Indianapolis." After reminding Stanton that he had recommended sending the men by way of Cincinnati, Smith went on to explain that marching the soldiers over a mile through town was the source of the problem.

What Smith failed to explain was that the reason for the march was to provide rations. Stanton assumed that the problem resulted from the tracks being separated, and he was determined to do something about it. Desiring that "the evil should be cured immediately," he directed Scott to go to Indianapolis and "cause a track to be put down, if practicable, in as few hours as can be done." If the railroads would not perform the work, Scott was authorized to seize whatever materials and impress whatever labor was necessary to do the job. Stanton also sent a message to Garrett, asking him to go and help.

Garrett checked with Cole at Indianapolis and informed Stanton of the true cause of the delay. The Indiana Central and the Jeffersonville lines were of different gauges, he explained, but they ran close enough together that transfers were made directly from one road's cars to the other. That view was confirmed by Scott, who made a hasty trip to Indianapolis, agreeing that the march to the Soldiers' Home, arranged by military officials, was the only cause of the delays.[33]

Although he said nothing, Scott may have viewed his trip to Indianapolis as further evidence that when the military and the railroads worked together, the latter could perform much more efficiently if not impeded by the former. If so, events of the next several days worked to reinforce that view. When he entered Kentucky, Scott found himself squarely in the middle of a long-standing controversy between the Louisville & Nashville Railroad and military authorities. It dated back to the February 1862 conference between army, government, and railroad officials that had resulted in the government's 10 percent discount. The L&N's Guthrie had long argued that the arrangement placed an undue burden on his line. Writing to Quartermaster General Meigs, he complained that the lower rates barely allowed his company, operating in a war zone, to pay for damages. In addition, as the road took on more and more government business, it lost both profits and goodwill from the private customers it could no longer serve.

Guthrie's arguments did not impress military officials. They knew only that the L&N charged considerably more than most other railroads and that it still failed to deliver all that the armies needed. Further, they charged Guthrie with giving preference to more lucrative commercial business, often sending it through secretly, at the expense of the military. Guthrie retained the confidence of both Lincoln and Stanton—as well as the management of his line—but he and other L&N officials still bristled at the criticism. In the company's 1863 annual report, Fink sardonically observed, "It seemed to be taken for granted, that because the Road could not carry as much freight as the Army of the Cumberland . . . chanced to require, it must necessarily be badly managed."[34]

With the Army of the Cumberland on the verge of starvation at Chattanooga, the fragile iron supply line was more critical than ever. It was under these circumstances that Scott entered the picture. The movement he was to supervise, designed to help save the army, had the ironic side effect of using the engines and freight cars needed to carry the supplies that would keep it alive in the meantime. Complicating things further was Wheeler's raid, which cut off a portion of the Nashville & Chattanooga as the last of Hooker's men were arriving from the East.

All of this placed Scott in an uncomfortable position. Stanton was adamant in his insistence that Hooker's men and their equipment reach the front as quickly as possible. Rosecrans and his railroad officials were equally determined that their army be supplied. On 25 September, the day he arrived in Louisville, Scott contacted Col. William P. Innes, Rosecrans's superintendent of military railroads. He informed Innes of the urgency of the transfer and urged him to unload all cars in Nashville and return them to Louisville without delay. Citing the authority of the secretary of war, Scott maintained pressure on Innes during the next several days to keep the men moving and get all available rolling stock quickly back to Nashville. When he learned that more men were coming than originally expected, Scott advised Innes, "You must . . . devote all your energies to fill the requisition [for more cars] as it is deemed of the utmost importance by the authorities that no delay should occur."[35]

Scott reached an agreement with Innes to provide the railroad superintendent with twenty cars daily to supply rations and forage to the army at the front. He advised Rosecrans of the arrangement, adding, "I hope no orders will be given that will interfere with troops and their equipment coming from the east." Scott offered to remain at Louisville to "keep all the equipment in Government service." Apparently Scott was aware of the feelings in the Army of the Cumberland regarding the alleged covert activities of President Guthrie.[36]

Indeed, Scott might have been able to maintain harmonious relations with both Innes and Rosecrans had it not been for Wheeler's raid, which placed additional strain on everyone connected with the railroads, and for grievances that private railroad officials had with Innes. One of those officials, Superintendent Alfred Gaither of the L&N, charged that Innes had ignored the government's contract with the railroads. Specifically, he claimed, Innes impressed private cars for military use, then carried private freight in those cars, depriving his company of business that legitimately belonged to it.

Appreciating the importance of harmonious relations with the railroads, Stanton responded promptly to the charges. He instructed Quartermaster General Meigs, who was still studying the situation in Chattanooga, to "make a careful examination into the conduct of Colonel Innes." The secretary of war then informed Innes of the pending investigation and ordered him to cooperate fully with Meigs. In the meantime, Innes was to confine himself "strictly to your duties in relation to military transportation and abstain from improper interference with any private rights, and from any contracts or arrangements for private transportation."

Innes replied that he hoped the secretary would "promptly and freely investigate every charge mentioned" and do so "at the earliest possible moment." Scott told Stanton that the message had "raised quite a commotion in that camp." He further informed the secretary that a special messenger was on his way to Washington to present Innes's case. It was Scott's opinion that all contracts made for the transportation of supplies, except for government property, should be subject to the approval of the secretary of war. The arrangements, Scott advised, "should be in the hands of responsible parties, and not under the direct control of superintendents of military roads."[37]

Meanwhile, Innes was working to keep his immediate superiors on his side. On 7 October, one day after receiving Stanton's telegram, Innes told James Garfield, Rosecrans's chief of staff, that he was "working day and night" to repair the damage to the line resulting from the cavalry raid. He would "strain every nerve to reopen [the railroad] immediately." Meanwhile, he was forwarding troops and supplies from Nashville "as fast as they arrive." The next day Innes complained to Garfield that Scott had requested that one hundred cars be sent to Louisville daily "to transport the stuff down here." The loyal colonel, knowing the army was desperately in need of forage and rations, strongly disagreed with this plan. "I think," he wired, "justice to the army would say let the [XI and XII Corps] horses come along as soon as it can be done without detriment to the army in front." Innes further pointed out that he was still working day and night.[38]

Garfield agreed with Innes. He wired back that forage and beef cattle must be sent before any troops or equipment. Rosecrans, Garfield added, "fully approves the view expressed in your dispatch." The chief of staff authorized Innes to "communicate this to Colonel Scott." Meanwhile, Meigs was telling Scott that the "greatest exertions" should be made to get the transportation of the two eastern corps forward. From Washington the secretary of war asserted, "Everything must give way to military use of the road," meaning specifically the transfer of the two corps. Scott had planned to return to Washington, but Stanton asked him to stay on in Louisville "for some time longer." Scott agreed to remain, advising Stanton that he would visit Nashville to "see if matters cannot be improved."

Meanwhile, Rosecrans had gotten personally involved. On 12 October he wired Scott, "Colonel Innes telegraphs that he is pressed for cars. I know it. You want them at Louisville. Measure the capacity of the Louisville road," the general instructed, "and telegraph me. I will give instructions accordingly to Innes."

Scott replied that he was receiving about one hundred cars each day at Louisville. With these he had to forward all the supplies needed by the Army of the Cumberland as well as the transportation of the XI and XII Corps. He explained that there was enough rolling stock available to send 140 cars daily, "if they are handled promptly." Delays were caused, Scott pointed out, by the process of unloading the L&N cars at Nashville and transferring the freight onto the N&C, which was under Innes's control. He suggested that trains be run through from Louisville to Bridgeport to alleviate these slowdowns.[39]

As Scott prepared to visit Nashville, Innes pressed his case harder to Garfield. Responding to Meigs's message concerning the urgency of getting the transportation through, Scott had requested all the flatcars Innes could spare. Innes complained, "I receive telegrams every day to send cars to the rear. Can't the Louisville road do this kind of freighting without calling on us for cars?" Although the protest was likely sincere, his real concern may have been that he was being subjected to orders from a civilian. "I will, of course, cheerfully obey any instructions I receive," Innes informed Garfield, "but I should like them to come from department headquarters."[40]

Apparently, Innes's claims no longer impressed his commanding general. As Meigs made plans to return east, Rosecrans asked him to check out the situation in Nashville. Specifically, Meigs was to see Innes "about perfect accord with [the] Louisville and Nashville road as to through trains to Bridgeport." The army commander added that he wanted the transportation of the eastern corps sent through.[41]

Scott himself reached Nashville on the fifteenth and discovered a "great want of power and equipment" between there and the front. After examining the situation more closely, he determined that by borrowing two locomotives from the L&N he could keep Rosecrans supplied until new equipment already ordered by the government arrived. Apparently, he and Innes were able to reach a working agreement as well. Neither henceforth complained about the other in dispatches to their respective superiors. On 16 October, Innes notified Rosecrans, "I am making arrangements for through trains to Bridgeport; also hope to borrow two engines Monday." Stanton, too, seemed satisfied. He would eventually drop the charges against Innes at the request of Tennessee's military governor, Andrew Johnson.[42]

On 17 October both Meigs and Scott informed Stanton that all was well. The transportation was moving forward, Scott reported, and the gauge change on the Lexington road had been completed that day. Meigs noted that some of the animals had not stood the trip from Washington well. He had ordered that substitutes be taken from the stock on hand at Louisville.[43]

Scott returned east the following week, one month after he, Garrett, Smith, McCallum, and Felton had met with Stanton at the War Department to plan the unprecedented movement. As Stanton acknowledged, the railroad officials had worked with "energy and skill," and their accomplishment had been "a great achievement."[44]

Now it was out of their hands. Fighting Joe Hooker and the two least respected corps of his former army had been given an important assignment—and a second chance. Their actions in the weeks that followed would help determine the significance of the railroad men's efforts, the fate of the Army of the Cumberland, and their own place in history. They would not have much time to ponder these things, however. As they arrived, Joe Wheeler was on hand to greet them, and he was eager to demonstrate to these veterans of the Army of the Potomac that western Confederates could be every bit as problematic as those from the Army of Northern Virginia.

7

"We Are Nearly Out of the World"

As Fighting Joe Hooker entered Tennessee from the north, "Fighting Joe" Wheeler was approaching the Volunteer State from the south. On 1 October, one day before Hooker arrived at Stevenson, word reached Rosecrans that Wheeler had pushed across the Tennessee River north of Chattanooga with three divisions of cavalry raiders. Brig. Gen. George Crook, stationed at Washington, Tennessee, had been ordered to guard the section where the crossing occurred, but he had only two thousand men to patrol an area approximately fifty miles in length. As a result, he could do little more than slow the raiders a bit and send word to Rosecrans that the enemy was heading west toward McMinnville.[1]

On the second, Wheeler took a detachment of fifteen hundred men and headed south into the Sequatchie Valley toward Jasper. They soon overtook and captured a Federal supply train of thirty-two wagons, but that was only the start. Continuing south, Wheeler's troopers spotted a much bigger prize, a train of some eight hundred wagons spread out for nearly ten miles from the top of Walden's Ridge toward Jasper. The train, Wheeler reported, was "heavily loaded with ordinance, quartermaster's, and commissary stores." Destined for three divisions of the XIV Corps, it was instead soon the property of the Confederates. "After selecting such mules and wagons as we needed," Wheeler later reported, "we then destroyed the train by burning the wagons and sabering or shooting the mules." Wheeler failed to note that his undisciplined troopers also plundered ruthlessly, robbing sutlers' wagons and even their prisoners of clothing and other personal items. Wheeler and his men then headed for McMinnville, leaving not only the wagon train in ruins but, as things would develop, Rosecrans's career as well.[2]

The raid also changed Rosecrans's plans for Hooker and his men. Although he had originally intended for the eastern units to go "direct to Bridgeport" to reopen his tenuous supply line, on 3 October he sent instructions to Hooker at Stevenson to "order promptly all the Twelfth Corps to stop on the railroad," placing one division at Wartrace and another at Decherd, "till the raid blows over." Hooker was also to "see well to the safety of our depots at Stevenson and Bridgeport."[3] Any dreams Fighting Joe had of winning glory in the West would be at least temporarily delayed.

On 4 October, Hooker assumed command of the district embracing the line of the Nashville & Chattanooga between Wartrace and Bridgeport, with headquarters at Stevenson. Slocum's corps was responsible for guarding the N&C from Wartrace to Tantalon, a distance of approximately forty miles. Howard's corps was to take charge of the line from Tantalon to Bridgeport, some thirty miles in length. Brig. Gen. Robert S. Granger, the commanding officer at Nashville, was responsible for guarding the railroad from there to Wartrace. Through Butterfield, his chief of staff, Hooker sent orders to Howard to return north all XII Corps regiments that had already arrived at Bridgeport. Butterfield then directed Slocum to "report at once the whereabouts of your command," advising the corps commander that Hooker "has not received any reports from you since your command left Washington."[4]

For the men of the XII Corps, who thought their time on the rails had ended, all this meant climbing back aboard the freight cars and retracing their route over the N&C. Less than two hours after arriving at Stevenson, the Twenty-seventh Indiana booked passage on flatcars for what the unit historian termed the "utter folly and uselessness of employing infantry against cavalry when making . . . a raid." For the Fifth Connecticut the return journey was aboard "lumber cars very much crowded." The 107th New York reached Stevenson at 2:00 A.M. on 3 October, and Lt. John D. Hill wrote his friends, "It was a great relief to get out of the cars and lay on a solid foundation." The respite lasted little more than twenty-four hours. The next morning the unit was back on the cars, traveling thirty miles north to Decherd, where their job was to guard the N&C.[5]

Hill's outfit at least got to stay put at Decherd, but many units were not so lucky. William Sharp of the Forty-sixth Pennsylvania wrote that his regiment returned to Wartrace to prevent the Rebels from burning a bridge there, "but we were too late, they had burned it and left." The Forty-sixth went in pursuit, but the cavalry was too fast. "We scouted after them for a week or more," Sharp wrote, "and [then] returned tired and starved, being three days without rations."[6]

The experience of the Third Wisconsin was similar. After returning to Duck River by rail, they marched on successive days to Bell Buckle, Christiana, and Normandy, the last march covering twenty-five miles. Without rations, they "lived on the country and formed the acquaintance of an indigestible slug of baked meal called 'corn dodgers.'" Regimental historian Edwin E. Bryant recalled, "For some days we rambled about, having no sort of notion where we were." Bryant, however, was philosophical about the experience. "The climate was superb," he conceded, "the air had a rich freshness, so different from the humid heat of the Atlantic coast. Our marches lay through great forests of beech trees with . . . beech nuts an inch thick on the ground." Less understanding was Alonzo Quint, chaplain of the Second Massachusetts. After three days of long marches, one beginning at 4:00 A.M., the unforgiving clergyman decided "that the general conducting a march ought to go on foot, and . . . carry twenty-five pounds on his back."[7]

On 6 October Hooker received word that Wheeler's force had struck at Wartrace, where they tore up some N&C track and burned a bridge, and at Shelbyville, ten miles west. Slocum was in Nashville at the time, and the raid cut him off from his command. Hooker dispatched Butterfield to Decherd to take command of the XII Corps. Butterfield reached Decherd at 1:00 P.M., continuing north to the

Duck River Bridge with fifteen hundred infantry soldiers, who had gathered at Decherd under his orders.

His report to Hooker threw Fighting Joe into a rage. "I can scarcely retain the chagrin and mortification I feel," he wired Butterfield concerning the abandonment of Wartrace and the nearby Garrison's Fork Bridge. "It does not appear that a gun was fired in defense of either. Women would not act so badly," he concluded. Time would eventually show that the commanding officers at both locations had left under orders to protect more vital spots. Hooker was not assuaged, however. In his report he noted that the raid had cut communications for four days. "In my judgment," he added, "a much longer time will be required to repair the reputations of some of the officers to whom the defense of our communications had been intrusted."[8]

On the afternoon of 6 October, Butterfield ordered the First Michigan Engineers up to replace the Garrison's Fork Bridge. The next morning he took his infantry and headed toward Shelbyville, only to discover that Crook's cavalry was in hot pursuit. He then returned to the N&C and continued north through Bell Buckle, Fosterville, and Christiana. Hooker sent word to Slocum, who he assumed was at Murfreesboro, to leave a garrison at that point and "take all available forces at hand," leaving behind enough men to protect the railroad and bridges, and "push forward on the line of the railroad, attacking and dispersing the enemy wherever you find them." General Williams responded, informing Hooker that Slocum was in Nashville. He also reported that the enemy had long left the line of the railroad after destroying two small bridges and tearing up short sections of track and telegraph wire between there and Christiana. Williams then sent a wire to Slocum, apprising him of the situation and adding, "It is plain General Hooker knew nothing of the conditions of matters this way."[9]

Butterfield continued north to Stones River, where his men encountered two regiments of Geary's division guarding a work party at the railroad bridge. Butterfield remained in the vicinity

General Hooker (sixth from the right) and staff in Lookout Valley during the winter of 1863–64. Gen. Daniel Butterfield, chief of staff, is fifth from the left. (Courtesy Military Order of the Loyal Legion, Massachusetts Commandery, the U.S. Army Military History Institute.)

of Murfreesboro until 9 October, when he turned command of the XII Corps back over to Slocum and returned south. Telegraphic communication was restored between Nashville and Bridgeport on the eighth, and crews completed the last repairs on the railroad the next day. Meanwhile, Wheeler was racing against Crook's forces to escape destruction. Early on the ninth Butterfield informed Hooker that the raiders were "in full flight, Crook's command pursuing and gaining on them." Later that day Wheeler's column recrossed the Tennessee at Muscle Shoals.[10]

The only other damage to the railroad came on the morning of 10 October. A band of Rebel cavalry under the command of Brig. Gen. Philip A. Roddey threw rocks, timbers, and other obstructions into the tunnel just south of Cowan. They dropped the objects through shafts that had been bored to remove rocks from the tunnel during construction. Butterfield reported that the "conduct of the commanding officer of the [tunnel] guard was damnable." He ordered the officer's arrest and was "of a strong mind to drum-head and shoot him."[11]

General Williams, informing his daughter of the incident, suggested that any danger was more apparent than real. "As fortune would have it," he wrote, "a rock had lodged in one of the shafts and when the first train went through with General Butterfield, down it tumbled." Butterfield, he continued, "imagined the Rebs. were after him and telegraphed a firm order . . . for watchfulness, etc." Williams "had the whole country around scoured, but found no Rebs." He concluded, "I am bored to death by incessant stories brought in by citizens that rebel cavalry is moving to attack such and such points."[12] Apparently his boredom also extended to nervous major generals.

With the raid over and the railroad open, the XI and XII Corps were able to start reforming some semblance of military commands as supplies and tardy soldiers began trickling in. Battles at Chancellorsville and Gettysburg had left many men of both corps wounded, and some were still recovering when the transfer occurred. Among them was Rice C. Bull of the 123d New York. On 6 October, Bull and several other men who had been gathered at the convalescent camp near Alexandria, often termed "Camp Misery," received a final meal and started on their way. Like those who had preceded them west, they endured crowded boxcars, and many took to the roofs for relief. Unlike their predecessors, they were not fed along the way. On the fourth day they arrived at Columbus and had the opportunity to find a restaurant and enjoy their first meal, other than the hardtack in their haversacks, since they left. From Columbus the men went to Cincinnati, taking a boat from there to Louisville. The remainder of the journey was by rail, and Bull returned to his unit, which was guarding the N&C some forty miles south of Murfreesboro, about two weeks after leaving Virginia.[13]

Also arriving at various posts were officers and men left behind when the raiders hit the railroad. These included Maj. Charles H.

Howard, General Howard's brother and a member of his staff. On 7 October he wrote his mother that he and other staff members were stranded in Nashville. The XI Corps artillery horses were there as well. Even when they again started on their way, the going was slow. First their train got stuck on a steep grade between Wartrace and Tullahoma, remaining there several hours until a helper engine could be pressed into service. Then they were delayed by the obstructions the Confederates threw into the tunnel below Cowan. The next delay occurred at Stevenson, where the group transferred from one train to another, waiting for crews to assemble the train that was to take them the last ten miles of their journey. That train, it turned out, was too long for the locomotive to pull, and Howard and his comrades had to wait for the front section to be delivered to Bridgeport before the locomotive could return for them. All told, it took the group forty hours to travel 123 miles.[14]

The reopening of the railroad, along with the efficient work of Thomas Scott, also allowed badly needed supplies and equipment to start arriving. Organization was generally lost during the transfer, and many items arrived worse for wear—or not at all. David Mouat noted that he and many of his comrades from the Twenty-ninth Pennsylvania discovered that their "guns and accoutrements . . . got lost or some of the lads who had lost theirs confiscated ours." Mouat and friends solved their problem when they "found" several guns at the depot in Murfreesboro. When they fell into line for their first inspection in Tennessee, "Our captain looked at us pretty hard but said nothing."[15]

Supply problems took many forms. Dr. Hubbard sent a surgeon to Nashville from his Bridgeport headquarters for much needed medical supplies. Chaplain Quint of the Second Massachusetts made plans for a worship service soon after arriving in Tennessee, only to discover that the hymnals had not yet arrived. By the time he located some and returned to camp, orders had come to move out again. John Love of the Thirteenth New Jersey, a division surgeon under Williams, faced a different problem. On 13 October Love wrote to his wife to report that his black servant Dick had not arrived with the division's horses. He heard that Dick and two other servants had been straggling and were left behind at Washington, and he did not expect to see him again. Four days later, however, Dick showed up, having traveled all the way from Washington on his own without paying a dime in fares. According to Love, Dick explained, "'I would get on one train, and when they asked me for money I would say I had none. Well den dey would say "you must git off." All right I would git off, go round behind and jump on and thus I would get from one station to another.'" The process had taken two weeks, but Love concluded, "I think he will do, guess he can go almost anywhere."[16]

Love reported that his horse had come through in good condition except for missing some hair from his tail and sides caused by rubbing against the cars. Not all horses fared so well, however. General Williams reported that his stallion was "badly rubbed on both hips." His other horse, "Old Plug Ugly," arrived in even worse shape. Because of his length he rubbed at both ends of the car and his head and tail were bared to the bones. To make matters worse, "some indignant horse" had bitten his neck. "He looks worse," Williams concluded, "than after the shell exploded under him at Chancellorsville."[17]

Adding to the difficulties of those whose supplies did not make it through, Tennessee was a more difficult place than Virginia to locate needed items. Capt. John Griswold of the 154th New York told his wife, "I have seen nothing in the shape of fruit here." He had managed to track down a dry goods sutler, from whom he purchased a much needed shirt at what he reported to be a highly inflated price. John Love asked his wife to send some copies of the *New York Times*. Writing from Murfreesboro, he complained that the men received no papers "except the miserable sheets published in Nashville," which reported the same news he had read in eastern papers two weeks earlier.[18]

Love was also unimpressed with Murfreesboro. He conceded that it had at one time been "a beautiful, thriving town." The "once neat, stylish, and costly" homes, he added, "indicate that the owners were persons of wealth and taste." But after more than two years of war, the community had been "used up." All one passing through could now see, Love concluded, was "decay, desolation, filth, and niggers."[19]

If not charitable, Love's reflections were typical. Ezra Carman reported that his first view of Wartrace did not "strike me with favor," and he dismissed Stevenson as "a poor dirty hole." Dr. Hubbard, Howard's fastidious medical director, informed his wife that Bridgeport consisted of "less than half a dozen dilapidated shanties." According to Captain Griswold, the men stationed at Bridgeport "think we are nearly out of the world." Even Howard was depressed at the sight of his new command, ordering his men to start cleaning the village as soon as they arrived.[20]

If Tennessee's communities failed to impress the eastern soldiers, the Volunteer State's natives fared even worse in the men's estimation. It is not surprising that Hubbard dismissed the Tennesseans as "the most ignorant abject people it has ever been my misfortune to see." Yet even General Williams, whose opinions generally were more carefully measured, confided to his daughter that the people he had encountered "look shabby and forlorn." Horatio Chapman of the Twentieth Connecticut told of visiting a family of eight who lived in a one-room log cabin near Cowan. The cabin had two beds, which together took up half the space in the dwelling. He asked the "largest girl" her age, but she did not know. Her father guessed that she was eight or ten, but his wife corrected him, saying she was "right smart on to eleven she reckoned."[21]

The women made a special impression, particularly on the men of the Northeast. Nearly all of the females they encountered, recalled Sgt. Henry Morhous of the 123d New York, "chewed and smoked tobacco, dipped snuff, and swore at the Yankees." John

Love estimated that seven out of ten smoked, chewed, or dipped, "and frequently all three. Ladies delicate in appearance, beautiful in form," he continued, "take out their pouch and take out their chew and spit away like any tobacco useing biped of the male race." Even Hubbard, though disgusted by the practice, conceded that they "spit with great skill after the manner of masculine tobacco chewers."[22]

Two and a half years of war had, of course, contributed to the destitution of the residents. Sergeant Morhous said many had been "stripped of everything but land and houses by the Rebels." They received rations from the Union government, and many "had to work for Uncle Sam by the side . . . of their former slaves." Although no houses were in sight, Griswold wrote that occasionally a woman on horseback would emerge from the woods at Bridgeport. They were "so thin that it would take both horse and rider to make a good shadow." The women sought rations, "affirming their loyalty while in all probability their husbands and sons are engaged in the business of bushwhacking or guerrilla warfare." Still, "common humanity" required that they be fed.[23]

Most men agreed that Tennessee had a higher percentage of loyalists than Virginia. Still, many would have agreed with Chaplain Quint's assessment that it was "Border State" loyalty. "It is not," he observed, "the loyalty which regards slavery as of more consequence than the Union." Love found the residents around Tullahoma to be "mostly Union," willing to bring large quantities of supplies to the men "for the consideration of greenbacks." Still, he was quick to point out that many were "the genuine article," people who could not "do enough to help the good cause." Brown of the Twenty-seventh Indiana agreed, saying Tennessee lacked the "evident tone of hostility" that he had noticed everywhere in Virginia. In the Volunteer State, he remarked, "A Union soldier could feel somewhat at home."[24]

The eastern soldiers were largely unimpressed by their new comrades from the Army of the Cumberland. Not surprisingly, Hubbard found them to be "wild and rough," forming what he termed "a barbarous society for which I have no taste." Ario Pardee Jr. of the 147th Pennsylvania wrote home that the western soldiers were "mighty loose and negligent in all their military duty." George Metcalf of the 136th New York echoed this view. After the war he recalled that among western outfits there was "less attention paid to the uniforms of the soldiers, and a general letting down of rules and their enforcement."[25]

The negative feelings apparently were mutual. On 22 October Ohio soldier Henry Henney recorded simply in his diary, "The Army of the Cumberland doesn't like the Army of the Potomac very much." On the day that the 149th New York arrived in Nashville, they were hastily sent forward to Murfreesboro and stationed in a large fort along Stones River. There they and a group of western troops fell into position to repel an anticipated cavalry attack. Seeing no signs of cavalry, the New Yorkers relaxed and began making coffee and preparing food. Observing this nonchalant attitude, the westerners sneered that the Army of the Potomac "didn't know enough to be afraid when it was in danger." Then, noticing their eastern comrades' blackened shoes and neat uniforms, they dubbed the new arrivals "Paper-collar soldiers." The Army of the Potomac gave as good as it got, however. Just before dark the westerners sprang to arms and nearly opened fire when a group of horsemen approached. There was "considerable laughter in the ranks of the 149th" when they learned that the advancing horsemen were Union cavalry in pursuit of a retreating enemy.[26]

As time wore on, these views moderated—at least to an extent. Pardee noted that the Army of the Cumberland had "a more exalted opinion of the Army of the Potomac than I expected to find," adding, "This good opinion has increased since they met Longstreet." Chaplain Quint later recalled that a group of Michigan soldiers willingly shared their rations with the hungry men of the Second Massachusetts, shunning all offers of payment. Another Massachusetts soldier saw through what he considered a bold facade. Writing home, Charles Fessendon Morse observed of western officers, "No matter how rough they are, or how much they blow for their army . . . they are perfectly liberal in their ideas and are as hospitable as men can be, offering us horses, rations, or anything else we want."[27]

Still, there were tensions. Even the normally calm Williams, citing "a decided lack of harmony" between the eastern and western soldiers, found it necessary to address the situation. In an order issued on 21 October, he noted that on several occasions "this feeling has nearly resulted in a collision between small parties of the respective commands. It is earnestly hoped," the general continued, "the present state of feeling may immediately give place to a spirit of at least apparent harmony." Although these "little bandyings" had often been "playfully commenced," he threatened any officer or enlisted man who persisted in such behavior with arrest.[28]

Some commanders became concerned that their men were picking up some of the bad habits that seemed to characterize the western soldiers. On 15 October, Schurz issued a lengthy order on the subject. The general had noticed "with regret" that some of the regiments under his command "present a slovenly appearance, perform their duties in a negligent and careless way and show symptoms of lax discipline and unsoldierly spirit and a deplorable want of instruction." The solution, in his opinion, lay in "stimulating the zeal and activity of some officers." Both field and line officers would be responsible for the discipline of their commands; the personal cleanliness of their men and good condition of their arms and equipment; the conditions of their camps; and the "soldierly spirit and military bearing of their men," particularly their "demeanor toward their superiors." All officers who did not "succeed in raising their commands to the required standard of efficiency" risked dismissal.

Four days later Geary issued a similar, albeit much briefer, order on the subject of dress. All soldiers on duty were to "appear in the proper uniform of the Army, neat and clean," and knapsacks were to be "properly slung." Soldiers failing to comply would be "severely punished," and their company commanders would be "held responsible for the neglect of duty." Geary also became concerned after the enemy captured several pickets under his command. To correct the problem he ordered guard-mounting ceremonies "with much pomp and style" and put his own officers in charge of inspections. He also put the principal picket posts under the command of easterners. The western soldiers responded with "some heart-burnings and internal swearing," but no more pickets were captured.[29]

Meanwhile, Hooker was attempting to score points with one prominent easterner—the secretary of war. On 11 October he informed Stanton, "If you projected the late movement of the Eleventh and Twelfth Corps you may justly claim the merit of having saved Chattanooga to us." Hooker explained that the enemy's intention was to destroy the line of communications and supply "before my force came up." They "undoubtedly would have succeeded," he added, "but for a prompt movement on our part." As it was, the Confederates had done some damage and interrupted communications, "but it is now restored."

The next day Hooker communicated with a more prominent superior, returning to a familiar subject. In a message to the president he asked that Slocum be "tendered a command in Missouri or somewhere else." He offered no specifics but asserted, "Unless he gives more satisfaction in the discharge of his duties, he will soon find himself in deeper water than he has been wading in." Hooker said the XII Corps commander "now appears to be swayed entirely by passion in the exercise of his office," adding, "It seems he aspired to the command of the Army of the Potomac, and that mortal offense was given in not naming him first." He concluded, "I should rejoice to have the Twelfth Corps put in Butterfield's hands."[30]

Despite his commanding general's views, on 13 October Slocum formally assumed command of all troops guarding the Nashville & Chattanooga Railroad between Murfreesboro and Tantalon. Orders immediately went out from corps headquarters calling for proper works to be erected at bridges and other vulnerable portions of the road. "It is of vital importance to the Army," Slocum pointed out, "that there should be no interruption in the Rail Road communication." In case of attack, it was expected "that the men will defend themselves and their position." Officers were to report directly to Slocum any damage to the railroad or the telegraph lines and see to it that the damage was promptly repaired. Brigade and division commanders were to inspect all works within their commands at least twice each week and report the state of the defenses to corps headquarters.[31]

On 15 October, Slocum reported the dispositions of his command, thinly spread along the sixty-three miles of N&C track he was to protect. They were as follows:

First Battalion, Tenth Maine Volunteers (corps provost guard), at Wartrace.

First Division, Brig. Gen. A. S. Williams; headquarters at Decherd.

First Brigade, First Division, Brig. Gen. J. F. Knipe; headquarters at Decherd.

Twentieth Connecticut at Cowan; Third Maryland at tunnel, 2 miles beyond; Col. S. Ross commanding at Cowan and vicinity.

Forty-sixth Pennsylvania, Fifth Connecticut, One hundred and twenty-first and One hundred and forty-fifth New York Volunteers; Batteries F, Fourth United States, and M, First New York Artillery at Decherd; Brig. Gen. J. F. Knipe commanding post.

Third brigade, First Division, General T. H. Ruger; headquarters at Tullahoma.

Third Wisconsin, Second Massachusetts, eight companies One hundred and seventh New York, at Elk River; two companies One hundred and seventh New York at water-tank and culvert, Estill Springs; Col. William Hawley commanding post at Elk River and vicinity.

Twenty-seventh Indiana, Thirteenth New Jersey, and seven companies One hundred and fiftieth New York Volunteers, at Tullahoma.

Three companies One hundred and fiftieth New York at trestle-work, 3 miles south of Tullahoma.

Brig. Gen. T. H. Ruger commanding post at Tullahoma and vicinity.

Second Division, Brig. Gen. John W. Geary; headquarters Murfreesborough.

First Brigade, Second Division, Col. Charles Candy; headquarters Duck River.

Sixty-sixth Ohio between Wartrace and Bell Buckle, guarding bridges; Seventh Ohio guarding Garrison's Fork bridge; headquarters of both of these regiments at Wartrace.

Eighty-fifth Indiana, and Battery K, Fifth U.S. Artillery, at Wartrace; Col. W. R. Creighton commanding post at Wartrace.

Twenty-eighth and One hundred and forty-seventh Pennsylvania at Duck River with brigade headquarters.

Twenty-ninth Ohio and seven companies Fifth Ohio at Normandy trestle, Col. John H. Patrick commanding post.

One company Twenty-ninth Ohio at water-tank between Normandy and Tullahoma. The road is patrolled twice a day between Bell Buckle and within two miles of Tullahoma.

Second Brigade, Second Division, Col. George A. Cobham; headquarters at Christiana.

One hundred and Eleventh Pennsylvania, Lieut. Col. T. M. Walker, at Christiana, on picket duty and patrolling the railroad from within 3 miles of Murfreesborough to Murray's Cut.

One hundred and ninth Pennsylvania, Capt. F. L. Gimber, at the Millersburg and Columbus Cross-roads, on picket and patrolling railroad, to connect with One hundred and Eleventh Pennsylvania.

Twenty-ninth Pennsylvania, Col. W. Rickards, at Fosterville (two companies at Shelbyville) on picket, patrolling railroad to Bell Buckle and connecting with One hundred and ninth Pennsylvania.

Third Brigade, Second Division, Brig. Gen. George S. Greene; headquarters Murfreesborough.

Seventy-eighth New York Volunteers, Lieut. Col. H. von Hammerstein, on railroad bridge over west fork of Stone's River, about 3 miles south of Murfreesborough.

Sixtieth New York Volunteers, Col. A. Goddard, One hundred and second New York Volunteers, Colonel Lane, and Nineteenth Michigan Volunteers, Col. H. C. Gilbert, stationed at Murfreesborough, near railroad depot.

One hundred and forty-ninth New York Volunteers, Lieut. Col. C. B. Randall, Twenty-second Wisconsin Volunteers, Col. W. L. Utley, and detachments of convalescents, in Fortress Rosecrans.

One hundred and thirty-seventh New York Volunteers, Col. D. Ireland, guarding trains going to Tantalon.

Knap's E (Independent Pennsylvania), Battery, Capt. Charles A. Atwell, at Murfreesborough.

Fortress Rosecrans, Maj. C. Houghtaling, First Illinois Light Artillery, commanding.

Detachments of dismounted cavalry, Lieut. Col. J. J. Seibert, on court-house square, Murfreesborough.

Detachment of Fourth East Tennessee Cavalry, Lieut. Col. J. M. Thornburgh, at Murfreesborough, when not out on scouting duty.

Detachment of infantry, First Brigade, Fourth Division, Fourteenth Army Corps, Lieut G. W. Boggess, near Fort Rosecrans.[32]

The soldiers stationed at these scattered posts were generally satisfied with their assignments. George Edwards of the Twenty-seventh Indiana perhaps summed up the view of many. In a letter to his wife he wrote that he was on guard duty every other day. "I call that pretty heavy duty," he remarked, "but I guess we can stand it rather than go to the front." John Hill of the 107th New York agreed. He was guarding the Elk River Bridge and informed his family that the prospect of spending the winter there was "a very agreeable affair as we are very comfortably situated." (Unfortunately, only days after completing comfortable winter quarters, the 107th received orders to march to the front. They started off through rain and mud,

only to be sent back north two days later to Fosterville, forty miles
beyond the Elk River.)

After four days of chasing Wheeler's cavalry, Samuel Toombs of
the Thirteenth New Jersey reported that his regiment was happy to
halt at Tullahoma with the "joyful news" that "our ramblings were
now at an end." The men selected a campsite near the railroad, with
company streets "mathematically laid out," and then went "heartily
to work erecting stockades." A few days of "persistent toil" resulted
in a camp that "presented a very pretty sight."[33]

Like the XII Corps, the XI spent a good deal of its time guarding
the N&C, but its activities were more diverse. General Howard
was headquartered at Bridgeport, where the Confederates had destroyed the railroad bridge across the Tennessee. The Rebels occupied the south side of the river, but according to Charles Howard,
they seldom showed themselves, and when they did it was usually
on distant ridges. The general established his headquarters within
the enclosures of an abandoned Confederate fort. "We have reason
to be thankful," his brother noted, "that the enemy did so much
digging for us."[34]

On 6 October men from Schurz's division put a pontoon bridge
in place across the Tennessee. (Actually there were two pontoons,
one from Bridgeport to a large island in the river, the other continuing the rest of the way to the southern bank.) The next day
work began felling trees to replace the N&C trestle. Soon another
detachment from the active corps was widening and corduroying a
wagon road from Bridgeport to Jasper along the north bank. Heavy
rains virtually every day from 1 to 20 October rendered the work
more difficult yet also more important since the mud that resulted
made it even more difficult to transport supplies to Rosecrans's
army. Work on this project continued until 17 October, when Rosecrans terminated it. At the suggestion of XI Corps quartermaster
William Le Duc, the commanding general decided that it would be
more feasible to lay track on an adjacent roadbed that was already
graded.[35]

Work parties from the XI Corps put a pontoon bridge in place at Bridgeport, Alabama, adjacent to the N&C Railroad bridge, which had been destroyed by the Confederates. (Courtesy Military Order of the Loyal Legion, Massachusetts Commandery, the U.S. Army Military History Institute.)

Le Duc was also in charge of an 8 October foraging expedition that ventured five miles on the south side of the river. The party returned with 1,045 bushels of corn gathered in the field of a Mr. Poe, who was reported to be "a scout and guide in the employ of the Confederate States." A small cavalry detachment that accompanied the expedition returned with four prisoners, two Confederate soldiers and two private citizens. Of the latter pair, one man was accused of stealing government horses and one was believed to have concealed traitors.[36]

Howard's energetic quartermaster was also involved with Capt. Arthur Edwards in the latter's project to convert a flat-bottomed scow into a serviceable steamer to help supply the army in Chattanooga. Rosecrans was eager to have the job completed, and Howard supplied several caulkers and other workers for the project.

For nearly three weeks Le Duc divided his time between the steamer and the railroad to Jasper, perhaps, as Garfield once suggested, to the neglect of his other duties. (Still, Edwards and Le Duc would launch their little floating supply line on 24 October and, five days later, push two barges loaded with desperately needed rations to Rankin's Ferry.)[37]

Although Rosecrans was anxious to have the steamer put into service, he was not around to witness its completion. On 16 October the War Department issued General Orders 337, combining the Departments of the Ohio, the Cumberland, and the Tennessee into the Military Division of the Mississippi. Maj. Gen. Ulysses S. Grant was to command the division, and Maj. Gen. George H. Thomas, the hero of Chickamauga, succeeded Rosecrans as commander of the Army of the Cumberland.[38]

Rosecrans's days may have been numbered following the defeat at Chickamauga. Perhaps equally important were Secretary Stanton's dislike of him and Assistant Secretary Dana's eagerness to please his boss. On the evening of 20 September, as the disorganized remnants of the Army of the Cumberland were retreating back to Chattanooga after their defeat at Chickamauga, Dana had exonerated the commander. "I can testify," he wired Stanton, "to the conspicuous and steady gallantry of General Rosecrans on the field. He made all possible efforts to rally the broken columns; nor do I see that there was any fault in the disposition of his forces."

Soon, after Stanton dropped several loud hints about his disapproval of the commanding general, Dana's messages became quite different in tone. By 27 September he was reporting Rosecrans to be "greatly lacking in firmness and steadiness of will." In a 12 October dispatch Dana reported, "I have never seen a public man possessing talent with less administrative power, less clearness and steadiness in difficulty, and greater practical incapacity than General Rosecrans." Four days later Dana was referring to "our dazed and mazy commander [who] cannot perceive the catastrophe

that is close upon us, nor fix his mind upon the means of preventing it. I never saw anything which seemed so lamentable and
hopeless."[39]

If Dana's dispatches provided Stanton with evidence to lay before the commander in chief, Rosecrans was already in the process of convincing Lincoln by himself. On 3 October, as his army
approached starvation at Chattanooga, Rosecrans sent Lincoln a
message suggesting that the president "offer a general amnesty to all
officers and soldiers in the rebellion." Such an action, he asserted,
"would give us moral strength, and weaken them very much." Lincoln responded patiently that he was considering "something like
what you suggest" at the appropriate time. Meanwhile, "If we can
hold Chattanooga and East Tennessee, I think the rebellion must
dwindle and die. I think you and Burnside can do this," he continued, "and hence doing so is your main object." In a rambling
message on 12 October Rosecrans listed the many disadvantages
under which he was laboring, including a lack of transportation and
provisions, but concluded, "Every exertion will be made to hold
what we have and gain more, after which we must put our trust
in God, who never fails those who truly trust." Nevertheless, on
16 October, Rosecrans confided to Halleck his opinion that "our
future is not bright."[40]

All of this was enough to convince Lincoln, who later told Hay
that ever since the loss at Chickamauga Rosecrans had acted "con-
fused and stunned like a duck hit on the head." Officially, Grant
was given the option of retaining Rosecrans or replacing him with
Thomas, but there was little doubt which course he would choose.
Grant was on his way to Chattanooga, and Rosecrans was headed
into military oblivion.[41]

As Grant headed south along the Louisville & Nashville and the
Nashville & Chattanooga, several of his new subordinates turned
out to get a look at the hero of Vicksburg. Chaplain Quint was
present in Nashville when the general's train arrived on 22 October.
That evening a military band and a crowd of sightseers drew him out

of his hotel but could not persuade him to deliver a speech. Grant finally thanked them for their good wishes and told them "he never could talk, and he was now too old to begin." The crowd did get a speech from Andrew Johnson, the military governor of Tennessee, but Quint did not hear much of it. "I yielded to appetite," he later confessed, "and went off in search of beefsteak, rare done, and fried potatoes."[42]

On down the line, the Twenty-seventh Indiana was especially happy to welcome their fellow westerner into the ranks. "The sight of this plain, unassuming Western man, with his Western ways, brought our hearts right up into our throats," Edmund Brown recalled. Stopping briefly at Tullahoma, Grant wore "a faded coat, the buttons of which indicated the rank of brigadier-general." As at Nashville, the new commander spoke very briefly, and Brown noted, "What he said could not be heard a rod away."[43]

On 21 October, Grant arrived at Stevenson. Howard was present to greet him, but Hooker was not. Fighting Joe had sent a spring wagon to deliver the new commanding general, who was recovering from injuries sustained in a fall from his horse, to his headquarters. "Without the least disturbance of manner," Howard recalled, "Grant said [to Hooker's messenger], 'If General Hooker wishes to see me, he will find me on this train.'" The response, Howard concluded, "was General Grant's method of asserting himself where he thought a general who had had large commands and considerable self-assertion might be seeking an ascendancy over him." Hooker got the message and was soon on hand to pay his respects in person.[44]

Hooker remained behind as Grant continued on to Bridgeport, where he spent the night at Howard's headquarters. Interpreting his physical features, Dr. Hubbard informed his wife, "His thin, slightly compressed lips tell of firmness and perseverance in whatever he undertakes." Hubbard found the general's demeanor to be "quiet, self-possessed and not communicative, evidently avoiding all effort to impress any idea of greatness upon those around him."

At one point during the evening the commanding general spotted an empty whiskey flask in Howard's tent. "That flask is not mine," Howard quickly assured him. "It was left here by an officer to be returned to Chattanooga; I never drink."

"Neither do I," Grant responded. Howard believed him, noting that his appearance was "the contradiction of a thousand falsehoods which ambition and envy had industriously circulated against him." Hubbard agreed, assuring his wife, "He looks least of all like one addicted to intemperance." The doctor added that a "prominent member" of Grant's staff (possibly the protective John Rawlins) had told him that Grant was not only totally abstinent but so disapproving of strong drink that when staff members wished to indulge, "they do it clandestinely."[45]

The next morning Grant left for the last leg of his journey to Chattanooga. There he would meet with Thomas and initiate the movements that would eventually break the month-old siege. The first step would be to open a supply line into the city to sustain the nearly starved men of the Army of the Cumberland. Both Hooker and Howard would play prominent parts in that first step, giving them an opportunity to prove that Stanton's proposed rescue by rail had indeed "saved Chattanooga to us."

8

"You Have Opened Up Our Bread Line"

At daybreak on 22 October, Ulysses S. Grant and his party set out from Bridgeport for Chattanooga, following the same muddy, winding mountain road over which supplies had been trickling into the city. His painful leg injury made the two-day journey an especially difficult one for the new commander. He arrived on the evening of the twenty-third, "wet, dirty, and well," according to Dana.[1]

He was also in a mood to get right to work. There was something in the makeup of this man, historian Bruce Catton observed, "that when Grant showed up things began to happen." An officer at Chattanooga later put it this way: "We began to see things move. We felt that everything came from a plan." Horace Porter of Thomas's staff agreed. Although he found the new commander to be "slight in figure" and "carelessly dressed," still, "So intelligent were his inquiries, and so pertinent his suggestions, that he made a profound impression upon every one by the quickness of his perception and the knowledge which he had already acquired regarding important details of the army's condition." All were impressed, Porter later asserted, "by the exhibition they witnessed of his singular mental powers and his rare military qualities."[2]

While Grant brought a new initiative and energy with him to Chattanooga, that energy was devoted mainly to carrying out plans that others had already formulated, which he readily admitted in his memoirs. At Stevenson, for example, he had met briefly with Rosecrans, who "described very clearly the situation at Chattanooga." Grant generously added that Rosecrans "made some excellent suggestions as to what should be done," while noting less generously, "My only wonder was that he had not carried them out."[3]

On the morning of 24 October, his first full day in Chattanooga, Grant set out to learn firsthand what could be done to carry out the plans Rosecrans had discussed with him. Accompanying him were General Thomas and Gen. William Farrar Smith. The latter, known in army circles as "Baldy," had been with the Army of the Cumberland only a few weeks, arriving shortly after wearing out his welcome with the Army of the Potomac because of his sharp tongue. Named chief engineer by Rosecrans, Smith had performed routine duties. Much of his time, however, he had devoted to scouting out a reliable supply route between Bridgeport and Chattanooga.

He thought he had found one, and now Smith was ready to show it to his new commanding general. The party crossed the Tennessee via a pontoon bridge north of town, then headed west. This route took them across Moccasin Point, a peninsula formed by the river as it bends sharply south just west of Chattanooga before turning back to the north-northeast. They followed a dirt road to a crossing, known to the locals as Brown's Ferry, at the western end of the neck of the peninsula. Across the river the road continued, providing a link to Bridgeport through Lookout Valley. Taking advantage of an informal truce between pickets, the trio studied the site. Grant was impressed by what he saw and returned to Chattanooga to issue appropriate orders to put the plan in motion.[4]

That plan called for Smith to command an expedition to seize Brown's Ferry and drive away any Confederates stationed there. Engineers would follow and build a pontoon bridge across the river. At the same time Hooker and his easterners were to march from Bridgeport to link up with Smith's force. If they succeeded, the supply route from Bridgeport to Chattanooga would be opened.[5]

On the evening of 26 October, fifteen hundred specially selected men from the brigade of Gen. William B. Hazen were ready to move out. They did not know where they would be going or what they would be doing, but they had spent enough time in the army to know that the assignment they had drawn was going to be important and likely dangerous.

Chosen for their bravery in past campaigns, the men were to seize and secure Brown's Ferry and throw a pontoon bridge across the Tennessee at that point. They would reach Brown's Ferry by floating some eight miles down the river on fifty pontoon boats hastily assembled for their mission. The importance of the assignment was obvious. So, too, was the danger; the men would drift directly past Confederate pickets most of the way, with Rebel artillery staring down at them from Lookout Mountain. The rest of Hazen's brigade, along with the brigade of Gen. John B. Turchin, was to march in support, taking the same road across Moccasin Point that Grant and his party had used. Accompanying them would be Maj. John Mendenhall and three batteries of artillery.

At midnight, 27 October, the squads that had been selected a few hours earlier received orders to march through Chattanooga to the riverfront. There they learned their mode of transportation—and their destination. Three hours later they began their perilous mission. In the lead was Lt. Col. James Foy of the Twenty-third Kentucky, the officer who was to command the first landing party when the boats reached Brown's Ferry.

The first phase of the operation went smoothly, and sometime between 4:30 and 5:00 A.M. Foy and his men came ashore at their destination. They drove off a handful of Confederate pickets and quickly went to work building breastworks. As they began, Col. William C. Oates launched a counterattack with his Fifteenth Alabama Regiment. The Confederates pushed Foy's men back to the river, where they met reinforcements from Turchin's brigade, who had just crossed over on the abandoned pontoon boats. Together the two forces overwhelmed the attackers and secured Brown's Ferry for good. Later that day engineers completed the pontoon bridge, shortening considerably the supply line to Chattanooga.[6]

Now it was up to Hooker and his men to complete their part of the operation. On 23 October, Fighting Joe received his preliminary orders from army headquarters at Chattanooga. He was to move to the south side of the Tennessee with the XI Corps and one division of the XII. The other division was to remain behind and guard the line of the Nashville & Chattanooga. Further instructions, received the following day, informed Hooker that Williams's First Division would remain behind; Geary's Second Division would march with him and Howard. He also learned, doubtless to his delight, that Slocum would stay behind with Williams.

After crossing the river, Hooker and his three divisions were to proceed along the line of the N&C in the direction of Rankin's Ferry. "The object of the movement," Hooker was informed, "is to hold the road and gain possession of the river as far as Brown's Ferry."[7]

It was an assignment about which Hooker was less than sanguine. Howard later recalled that he "never saw Hooker apparently so apprehensive of disaster." He told the XI Corps commander, "Why, Howard, Longstreet is up on that Lookout Range with at least 10,000 fighting men. We will be obliged to make a flank march along the side and base of the mountain. I shall have scarcely so many men, and must take care of my trains. It is a very hazardous operation," Hooker concluded, "and almost certain to procure us a defeat."[8]

Howard recorded his commanding general's concerns four decades later, which leaves some doubt as to their accuracy. On 24 October, however, soon after he received his second set of instructions, Hooker expressed similar qualms in a message to army headquarters. He had been talking with "men who have grazed their stock on Lookout Mountain." They told him that there were numerous bridle paths leading down Lookout Mountain into the valley, perilously close to Hooker's right flank. Further, "infantry can descend the north slope of Lookout at many points." Hooker did not make any specific suggestions—he certainly did not recommend abandoning the mission—but clearly there were doubts in his mind.[9]

Despite his misgivings, Hooker acted diligently to carry out his instructions. Geary's command, which extended as far north as Murfreesboro, once again boarded the cars of the N&C, but as before, the going was rough. According to Geary, Hooker's orders "were immediately acted upon, but, owing to the limited transportation and difficulty in procuring the same, combined with numerous interferences with the road and trains by hostile parties, much delay was occasioned." Lt. Albert R. Greene of the Seventy-eighth New York later recalled of his unit's move to Bridgeport: "3 days and nights getting from Murfreesboro to Bridgeport—relaying track, building culverts and bridges, wet by rain all the time." As a result, when the movement got under way from Bridgeport, Geary had only four regiments with him.[10]

Also joining Geary at Bridgeport was a portion of Independent Battery E, Pennsylvania Light Artillery. This was Knap's Battery, named for its founder, which had accompanied the Twenty-eighth Pennsylvania throughout the war. Commanding the outfit's four guns was Capt. Charles Atwell, assisted by Geary's son, Lt. Edward Geary. Writing from Bridgeport on 25 October, Geary told his wife, "Edward is here and is well." The proud father informed the young man's stepmother, "He has been chosen captain of Battery [F] . . . and nothing remains but for [Pennsylvania governor Andrew] Curtin to issue the commission." That meant Edward would be returning to the Army of the Potomac, "and although I dislike the idea of separation from him," Geary wrote, "still I will not let anything stand in the way of his promotion, for he is a noble boy, and well he has earned it."[11]

The movement was originally scheduled to commence at 9:00 A.M. on 26 October. Howard was to take the lead with his corps, picking up units already on the south side of the Tennessee as the march progressed. Geary's division would follow. Despite any doubts he may have harbored, Hooker had resigned himself to the task at hand and was determined to get on with it. When Howard requested a delay, offering excuses about his artillery not being ready, Hooker reacted sharply. "I am surprised to learn," the commanding general replied, "that you have but one reliable battery out of five. We will march to-morrow if we go without any." Despite this bluster, Hooker modified his plans when he learned of the difficulties Geary was encountering getting his men to Bridgeport. Two hours after his outburst, Hooker altered his instructions to Howard, wiring, "Let everything be in readiness for an early start the following morning."[12]

That early start came at 6:30 A.M. on 27 September, when Steinwehr's Second Division left camp, crossing the pontoon bridges at Bridgeport. The rear of the XI Corps column cleared the Tennessee two and one-half hours later, and Geary's division followed. Out in front were two companies of cavalry, loyalist outfits from Alabama and Tennessee, that had been assigned to Howard. Hooker, perhaps still harboring thoughts of Chancellorsville, traveled with Howard. The men marched northeast along the roadbed of the N&C toward Shellmound, some five miles away. From there they followed the south bank of the river for about three miles before turning southeast toward the community of Whiteside. There, following a march of about fifteen miles, the XI Corps made camp for the night. Geary's division went into camp at Shellmound, where three more of his regiments caught up with him.[13]

The first day's march had not been easy. The roads were muddy from the recent heavy rains, and rocks blocked the way. "The whole country," Dr. Hubbard wrote, "is divided into valleys and narrow defile[s] by ranges of mountains running at various angles to each other and not infrequently for a long distance parallel. Our road," he went on, "was along these valleys and defiles or along the river bank underneath overhanging ledges and cliffs of limestone towering hundreds of feet and apparently threatening to topple from their insecure bases upon our devoted heads." The defiles were often only fifty yards wide, and the roads were "exceedingly difficult." The only signs of civilization marking their path, the good doctor remarked, were "the same miserable log shanties with the same wretchedly

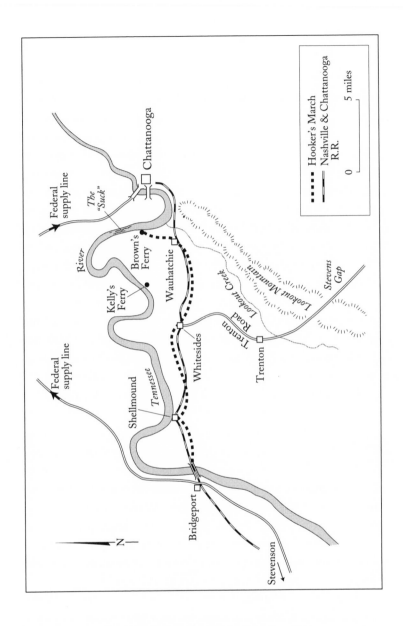

Hooker's march from Bridgeport to Wauhatchie and Brown's Ferry, 27–28
October 1863. (From a sketch by Douglas Cubbison.)

ignorant and dirty inmates as everywhere thus far down in Dixie abound."[14]

Still, after a month of monotonous guard duty, the men were again on the move, and according to Howard, they were glad to be. "Just what was before us nobody knew," the general wrote, "[but] it was at least a change." Helping lift their spirits were breathtaking vistas of "mountain sides ablaze with the colors of October." At Shellmound many took advantage of the opportunity to explore the Nickajack Cave. The Confederates had mined saltpeter extensively there until Rosecrans and his army drove them away. Now men of the Union XI and XII Corps "by the hundreds" were enjoying its beauty, some penetrating more than a mile inside to explore the "numberless chambers." The Fifty-fifth Ohio's regimental band also found its acoustics to be favorable. "We went in . . . and played several tunes in there," wrote bandsman Henry Henney. Among the sightseers was General Geary himself. Many followed a large stream that flowed through the cave. It was reported that explorers had followed it in a boat as far as six miles but had been unable to locate its source.[15]

Both Howard and Geary had their commands moving at daylight the next morning. The XI Corps headed generally to the east toward Wauhatchie Junction, where the N&C intersected with the Trenton Railroad. From there Howard's force would march northeast to Brown's Ferry. Geary was under orders from Hooker to "push on vigorously until you come up with the rear of the Eleventh Corps." The roads Howard's men traversed were even rougher than they had been the day before, resulting in broken artillery wheels and a scattering of the command. At about noon, as his men entered Wauhatchie Junction in Lookout Valley, Howard called a halt "and the troops massed until the [entire] corps came up."[16]

Soon after that Howard's men had their first encounter with the enemy. As the advance scouts reached the fork of the Brown's Ferry and Chattanooga Road, they came under fire from Confederates hiding in thick underbrush near the riverbank. Because of their concealment, it was "impossible at first," Howard later reported, "to tell the strength of the enemy." Under orders from Hooker, he sent Steinwehr straight ahead with a brigade, covered by skirmishers. Steinwehr's other brigade was dispatched to the left flank of the enemy position and one of Schurz's brigades to the right. The precautions proved unnecessary. The resisting force was a lone South Carolina regiment. The Seventy-third Ohio and the Seventy-third Pennsylvania fired a few volleys, then charged, driving away their foes.[17]

Thus ended the first skirmish west of the Appalachians between these veterans of the Army of the Potomac and the Army of Northern Virginia. Tactically the affair barely deserved to be dignified as a skirmish. Its significance, however, should not be overlooked. The last time these men had engaged each other in combat was at Gettysburg, almost four months before and several hundred miles away. Their very presence indicated that both governments had realized the importance of the war in the West. It also verified that railroads had come of age as tools of war. The men in Lookout Valley had indeed come a long way to get where they were that afternoon. Now they were simply doing the same thing they had done for the last three years—shooting at each other. But the very fact that they were doing it at this place showed that warfare had also come a long way.

The South Carolinians were not the only Confederates aware of the Union force's presence in the valley. Watching from atop Lookout Mountain were Generals Longstreet and Bragg. As they looked down at the blue-clad column advancing toward Wauhatchie, these stubborn officers beheld the fruits of a strained relationship and the dearth of personal communication it had produced.

It had all begun soon after Longstreet arrived from the East. In the wake of the victory at Chickamauga, Longstreet fell in with the sizable anti-Bragg contingent in the Army of Tennessee. Soon, according to his most recent biographer, the Georgian became "the faction's leader." On 26 September, Longstreet sent a letter to Secretary of War James Seddon, criticizing virtually everything Bragg had done (and not done) since Longstreet's arrival. "It seems," Longstreet complained, "that [Bragg] cannot adopt and adhere to any plan or course, whether of his own or someone else."[18]

On 9 October, President Davis, a staunch supporter of Bragg, arrived in Tennessee to try to straighten out the dispute. The idea miscarried when, in Bragg's presence, Longstreet informed the president that Bragg was "incompetent to manage an army or put men into a fight." That sentiment was then repeated by Gens. Simon B. Buckner, Benjamin Cheatam, and Daniel Harvey Hill. Three days later, despite their verdict, Davis announced that Bragg would remain in command. Soon after that, the triumphant general removed Hill from command, reduced Buckner from a corps to a division commander, and reduced the size of Longstreet's command so it included only the units he had brought with him from Virginia.[19]

Another result of the imbroglio was a virtually isolated command on Lookout Mountain for Lee's veteran corps commander, with only occasional written communications passing between him and Bragg. The situation seemed to produce a lethargy in Longstreet that became dangerous when he discounted the importance of Lookout Creek Valley as a potential supply route for the Army of the Cumberland. Although he ordered two regiments to the north bank of the Tennessee below Raccoon Mountain on 9 October, Longstreet ignored the valley and the Trenton Road that crossed through it.

On 25 October, Bragg received a scouting report informing him of Hooker's impending crossing at Bridgeport. Ordered by Bragg to make a reconnaissance, Longstreet did nothing. He had become convinced that the objective of any Federal movement from Bridgeport was not Lookout Valley. Instead, he reasoned, the Union forces would cross Lookout Mountain well to the south to get at his flank and rear. It was an unsupportable theory, but Longstreet stuck to it even after the assault on Brown's Ferry made the northerners' intentions obvious.

In fact, Longstreet did not even bother to report that the Federals had taken Brown's Ferry. Bragg learned of it only after sending Gen. St. John Liddell to Lookout Mountain to see what all the shooting was about. Meanwhile, Longstreet continued to brush off scouts' reports warning him of Hooker's advance into Lookout Valley. To Bragg he explained that the operation at Brown's Ferry was merely a diversion designed to mask the flanking movement he was still convinced was on the way.

That theory was finally exploded the following day, 28 October. Determined to learn the true situation, Bragg ordered Longstreet to meet him in person atop Lookout Mountain. As the pair beheld General Smith's pontoon bridges, some two miles away, a messenger arrived to report a large Federal column advancing through Lookout Valley. Not believing the news, Bragg and Longstreet accompanied the messenger to the western rim of the mountain. From there they watched as Hooker neared Wauhatchie. The threat to Longstreet's flank did not exist, and all that could be done now was to bring up Porter Alexander's artillery to throw some shells at long range in the direction of the Union forces.[20]

Those shells had little effect and were certainly not unexpected. By the time the men reached Wauhatchie, the peak of Lookout Mountain "stood out in bold view." On it the men could plainly see waving signal flags and Confederate guns. "A blue puff of smoke, and then the report, told us the advance of our column had come under their aim," recalled George Metcalf of the 136th New York. Fortunately, the Rebels' aim was not accurate at that range. Most of the shells overshot their mark, and casualties totaled one man killed and one wounded. Still, enough shells fell close enough to the line, Howard later remarked, "to make our men long for shelter, and to cause them to hasten their steps in order to gain a safer distance." For a time the column would enjoy the partial protection of a wooded area, then come to an open field, where they were in plain view. Whenever they emerged, Dr. Hubbard observed, the Confederate gunners "were not slow to improve on these opportunities."

Hooker stationed himself in the thick of it, displaying once again his famed coolness under fire. Col. James Wood of the 136th New York said he found the commanding general at "the point most exposed to the fire . . . notifying the men as they passed that there was no danger from the artillery firing, and testifying by his presence and position that he believed what he said." Metcalf recalled, "I saw one solid shot pass under his horse and go bounding away for rods beyond, but he appeared in no hurry."[21]

As Howard's men got beyond the range of the Confederate gunners they were "startled to see a considerable force crowning some round hills which suddenly rose up in our pathway." They could see red, white, and blue flags, but since those were also the colors of the Confederacy the sight was not reassuring. As Howard prepared to advance his men cautiously, "we heard a welcome sound." It was Hazen's men, advancing to greet them and shouting, "Hurrah! Hurrah! You have opened up our bread line!" According to Samuel Hurst of the Seventy-third Ohio, "As our column advanced along the valley, greeted and greeting, the shout was passed from hill-top to hill-top—the bands played, flags waved, and the very heavens rang with shouts such as are only heard in the army; and their shouts were answered back by our men with real soldierly enthusiasm." Seven days later an unidentified soldier from the 136th New York summed up the situation succinctly: "Grant's men were glad to see us and well they might be. We found them living on three hard crackers per day, and our move has opened the river so that steamers are now running regularly with supplies."[22]

As Howard reached Brown's Ferry, Geary and his Second Division were arriving at Wauhatchie, where Hooker had ordered them to encamp. Under orders from the commanding general, Geary had detached the 60th New York near Whiteside to guard the pass and branch road leading south to Trenton, Georgia. This left him with two brigades, a total of six regiments. Col. George A. Cobham's

Second Brigade, comprising the 29th, 109th, and 111th Pennsylvania, arrived at Wauhatchie intact. Gen. George S. Greene's Third Brigade was short two regiments, the 60th New York and the 102d New York, which had remained behind to escort the division ambulance train. Greene's brigade now consisted of the 78th, 137th, and 149th New York. All told, Geary went into camp at Wauhatchie with ninety-three officers and fourteen hundred men.[23]

Geary's men undoubtedly welcomed the change in orders which allowed them to halt at Wauhatchie rather then continue on and close up with Howard's corps. Many of them had spent the previous evening putting pontoons across the Tennessee at Shellmound. They had not completed the job until 1:00 A.M., three hours ahead of reveille and four hours before they resumed their march. General Hazen was less pleased with the decision, feeling Geary's isolated force was vulnerable to attack. Hazen went to Hooker "and endeavored to get him to take up a compact line across the valley, and to bring his forces together." This Fighting Joe refused to do; his orders were to "command the road from Kelly's Ferry to Brown's Ferry." Because the Tennessee was not navigable beyond Kelly's Ferry, keeping the road open was vital. Doing so required him to post a force at Wauhatchie. Besides, the only enemy he had seen in two days had been a mere two regiments. Hazen gave up but remained concerned.[24]

Geary, too, was concerned. Like Howard, he could easily see the "active signaling" on Lookout Mountain. He ordered his men to bivouac on their arms and to leave their cartridge boxes on. Geary also had the four guns of Knap's Battery posted on a knoll that commanded the points from which an attack was likely to come. Finally, he gave his officers instructions "to have their men spring to arms upon any alarm." Then, with pickets well thrown out, the weary men of the White Star Division settled in for what they hoped would be a restful night.[25]

9

Wauhatchie

Joseph Hooker had offered the Confederates one last chance to retrieve their fortunes in Lookout Valley. By carelessly leaving Geary's division isolated and failing to cover the approaches for a possible attack, he had handed the Rebels the opportunity to drive a wedge between his forces and block the newly opened supply line.[1]

This the Confederates might easily have accomplished had it not been for the petty rivalries among the various commanders responsible for the operation. Both Bragg and Longstreet agreed that an attack would be made against the blue-clad visitors in the valley. Beyond that simple point there appears to have been no agreement whatsoever. Bragg evidently intended for Longstreet to attack the main force at Brown's Ferry, assuring him that all three divisions of his corps were at his disposal. Instead, either because he misunderstood Bragg's wishes or, more likely, because he wanted to do things his own way, Longstreet chose to attack Geary's smaller command at Wauhatchie.[2]

The attack was to be carried out by Hood's division, in which yet another personal controversy was playing out. When he took his corps west, Longstreet had requested and received the brigade of Gen. Micah Jenkins and assigned it to Hood's division. When Hood was seriously wounded at Chickamauga, Longstreet put Jenkins in command of the division. In doing so he passed over Gen. Evander M. Law, a popular brigade commander, who had led the division after Hood's wounding at Gettysburg. Law had reportedly served ably as commander; he had certainly been with the division much longer. Jenkins, however, held a two-and-one-half-month advantage over his rival in date of rank. More to the point, he was Longstreet's choice for the assignment.[3]

Longstreet's plan called for Jenkins's brigade, commanded by Col. John Bratton, to attack Geary, with Henry Benning's Georgians in reserve. Law was to move his brigade, commanded by Col. James Sheffield, along with Jerome Robertson's brigade, to a point between Brown's Ferry and the Union rear guard to prevent reinforcements from reaching Wauhatchie.[4]

At about sunset, as Jenkins was beginning to issue orders to his division, Capt. J. L. Coker of the Sixth South Carolina arrived at headquarters. Jenkins had sent Coker over Lookout Mountain that morning to gather information about the Union movement. Jenkins informed his scout that he planned to divide his force and take one brigade "to capture a large wagon train" in the valley. "My report indicated that one brigade would be insufficient," Coker later recounted, "that a heavy body of infantry with artillery was with the wagon train mentioned." Jenkins went to Longstreet with the information, "but the plan as originally made was insisted upon, and the movement proceeded."[5]

While Jenkins and Coker met, Geary was conferring with Col. William Rickards Jr. of the Twenty-ninth Pennsylvania. Rickards's regiment had drawn picket duty and he was officer of the day. Both Rickards and Geary had made inquiries of local residents and had been informed at all stops that there was no enemy force between them and Lookout Mountain. Rickards was not convinced, however, and after posting his pickets he visited the log cabin home of a magistrate named Rowden. There, "in conversation with a woman," he learned that a portion of Longstreet's corps had been there the day before. Rickards took Rowden to Geary, and "after threats" the judge informed both officers that Longstreet's men lay across Lookout Creek near a bridge just over a mile from Geary's camp. Rickards hurried to his pickets, found the road leading to the bridge, and posted his men along it "with instructions to be very watchful."[6]

Since Howard's men had advanced northward to Brown's Ferry with virtually no resistance, Geary assumed that any attack was likely to come from the south. He therefore stationed most of his pickets along a wagon road running southwest, paralleling the N&C tracks, although he posted pickets in all directions. Knap's Battery he placed atop a knoll just west of the road and south of the Rowden cabin. From there the guns commanded not only the wagon road but also a field to the north beyond some trees, where corn had been recently harvested.[7]

At about 10:30 P.M., according to Geary's subsequent report, the sounds of picket firing were heard to the north. "The entire command was put under arms at once," but the firing quickly died out. After an hour of silence, Geary allowed the men to return to their rest, lying down in battle lines and under arms.

The scattering of shots had apparently come from a patrol of the 141st New York sent out by Howard to intercept Confederate sharpshooters. They bumped into some of Law's skirmishers, producing the brief fire that startled the already edgy White Star Division. If the skirmish accomplished nothing else, it at least reminded Geary's men of the potential danger of their position.[8]

That potential danger became real some ninety minutes later, when Bratton's skirmishers reached Geary's pickets north of the Rowden cornfield. After crossing Lookout Creek, Bratton ordered skirmishers from the Sixth South Carolina to advance, followed closely by the First and Fifth South Carolina and the Second South Carolina Rifles. The Palmetto Sharpshooters were to move left and take a position along the railroad, where Bratton believed Geary's right rested. The skirmishers were under orders to capture the Union pickets, then advance rapidly and engage the main force. With the battle line following closely behind, the skirmishers were to fall in and fight with whatever regiment was nearest.[9]

It was about midnight or shortly after when Pvt. David Mouat of Company G, Twenty-ninth Pennsylvania, one of Rickards's pickets, thought he heard troops moving to the north. He called to his acting corporal, Elisha Jones, to come up. "We listened and nothing occurring he left me saying keep a sharp look out," Mouat later recalled. The private cocked his weapon.

Soon he heard the command, "Forward guide centre," followed by a challenge of "Who goes there?" from Joseph Strang of Company C. Strang's sergeant, Johnny Green, said, "If they don't answer give it to them Strangy." Strang fired, and his shot was answered by a volley that left him mortally wounded and his sergeant missing a tuft of hair. Mouat remained at his post until Jack MacLaughlin ran up, shouting, "For God's sake Dave come on the woods are full of Rebs."

As Mouat and MacLaughlin reached camp, the 109th and 111th Pennsylvania were improvising breastworks from a rail fence. Mouat overheard Geary ask Lt. Col. Thomas M. Walker of the 111th what all the trouble was. "The pickets have been firing and I guess the enemy are coming," Walker answered. "There's no Rebs there," Geary replied, prompting Mouat to inform his commanding general, "You'll damn soon find out."[10]

He did, but thanks to the obstinacy of his pickets, Geary and his brigade commanders had time to redeploy three regiments into a line facing north to receive the attack. On the right, its flank resting along the railroad, was the 111th Pennsylvania. This was Colonel Cobham's old regiment, now led by Lieutenant Colonel Walker. The 111th had been facing east, but with shots ringing out to the north, Walker changed its front. As the 111th came into position, the 109th Pennsylvania received orders from Cobham to "move by the left flank" to occupy a position to the left of the 111th.[11]

To secure his left, Geary called on two regiments of Greene's Third Brigade, the 137th and 149th New York. The division commander personally directed the movement of the 137th as they advanced northwest behind the 109th Pennsylvania to take their position.

They had no sooner arrived than the Confederates swept across the cornfield in front of them and opened fire. They could be plainly seen under what most participants described as a bright moon.[12] Still, Geary's men were not fully prepared for the surprise of a night attack. Observing his enemy, James Hagood of the First South

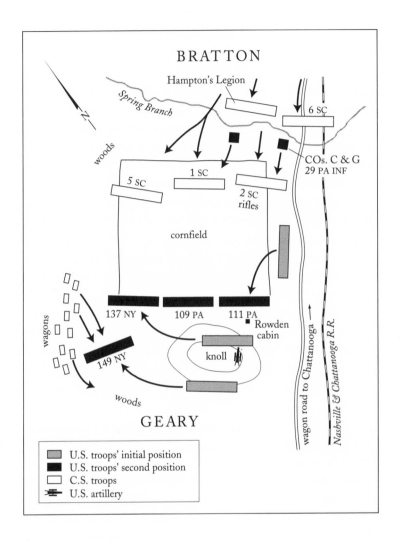

Early phase of the Engagement at Wauhatchie, 12:00 A.M. to 1:00 A.M., 29
October 1863. (From a sketch by Douglas Cubbison.)

Carolina later recalled, "An indescribable confusion now ensued, the Yankee soldiers firing their guns in every direction . . . or fleeing in a panic which promised soon to become general. All this was plainly visible to the Confederate troops destined to make the attack."[13]

As a part of the confusion Hagood described, mounted members of division and brigade staffs went galloping to the rear just as the 149th New York was advancing into position. The staff members "pass[ed] through my regiment in a dozen different places," Lt. Col. Charles B. Randall would later report. Behind them came ambulances, wagons, and horses from the "wagon train" that had been the object of the Confederate assault. "The regiment was thus entirely broken to pieces and disorganized," Randall confessed, "with no company formations whatever, and all exposed to a terrific fire." The disgusted commander pulled his men behind the 137th New York and tried to straighten things out.[14]

In front of them the three regiments were facing a heavy fire from Bratton's men. According to the historian of the 111th Pennsylvania, they "piled about their heads the rails from the dooryard fence of the [Rowden] cabin, and prostrate on the ground, bravely obeyed their instructions." Those instructions were simple and to the point: the men were to "lie down, and fire deliberately and low."[15]

General Greene was prowling the line, sending in the inevitable few stragglers, when a rifle ball struck him in the face. The ball entered the left side of his face, just below the nose, passed through his mouth, and exited through his right cheek after breaking his upper jaw. The wound would keep him out of action for over a year. As he was carried back to a makeshift hospital, Greene sent orders to Col. David Ireland of the 137th New York to assume command of the brigade.[16]

Down the line the officers of the 111th Pennsylvania were also having a rough time of it. A bullet struck Lieutenant Colonel Walker "squarely in the forehead," but his hat cord reportedly deflected it, saving his life. Maj. John Boyle was not so lucky; he was "killed beneath the colors" by a minié ball. Four days later, James T. Miller would inform his father that Company B of the 111th had suffered four killed and fourteen wounded of the thirty men it carried into the fight.[17]

The fire was coming from three South Carolina regiments, the Second Rifles, the First, and the Fifth. The Fifth was on the right, the First to their left, and the Second Rifles on the left. Raising the Rebel Yell, they charged across the cornfield in the face of what one member of the Fifth termed a "galling fire." That regiment advanced for about three hundred yards, passed beside the Union wagons, then paused at a gully and opened fire. When the First Regiment caught up with them, both units advanced until they were within about one hundred yards of the enemy. There Union fire forced them to hit the ground, a position they would hold for over an hour.

At this point Col. Franklin Kilpatrick of the First South Carolina discovered that his left was unsupported. The Second Rifles had received the brunt of the fire from Geary's line and had recoiled several feet behind. Kilpatrick dispatched his adjutant to request that Col. Thomas Thomson of the Second Rifles bring his men up. According to Lieutenant Hagood, Thomson's men "refused to be persuaded of the advantage of this step, notwithstanding their Colonel's eloquence (whose views coincided with Kilpatrick's)." Kilpatrick decided to resume the charge without them, but as he arose to give the command he immediately fell with a bullet in his heart. If the attackers ever had any chance of breaking Geary's front, it died with Kilpatrick. Meanwhile, the three Union regiments kept up a heavy fire. The commander of Company E, Fifth South Carolina, testified to its effectiveness. The next day he would report twenty-seven casualties out of the forty-one men he took into battle.[18]

Much of the Confederates' difficulty was attributable to Knap's Battery. Geary's decision to post his four guns atop the knoll behind the Rowden cabin was paying dividends. Firing thirty to forty yards behind the infantry, the gunners could not use canister, but they did use spherical case to maximum effect. The gunners trimmed their fuses to two inches, basing their range in the darkness on the flashes of Confederate muskets, and sprayed shrapnel through the enemy ranks.[19]

Although effective, the artillery fire also claimed the lives of several officers and men from the 111th Pennsylvania when shells exploded prematurely. One of them decapitated Lt. Marvin Pettit. Another inflicted horrible leg wounds on Lt. Albert Black. In a letter to his father, James Miller said his comrade Myron Smith "has a severe wound on the right arm caused by the premature bursting of one of our own shells."[20]

Bratton brought up the Sixth South Carolina to take the place of the Second Rifles and sent Hampton's Legion around to flank Geary's left. As the Legion advanced it passed the detail bearing the body of Colonel Kilpatrick to the rear. Col. Martin Gary ordered his men to continue forward, but the Union fire was hot, and they refused. "I believe," recalled Pvt. Elijah Tollison, "[that] if my hat had been iron I could have caught it full of bullets." Finally, Gary ordered his reluctant regiment to crawl on all fours to a wooded area at the west edge of the cornfield, where the men formed. From there they advanced to a gully, staying put until the order came to move forward. According to Tollison, "Everyone was afraid so each one told the other to move forward." Finally, they advanced "and drove [Geary's men] through their wagon yard, and it was said the men who had charge of [the] wagons were covered with blankets and didn't move."[21]

Gary's unit was now in position to threaten Geary's "entirely unprotected" left. Sizing up the threat, Lt. James E. Mix, adjutant of the 137th New York, refused the flank by turning Companies G and B to the west. The two companies opened fire, "creating confusion in [the Confederate] lines, and driving them back." Tollison took refuge behind a tree, claiming later that "every time I looked to the left I saw a man fall."[22]

As the threat to Geary's left eased, another developed on the right. Bratton sent the Palmetto Sharpshooters to the east side of the railroad, where they halted and opened fire. "If they had come on," Private Mouat later conceded, "it would have been all up with us as we had no troops on our side of the track only the one gun of the battery."[23]

Captain Atwell, the battery commander, had ordered that gun to the right to meet the threat. Commanding it was Lieutenant Geary. By then the battery, supported by the pickets of Companies C and G of the Twenty-ninth Pennsylvania, had become the object of the attacking Confederates. Located atop the knoll, with the flashes of their guns pinpointing their position, they were an inviting and vulnerable target, and the Confederates knew that and shouted, "Pick off the artillerists" and "Shoot the gunners." Indeed, a member of the Palmetto Sharpshooters, writing to his mother the next day, reported that Col. Joseph Walker "commanded us to concentrate our fire on [the battery]." A few days later, Sgt. David Nichol of Knap's Battery wrote his sister: "Seemed to me, every shot was fired at us. We were on a knoll & every shot fired too high for the Infantry came right for us." Lieutenant Geary had just raised from sighting his piece and shouted the order to fire when he fell dead with a bullet in his brain. Shortly after, Captain Atwell was mortally wounded when he was hit by a single bullet that passed through his hip and abdomen to his spine. One month earlier both officers had taken time as their trains reached Bellaire to visit with family members. "Little did Mrs. Atwell think . . . that was the last time she would see her husband," Nichol wrote. "But he fell in a good cause worthy of a soldier."[24]

So did many others, and the battery ran up horrible casualty figures both in men and horses. Eventually, even with the assistance of the men from Companies C and G, only enough men remained to operate two of the four guns of the battery.

At that point the 149th New York, its ranks reorganized, fell into position along the wagon road facing east, perpendicular to

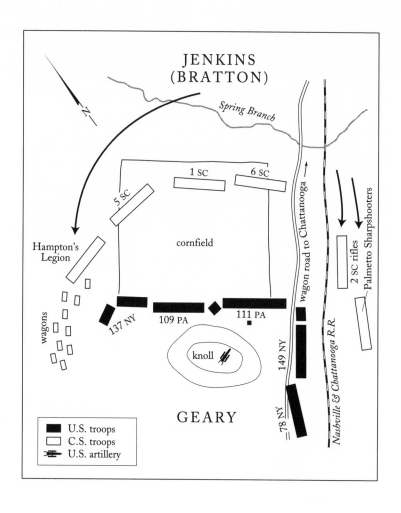

Later phase of the Engagement at Wauhatchie, 1:00 A.M. to 3:00 A.M., 29
October 1863. (From a sketch by Douglas Cubbison.)

the main line of battle. Lieutenant Colonel Randall then inched them forward to the railroad embankment, where they opened fire, shooting beneath the rails and between the widely spaced ties of the N&C.[25]

As they were arriving, Colonel Rickards ordered Lieutenant Geary's gun moved south along the wagon road to a grade crossing at the rear. From there it could enfilade the bank. Maj. John A. Reynolds, artillery chief of the XII Corps, objected. Reynolds had assumed command of Knap's Battery after Captain Atwell went down. He feared the enemy would capture the piece and also pointed out that he did not have any horses to pull it. Rickards said he would take responsibility and supply men from Companies C and G to haul both the gun and the ammunition.

"Pretty soon," Mouat later recalled, "Capt. Millison came to the log shanty and ordered [us] to drag the gun at which young Geary had been killed along the Rail road track and ordered us to stay with the gun at all hazards." Mouat's sergeant replied that "if the Rebs took the gun they would take him dead." It took two or three shots before the gunners could find their range, but when they did they "swept the enemy from the bank. This seemed to have a depressing effect upon the enemy," Rickards dryly observed.[26]

Indeed, the fire was slackening all along the line, much to the relief of Geary's beleaguered force. Ammunition was critically low. The 137th New York had sent to the field hospital for more and cut cartridge boxes from the dead and wounded, but "when the firing ceased there were not 200 cartridges in the regiment." Geary had "determined to rely on the bayonet should our ammunition fail, and hold our positions until relieved."

This did not prove necessary. Bratton had agreed that his opponents' circumstances were desperate, saying of their contracted lines, "The position of things at this time [about 2:30 a.m.] was entirely favorable to a grand charge." As he made his preparations, orders arrived from Jenkins to withdraw. Law's forces were under attack from Union reinforcements from Brown's Ferry, and

Bratton was informed that his command was in danger of being isolated.[27]

Those reinforcements, of course, belonged to the XI Corps. The sound of musketry, "with its unmistakable rattle," had awakened Howard three miles away at Brown's Ferry. He was no more than on his feet when a message arrived from Hooker imploring him to "hurry, or you can not save Geary. He has been attacked." Howard put Schurz's three brigades under arms, then went to find Hooker.[28]

Howard located Hooker and later recalled that the commanding general "seemed quite anxious." Hooker would later admit in his report that "no attempt [had been] made to establish and preserve a communication between [Geary and Howard's forces]." His explanation was that "the commands were too small to keep up a substantial communication that distance, and I deemed it more prudent to hold the men well in hand than to have a feeble one." Now, the "mutterings of heavy musketry" to the south suggested that the course he had followed had been less than prudent.[29]

Hooker ordered Howard to send one brigade to Geary's relief and another "to the position of the skirmish of the day before." Howard passed the order along to Schurz, whose division was "already under arms" and closer to Wauhatchie. Meanwhile, Hooker sent an aide, Capt. Robert H. Hall, to Schurz with an order for the division commander to move his nearest brigade to Geary's relief. Another of Hooker's staff officers, Lt. Paul A. Oliver, then arrived with orders for Schurz to "get his division or brigade . . . under arms, and occupy the hill (Tyndale's Hill) where we had the skirmish with one brigade." Finally, Hooker himself passed Schurz's camp and asked the division commander "if one brigade had been sent forward and the others ordered to follow up in the road." Schurz replied that the First Brigade was "marching accordingly."[30]

Ahead of it were the two brigades of General Steinwehr's division, Col. Orland Smith's Second Brigade in the lead, followed by the First Brigade, commanded by Col. Adolphus Buschbeck.

Schurz's lead brigade was Gen. Hector Tyndale's First Brigade. Behind it was the Second Brigade, led by Col. Wladimir Krzyzanowski. Col. Frederick Hecker's Third Brigade brought up the rear.[31]

Law was waiting for them. Upon learning that Bratton was in motion, he had ordered his line forward on a wooded slope (soon to be known as Smith's Hill) overlooking the road over which any reinforcements from the XI Corps would have to march. Since Law was commanding both his and Robertson's brigades, he turned command of his brigade over to Col. James L. Sheffield of the Forty-Eighth Alabama. Sheffield placed his regiment on the left. As the other regiments of the brigade arrived, each was placed in position to extend the line to the right—the Forty-seventh, Fourth, Forty-fourth, and Fifteenth Alabama in that order. The line went somewhat diagonally from the road, the left resting 30 to 40 yards away, the right 150 to 200 yards.[32]

Once in position, the men went to work throwing up rail and log breastworks, a task that consumed about an hour, as pickets went forward toward the road. To the left the men could hear "quite a lively engagement . . . in progress" as Bratton began his attack. Benning's brigade of Georgians was stationed on a hill (known soon after as Tyndale's Hill) between Law and Bratton, affording adequate protection in that direction. Sheffield was concerned, however, about his right. The Tennessee River flowed about a mile to the right and rear of Sheffield's position, and he dispatched two companies, the rightmost of the Forty-fourth Alabama and the leftmost of the Fifteenth Alabama, in that direction as pickets. This maneuver created a gap in his line that would eventually prove critical.[33]

Soon after the fighting on the left began, Sheffield notified Law that a column of troops was moving from right to left along the road in front of them. Law pulled his skirmishers back toward the line of battle and issued orders to withhold fire until the column had reached a position opposite the left of the line. When it did the entire brigade cut loose with a volley that, according to one

Confederate, "created a great deal of confusion in the enemy's ranks and sent them back."[34]

It was now obvious to Hooker that he had more to worry about than the attack on Geary. Steinwehr immediately received orders to capture the hill. To do the work he selected Smith's brigade. That outfit was woefully undersized. With the Fifty-fifth Ohio on picket duty, Smith was down to three regiments, the Thirty-third Massachusetts, the Seventy-third Ohio, and the 136th New York. Unknown to Smith, Howard had sent three companies of the Thirty-third off on the hunt of a Confederate regiment believed to be prowling around on the banks of the Tennessee. All told, he had about seven hundred men to dislodge an entrenched line with more than double that number.[35]

Smith ordered the Seventy-third Ohio and the Thirty-third Massachusetts to take the hill, the Ohioans on the right, the New Englanders on the left. The 136th New York he held in reserve at the foot of the hill. Riders were ordered to dismount as the two regiments began their ascent of the steep, slippery, and heavily wooded hill. In many places, recalled Maj. Samuel Hurst, the commander of the Seventy-third, "we could only advance by holding on to or pulling ourselves up by the underbrush."[36]

Despite being fired on by Rebel skirmishers, the Thirty-third advanced in good order until it reached a "crooked ravine some 20 feet deep running parallel with the hillside, the sides of which were almost perpendicular, slippery with leaves and clay, and covered with brush." This obstacle rendered it "impossible to preserve a perfect line," according to Lt. Col. Godfrey Rider, "but the regiment gallantly plunged into it—the dead and living rolling down together—climbed the opposite side and halted in some disorder."[37]

By this time the men had lost all contact with the Ohioans, and when the Thirty-third heard cries from their front of "Don't fire on us," they could not be sure if they were coming from friends or foes. Hoping to prevent a fatal error, Lt. William P. Mudge, adjutant of the Thirty-third, shouted, "Who is it?" "Who are you?" came the reply. "The Thirty-third Massachusetts," Mudge answered. With that, a hail of bullets settled the question of who they were facing.[38]

Still, the Thirty-third advanced, unsure where the regiment supporting them might be. Finally, virtually out of breath, they reached the crest of the hill, some sixty yards from the Confederate entrenchments. His ranks already decimated, Col. Adin B. Underwood prepared to lead his men in the final thrust. He got no further than "Remember Massachusetts, fix . . ." before a bullet cut him down with a shattered thigh bone. Isolated, their colonel a casualty, and under tremendous fire, "some confusion naturally ensued," stated Lieutenant Colonel Rider in one of the great understatements of the campaign. There was nothing to do but return down the slope and attempt to regroup.[39]

Meanwhile, the Ohioans were faring little better. They advanced only a few hundred yards before Sheffield's skirmishers opened fire on their left and front. At first, most of the fire passed over their heads, but as they continued up the slope it "grew heavier and more effective," Hurst recalled. The commander received orders to wheel to the left to connect with the Thirty-third. As his skirmishers (Company A) moved to the left in advance of the new front, a heavy volley shattered its rank, mortally wounding Capt. Luther Buchwalter.

The regiment continued up the hill, advancing in the face of "an irregular fire." As they neared the crest, "a most murderous fire" opened up on their right, "completely enfilading our line." Meanwhile, shouts of "Don't fire into your own men!" and "You are killing your own friends!" could be heard from the left. Unsure of the position of the Massachusetts regiment, Hurst "deemed it rash to advance farther until I knew that one, at least, of my flanks was protected." He drew his command back a short distance and sent an officer to determine the "position and movements" of the Thirty-third.[40]

The position of the Massachusetts men was at the foot of the hill, but the regiment was preparing to resume the attack. Colonel

Smith informed them, "We must take that hill at any cost. Now, when you reach the top again don't stop to fire but rush for them with the bayonet and yell for all you are worth at the same time. It will make them think you have had a reinforcement."[41]

In fact, they did. Steinwehr ordered Smith's remaining regiment, the 136th New York, to advance up the hill to the left of the Thirty-third. He, too, instructed the men not to fire as they advanced. "If you do," he explained, "that will give them the range to shoot you."[42]

The 136th advanced toward what should have been the left flank of the Confederate line. It no longer was, however, because Law had brought in reinforcements of his own. Using Robertson's brigade, he placed the Third Arkansas and the First Texas on his left and sent the Fourth Texas to extend the right.[43]

Once again the Thirty-third began its climb. Adjutant Mudge stepped to the front of the line, shouted, "Forward, boys, and avenge our colonel," and fell dead, a bullet through his heart. Thus inspired, with bayonets fixed, the Thirty-third proceeded to do just what the fallen officer had asked of them. According to the stoic Lieutenant Colonel Rider, his regiment advanced "directly up the face of the hill until, within a few yards of the breastworks, it drew the enemy's fire, when, with a cheer, it turned by the right flank, gained the crest, crossed the rifle-pits, and charged upon the enemy's flank with the bayonet, at the same time pouring a volley into his retreating ranks." Learning of this turn of events, Major Hurst "immediately charged forward again [and] took and occupied the works and hill in our own front, from which the enemy rapidly fled."[44]

Soon the 136th New York came in on the Confederate right. True to Steinwehr's orders, the men did not fire. One of them, George Metcalf, later claimed that the other regiments had not been as disciplined, firing occasionally as they advanced. "This did the mischief for them," he asserted. "The enemy ahead of us and those ahead of them, seeing them coming by the flash of their guns, turned down upon them a deadly fire."

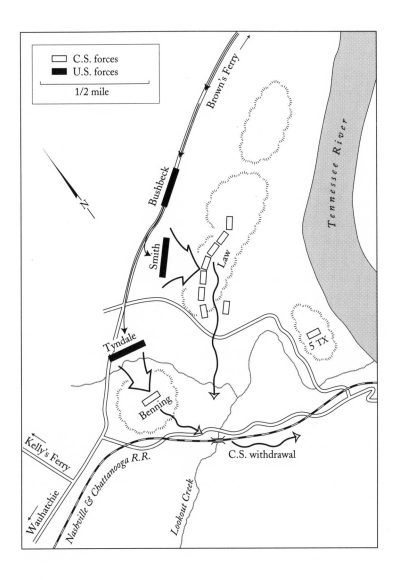

Smith's Hill and Tyndale's Hill, 2:45 A.M., 29 October 1863. (From a sketch by Douglas Cubbison.)

Metcalf and his comrades soon found themselves upon the Confederate line. "We gave out a most unearthly yell," he recalled, confessing, "If the rebels were not frightened, I was. We ran toward them with our bayonets. They never stopped to ask who we were, or how we got there, or how long we had come to stay, or how many there were of us, or to bid us good-by. They just ran." Another member of Metcalf's regiment, writing less than a week after the battle, expressed a similar view. "The Rebs didn't stop to take a second look," he noted, "but run leaving guns, knapsacks, picks, shovels, axes, and hats without number. Our boys picked up hats enough on the other side of the hill to furnish my whole company."[45]

If those accounts were somewhat laced with hyperbole, they were largely corroborated by Miles Vance Smith of the Fourth Texas. According to Smith, as the 136th advanced, "with our ears . . . wide open, we believed we heard Yanks crawling up the opposite slope just in front." Adding to this "intense strain of excitability" was the knowledge that the Alabamians on their left "had broken and were hunting 'tall timber' in their rear." This "rush to the rear came down the line like the swinging of a gate," taking the Texans with it. "A loneliness had taken possession of them," Smith wrote of his own regiment, "and it seemed with a unanimity they believed, if they were going to serve their country in the future they also had better right about face, and make a speedy march to the rear. Speedy does not express the velocity with which they went."[46]

The breakthrough occurred at the gap made between the Forty-fourth and Fifteenth Alabama when the two companies were removed to picket the right flank. "Right here was the main secret of our failure," a captain of the Fifteenth wrote after the war. In a postwar letter to Gen. Ezra Carman he estimated the space at thirty yards or more, "and through this your troops finally made an entrance and broke our line." He had taken his company to defend the breech "but was soon assaulted in the rear by troops crossing the works I had left." Finally, the situation forced him to order his company to retire, "which acted as a signal for my regiment, and we all went out faster than we came in."[47]

While Smith's three regiments certainly had the effect of hurrying the Confederates along, the decision to abandon the position appears to have been made independent of their arrival. According to Law's after-action report, he received a message from Jenkins before the second assault saying Bratton was withdrawing "and that he wished me to withhold my position until he could retire." Soon, as the second attack was commencing, Law received notification that Bratton was either crossing or about to cross the creek to safety. With that news he waited until "the firing had almost ceased [and] gave orders for the whole line to retire. . . . The movement," he added, "was executed in a quiet and leisurely manner, the enemy in front making no effort to follow."[48]

As this drama unfolded atop Smith's Hill, the latest installment of the Hooker-Schurz melodrama was taking place in the valley below. A sorry and confusing spectacle, it would finally be played out before a court of inquiry. The court would eventually side with Schurz, at Hooker's expense, but a great deal of the blame rested with a third party, Colonel Krzyzanowski.

After getting started behind Steinwehr, Schurz rode to the head of Tyndale's column, sending his chief of staff, Lt. Col. August Otto, back to both Krzyzanowski and Hecker with orders for their brigades to follow. When they reached the hill Hooker had ordered Schurz to occupy, he sent Tyndale's brigade forward to take the position. By then Benning had received orders to pull his Georgians back, and Tyndale captured his namesake hill with little difficulty.[49]

At this point the accounts become muddled. For reasons never explained, Krzyzanowski had called a halt upon reaching the vicinity of Smith's Hill. Hecker sent a staff officer forward to find out the cause of the delay. The officer reported back that the Second Brigade had received orders to halt, from whom it was not known. Hecker replied that he had received no such orders, and he sent his brigade around Krzyzanowski's. Major Howard then appeared and told Hecker he should march ahead to a nearby crossroads and halt there.

Hooker was at the crossroads, and he asked Hecker what troops those were. When Hecker informed him that they were the Third Brigade, Third Division, XI Corps, Hooker asked where Schurz was. Hecker assumed that he was somewhere toward the front because one of his staff officers, wounded by a stray shot from the Smith's Hill fight, had just been brought back. Hooker then asked what outfit was to his rear, and Hecker told him it was the Second Division, XI Corps. With that, Hooker told Hecker to "stay here," then rode away.⁵⁰

In the meantime, confusing and contradictory orders were flying about. Although no one intended it, their result would be to freeze Schurz's three brigades in place, preventing reinforcements from reaching Geary. The sequence began when General Butterfield sent orders with Captain Hall to Krzyzanowski to take a group of prisoners to Chattanooga. Misunderstanding the directive, Hall ordered Krzyzanowski to march his entire brigade to Chattanooga. Hall quickly returned to correct the mistake, but not before Schurz had received word from Capt. Louis Orlemann of Krzyzanowski's staff that the brigade was heading to Chattanooga under Hooker's orders. When Hall returned to revise the orders, Krzyzanowski did not bother to notify Schurz of the modification.

Major Howard then appeared and informed Schurz that Hecker's brigade was halted at Smith's Hill "and was under instructions from General Hooker." Unaware of the modification in Krzyzanowski's orders, Schurz naturally assumed that two of his brigades had been detached from his immediate command. As Schurz thought about that development, Lieutenant Oliver arrived with orders from Hooker to take Tyndale's Hill with the remaining brigade. This left the division commander with no one to march to Geary's aid. By then the firing in the direction of Wauhatchie had abated, leaving Schurz to assume that "circumstances might have changed. . . . The enemy had perhaps made a new movement," he later reflected.[51]

Soon after, about 2:00 A.M., Hooker rode up to Schurz, and Schurz reported that he had taken the hill and posted skirmishers in front. Hooker was less than pleased. In the words of one witness, "General Hooker seemed to be very angry, and asked him 'What were your orders, General Schurz—to press on to General Geary immediately?'" Schurz tried to explain his dilemma, but Hooker was in no mood to listen. Schurz then asked if he could have his other two brigades back to make the move. Hooker told him to "take them and push through with all speed."[52]

Schurz ordered the dilatory Krzyzanowski into the gap between Smith's and Tyndale's Hills and sent Hecker ahead to Geary. Hecker reached Wauhatchie at about 5:30 that morning, and Krzyzanowski arrived an hour or two later. Both, of course, showed up long after the fighting there had ended. It appears doubtful that they would have arrived in time to offer any assistance even if no delay had occurred.[53]

One officer who did press ahead to Geary's relief was General Howard. Early in the fight Howard asked and received Hooker's permission to "take . . . two companies of cavalry and push through to Wauhatchie." Even riding with cavalry, Howard did not reach Geary's position until 3:00 or 3:30 A.M. By then, "The firing was all over and quiet reigned." As he approached the camp he observed some men moving about. "Who goes there?" Howard shouted. They replied that they were Jenkins's men. Knowing no Union commander of that name, the suspicious general said, "All right, have you whipped the Yankees?" The same voice responded, "We were on their flank, but our men in front have gone, and we cannot find our way." Howard's troopers advanced slowly, bagging a large contingent of prisoners.

Entering Geary's camp, Howard first stopped at the tent of the "frightfully wounded" General Greene. "After a moment's delay for inquiry and sympathy," some of Greene's men conducted him to Geary. "Geary's hand trembled," Howard later wrote, "and his tall, strong frame shook with emotion as he held me by the hand and spoke of the death of his son, during that fearful night. . . . In this way," Howard concluded, "the soldier remembers that the exhilaration of victory was very often dampened, or entirely quenched, by real grief over its cost, a cost that cannot be estimated!"[54]

EPILOGUE

Aftermath of Battle

It is possible that every company of every army that ever marched numbered at least one David Mouat among its ranks. Certainly one can hope so.

The morning following the engagement at Wauhatchie Mouat fell into conversation with one of the western soldiers. "You fellows must have had a tough fight down here last night," the westerner observed.

"Where?" Mouat calmly replied.

"Why here wasn't you in it?" the man asked.

"Oh," Mouat answered, "that was no fight only a little kind of scrimmage."

"Well I don't know what you call a fight," the indignant soldier shot back, "but it looks to me with all them dead Rebs as if one had been going on here and the shooting sounded as if all hell was loose."

"Oh we're from the Potomac," Mouat replied, maintaining his nonchalant demeanor, "and we used to have those kind of rows nearly every morning to get up an appetite for breakfast."

The man "looked at me pretty hard," Mouat later recorded, "and said 'The hell you did. That'll do.'"[1]

Mouat's tongue-in-cheek appraisal notwithstanding, the performance of the two corps impressed their superiors. Of the fighting at Smith's Hill, Meigs informed Stanton, "Thirty-one dead soldiers attest to the difficulty of the assault and the valor and steadiness of the troops, which in a night attack accomplished one of the most brilliant feats of the campaign." In a congratulatory order issued 7 November, General Thomas went further: "The bayonet charge, made by the troops of General Howard, up a steep and difficult hill, over 200 feet high, completely routing the enemy and driving him from his barricades on its top, and the repulse, by General Geary's command, of greatly superior numbers, who attempted to surprise him, will rank among the most distinguished feats of arms of this war."[2]

From Murfreesboro Slocum sent word to Geary, "I am very happy to hear the good reports which reach me from all sides, relative to the conduct of your command in the recent action." Since he had not been present, Slocum explained, he could not "with good taste" issue a congratulatory order, "but I wish you and your command to know that I have been informed of all the facts in the case, and that I feel deeply grateful for their gallant conduct and for the new laurels they have brought to our Corps."[3]

Grant, too, was pleased at the reopening of the "cracker line," but he was less than satisfied with the commander of the XI and XII Corps. On the evening of 28 October, Colonel Wilson had reported "the disorderly and scattered condition of Hooker's camp." Grant had considered sending him back with orders to consolidate the command at Brown's Ferry, "but upon reflection, concluded to leave matters as they were."

The next morning, riding with Wilson over the field at Wauhatchie, Hooker was full of boasts and exaggerations. Among them was the claim that Geary's men had captured over one thousand muskets in the fight. Wilson "asked the general to show them to me, but it is hardly necessary to state that they had disappeared." Hooker also claimed that some of Geary's mules had gotten loose during the contest "and galloped down upon the rebels like a charge of cavalry." As Wilson noted, the mule charge story later grew to be "semi-historical," but he added, "I have always supposed that the repulse of the attack was due mainly to the courage and steadiness of Geary and his men."[4]

Wilson undoubtedly reported his conversation to Grant. Already frustrated by the Hooker-Slocum feud, Grant had recently recommended that Hooker be given the XII Corps and Slocum "relieved from further duty." In the wake of Wauhatchie, he wanted rid of both officers and the two corps consolidated under Howard. On 29 October Dana informed Stanton that Hooker had "behaved badly" since arriving from the East and Slocum had sent "a very disorderly communication," reiterating his desire to be separated from Hooker. "Grant feels that their presence here is replete with both trouble and danger," Dana added. All that prevented Grant from issuing the order himself was that both generals had been sent there by order of President Lincoln.[5]

The same day Dana forwarded Grant's wishes to Stanton, Confederate general Bratton wrote a letter to his wife. Describing his attempt to capture the Union wagons, he noted, "We tried honestly and fought hard but did not succeed." The enemy, he believed, "greatly outnumbered us, but how many it is impossible for me to estimate as I could only see the spurts of fire from their guns and not the men themselves." He bemoaned the wounding of Captain Coker of his staff and the death of Colonel Kilpatrick of the First South Carolina. His only consolation seemed to be that "we shot down a great many of the [enemy's] horses and mules."[6]

Bratton would eventually report 31 dead, 286 wounded, and 39 missing in the fight for a total casualty figure of 356. Of this official total, 102 came from the Fifth South Carolina. Geary, however, reported 153 Confederates buried on the field and 102 captured. At least one historian of the engagement, after exhaustive research into the primary sources, has concluded that Bratton "woefully minimized his casualties."[7]

Geary reported 34 killed, 174 wounded, and 8 missing, total casualties of 216. The 137th New York sustained the greatest loss with 15 killed and 75 wounded, this one regiment accounting for nearly 42 percent of the total casualties.[8]

The casualty report for the XI Corps came to 45 killed, 150 wounded, and 9 missing. Of those 204 casualties, Smith's Second Brigade sustained 162. The Thirty-third Massachusetts reported 88 casualties, including 26 dead. The total for the Seventy-third Ohio was 68. The 136th New York reported 2 killed and 4 wounded.[9]

The casualty figures reported by Sheffield and Robertson also seem questionable in light of the fierce struggle described by participants on both sides. Sheffield reported 3 killed, 18 wounded, and 22 missing in Law's brigade. Of those 43 total reported casualties, 38, including all of the missing, came from the Fifteenth and Forty-fourth Alabama. Robertson reported only 1 man wounded and 8 missing.[10]

As soon as it became obvious that the XI Corps was going to suffer large numbers of wounded, Dr. Hubbard selected a site about a mile north of Tyndale's Hill for a field hospital. Dr. Daniel Brinton, medical director for the XI Corps, who had only recently returned from leave, joined him there. According to Brinton, preparations at the makeshift hospital included "fires built, candles procured, straw collected from a neighboring barn for beds, amputating tables knocked together, and all the stores of the different regiments deposited there." Meanwhile, Hubbard "sent to Chattanooga for a barrel of whiskey and other supplies."[11]

The hospital received 109 wounded, including 3 Confederates. Eight died there, and 4 amputations were performed. Although there reportedly was a great deal of hand-to-hand fighting, the hospital did not treat a single bayonet wound. "I looked for them," Brinton recorded, "but neither saw nor heard of any. There was none." Hubbard wrote his wife that he had "never seen in proportion to the number injured, men so severely wounded." This he attributed to "the short range at which the fire was received as is the case in most night attacks."[12]

Many of the wounded were still lying in field hospitals the next day, 30 October, when the drenching rains that had fallen most of the month returned. "Severe on the wounded men, a number died—mostly Confederates," noted a diarist of the Twenty-ninth Ohio, whose regiment arrived at Geary's camp on 29 October.

James T. Miller of the 111th Pennsylvania had received a slight
wound to the calf area of his lower right leg. A week after the battle
he wrote his brother, "We laid in the rain one night in the field
hospital after the fight and then we were brought to Bridgeport on
a flat boat and we staid there three days and they came near starving
us and then they sent us here [Nashville] in cattle cars and it took
them forty hours to run 122 miles and our wounds were not dressed
in that time and they feel some sore this morning."[13]

Uncertain of what lay ahead, the men of both corps dug in and
prepared as best they could. After driving the Confederates from
Smith's Hill, the men of the Second Brigade "lay in line of battle on
the summit of this ridge, anxiously waiting for morning to come."
While they waited they put the entrenching tools the Confederates
had left behind to good use and soon had a line of breastworks
facing the opposite direction. The enemy threw some shells from
Lookout Mountain, but they did little harm. One solid shot did
strike within ten feet of a fire at which members of the Thirty-third
Massachusetts were preparing breakfast, "overturning our dippers
of coffee, and filling our eyes with dirt, causing a sudden change of
base."[14]

From Wauhatchie Geary appealed to Butterfield for seventy
thousand rounds of ammunition. Meanwhile, his men "carried
sticks, stones, and everything that could be carried to strengthen
the line." They rousted the occupants of the Rowden cabin, "nearly
frightened to death but unharmed," out of the structure and soon
had it torn down, using the timbers to reinforce the line. The 111th
Pennsylvania salvaged some fence boards for a different purpose—
to fabricate a coffin for Major Boyle. It was sent under guard on a
flatboat to Bridgeport, where the major's remains were embalmed
and shipped to his family.[15]

Among all this activity at Wauhatchie, the scene that stood out
most starkly was the commanding general's grief. Nearly thirty years
later, George Collins of the 149th New York remembered the "tall

and portly form of General Geary, standing with bowed head on the summit of the knoll . . . while before him lay the lifeless form of a lieutenant of artillery." The men "stood at a respectable distance while he communed with his grief."[16]

Geary poured out that grief in a stream of letters to his wife. "The death of my dear Eddie makes me sad and gloomy, and nothing keeps me up but the deep responsibilities which surround me on every side," the general wrote. "Time may wear much of this away, but never can I forget my darling boy." In another letter he wrote: "None knew him who did not love him. His praise was on every tongue." Trying to find an explanation for the unexplainable, the devout Geary suggested that it was God's "chastisement for the pride I took in him." Of his son Willie, Geary wrote, "I hope he will emulate his brother's many virtues and be just like him."[17]

The Battles of Wauhatchie and Smith's Hill had been unnecessary, the results of careless troop placement and little else. Still, the men of the XI and XII Corps had achieved two things. They preserved the vital supply line that they had helped to reopen. And, perhaps no less important, they had demonstrated that these "paper collar" easterners could fight.

That was fortunate because they had come west to stay, and many more tests lay ahead, including a "Battle Above the Clouds," a campaign to take Atlanta, and a March to the Sea.

Yet in the overall story of military history the most remarkable thing about these two tiny corps was the simple fact that they were where they were—and that they had been moved there so quickly and efficiently. Six weeks earlier they had been in Virginia, languishing both in activity and reputation. Now, thanks to the foresight of the secretary of war, they were doing important work and gaining at least the grudging acceptance of their new comrades.

Ten years earlier it would not have been possible for the XI and XII Corps to reach Tennessee in time for the battle they fought; nor, for that matter, would it have been possible for Longstreet's corps to arrive to provide the opposition. Railroads clearly had come of age, changing forever the logistics of warfare. Realizing this, Stanton, the former railroad attorney, had clearly proven his point. Perhaps, as he received word that supplies were flowing into Chattanooga to sustain Thomas's beleaguered army, the secretary of war even found the time to allow himself a brief smile.

ABBREVIATIONS TO NOTES

CCNMP   Chickamauga-Chattanooga National Military Park

CL   Schoff Civil War Collection, William L. Clements
            Library, the University of Michigan, Ann Arbor,
            Michigan

CWMC   Civil War Miscellaneous Collection

CWRT   Civil War Round Table

CWTI   *Civil War Times Illustrated*

INHS   Indiana Historical Society

LC   Library of Congress

MHS   Maryland Historical Society

MOLLUS   Military Order of the Loyal Legion of the U.S.

NA   National Archives

NJHS   New Jersey Historical Society

OHS   Ohio Historical Society

OR   U.S. War Department, *The War of the Rebellion: A
            Compilation of the Official Records of the Union and
            Confederate Armies*, 128 vols. Washington DC: U.S.
            Government Printing Office, 1880–1901.

RG   Record Group

SHC, UNC   Southern Historical Collection, Manuscript
            Department, Wilson Library, the University of North
            Carolina, Chapel Hill, North Carolina

USAMHI   United States Army Military History Institute

NOTES

PROLOGUE: MR. STANTON'S PROPOSAL

1. Tyler Dennett, ed., *Lincoln and the Civil War in the Diaries and Letters of John Hay* (New York: Dodd, Mead, 1939), 93.
2. Bruce Catton, *Never Call Retreat* (Garden City NY: Doubleday, 1965), 36–46, 208–10, 238–50; James Lee McDonough, *Chattanooga: A Death Grip on the Confederacy* (Knoxville: University of Tennessee Press, 1984), 41–42.
3. Margaret Leech and Harry J. Brown, *The Garfield Orbit* (New York: Harper & Row, 1978), 141, 149–50; Benjamin P. Thomas and Harold M. Hyman, *Stanton: The Life and Times of Lincoln's Secretary of War* (New York: Knopf, 1962), 286; Charles Dana to Edwin M. Stanton, 20, 22, 23 September 1863, Stanton to Dana, 23 September 1863, Edwin M. Stanton Papers, LC.
4. Dennett, ed., *Lincoln and the Civil War*, 93; David Donald, ed., *Inside Lincoln's Cabinet: The Civil War Diaries of Salmon P. Chase* (New York: Longmans, Green, 1954), 201–3; Walter H. Hebert, *Fighting Joe Hooker* (Indianapolis: Bobbs-Merrill, 1944), 250–51.
5. Donald, ed., *Inside Lincoln's Cabinet*, 201–3; Thomas and Hyman, *Stanton*, 286–87.
6. George C. Gorham, *Life and Public Services of Edwin M. Stanton*, 2 vols. (Boston: Houghton Mifflin, 1899), 2:122–25; Frank Abial Flower, *Edwin McMasters Stanton: The Autocrat of Rebellion, Emancipation, and Reconstruction* (Akron: Saalfield Publishing, 1905), 203–5.
7. Dennett, ed., *Lincoln and the Civil War*, 93.

1. NETWORK OF IRON

1. John F. Stover, *Iron Road to the West: American Railroads in the 1850s* (New York: Columbia University Press, 1978), xi, 5, 16, 197; George Rogers Taylor, *The Transportation Revolution, 1815–1860* (New York: Holt, Rinehart and Winston, 1966), 79; Alfred D. Chandler, *The Visible Hand: The Managerial Revolution in American Business* (Cambridge MA: Belknap Press of Harvard University Press, 1977), 83.
2. *American Railroad Journal*, 28 February 1857.
3. John F. Stover, *History of the Baltimore and Ohio Railroad* (West Lafayette IN: Purdue University Press, 1987), 71, 74–75.
4. Taylor, *Transportation Revolution*, 79.

5. Alfred D. Chandler, "The Railroads: Pioneers in Modern Corporate Management," *Business History Review* 39 (spring 1965): 17.

6. Chandler, "The Railroads," 17–18; Chandler, *Visible Hand*, 90–92. For government subsidies of railroads. see Taylor, *Transportation Revolution*, 88–94.

7. Chandler, "The Railroads," 18–19.

8. Daniel C. McCallum, "Superintendent's Report," 25 March 1856, in *Annual Report of the New York and Erie Railroad Company for 1855* (New York, 1855), quoted in Alfred D. Chandler, ed., *The Railroads: The Nation's First Big Business, Sources and Readings* (New York: Harcourt, Brace & World, 1965), 101.

9. Chandler, "The Railroads," 19–21; Chandler, *Visible Hand*, 87.

10. Chandler, "The Railroads," 22–27.

11. Chandler, "The Railroads," 27–28.

12. Chandler, "The Railroads," 27–28; Edward Hungerford, *Men of Erie: A Story of Human Effort* (New York: Random House, 1946), 139–40.

13. McCallum, "Superintendent's Report," in Chandler, ed., *The Railroads*, 102.

14. McCallum, "Superintendent's Report," in Chandler, ed., *The Railroads*, 103–7; Chandler, "The Railroads," 29–32.

15. *American Railroad Journal*, 2 September 1854.

16. *American Railroad Journal*, 24 June 1854, 11 October 1856; Hungerford, *Men of Erie*, 140–43.

17. *American Railroad Journal*, 28 March 1857.

18. Chandler, "The Railroads," 33.

19. Chandler, "The Railroads," 33–37.

20. Stover, *Iron Road to the West*, 22; *American Railroad Journal*, 4 August 1860.

21. *American Railroad Journal*, 4 August 1860; Chandler, *Visible Hand*, 103.

22. Robert C. Black III, *The Railroads of the Confederacy* (Chapel Hill: University of North Carolina Press, 1952), 9.

23. Stover, *Iron Road to the West*, 90–92; George Rogers Taylor and Irene D. Neu, *The American Railroad Network, 1861–1890* (Cambridge MA: Harvard University Press, 1956), 45–46.

24. Stover, *Iron Road to the West*, 90–91; census figures cited in Carl Russell Fish, "The Northern Railroads, April, 1861," *American Historical Review* 22 (1917): 790.

25. *American Railroad Journal*, 19 September 1857.

26. OR, Ser. 1, vol. 5, pp. 7–8. Unless otherwise noted, all subsequent references are to Series 1.

27. OR, Ser. 3, vol. 1, p. 879.

28. OR, Ser. 3, vol. 2, pp. 795–96, 838–39; vol. 5, pp. 976–77.

29. OR, 5:974.

30. OR, 5:974.

31. OR, 3:851–52; 5:975–76.

32. OR, 3:851–53.

33. OR, 5:976; *American Railroad Journal*, 24 May 1862.

34. George Edgar Turner, *Victory Rode the Rails: The Strategic Place of Railroads in the Civil War* (Indianapolis: Bobbs-Merrill, 1953), 153, 311–12; Thomas Weber, *Northern Railroads in the Civil War* (New York: Columbia University Press, 1952), 137–68; OR, Ser. 3, vol. 3, pp. 1–2.

35. Black, *Railroads of the Confederacy*, 51–53, 64, 85–91.

36. Black, *Railroads of the Confederacy*, 65–70.

37. Black, *Railroads of the Confederacy*, 107–23; OR, Ser. 4, vol. 2, pp. 225, 270–78.

38. Black, *Railroads of the Confederacy*, 166–70; OR, Ser. 4, vol. 2, pp. 579, 881–82.

2. REBELS RIDE THE RAILS

1. James A. Longstreet, *From Manassas to Appomattox: Memoirs of the Civil War in America*, ed. James I. Robertson Jr. (Bloomington: Indiana University Press, 1960), 433–34.

2. Jeffry D. Wert, *General James Longstreet: The Confederacy's Most Controversial Soldier, A Biography* (New York: Simon & Schuster, 1993), 301–2; OR, vol. 29, pt. 2, pp. 699–701.

3. OR, vol. 29, pt. 2, pp. 700–701.

4. Douglas Southall Freeman, *Lee's Lieutenants: A Study in Command*, 3 vols. (New York: Charles Scribner's Sons, 1942–44), 3:225; E. Porter Alexander, *Military Memoirs of a Confederate*, ed. T. Harry Williams (Bloomington: Indiana University Press, 1962), 448.

5. Black, *Railroads of the Confederacy*, 185–86; H. J. Peake to Sims, 16 September 1863, Telegrams to and from Frederick W. Sims, Valentine Museum, Richmond VA.

6. For starting points of various units, see John Dykes Taylor, *History of the 48th Alabama Volunteer Infantry Regiment, C.S.A.* (Montgomery: N.p., 1902), 20; Frank Mixon, *Reminiscences of a Private* (Columbia SC: State Company, 1910), 42; Mac Wyckoff, *A History of the 2nd South Carolina Infantry, 1861–65* (Fredericksburg VA: Sgt. Kirkland, 1994), 87; Mac Wyckoff, *A History of the Third South Carolina Infantry, 1861–1865* (Fredericksburg VA: Sgt. Kirkland, 1995), 133; James W. Silver, ed., *A Life for the Confederacy:*

As Recorded in the Pocket Diaries of Pvt. Robert A. Moore (Jackson TN: McCowat-Mercer Press, 1959), 164; Constance Pendleton, ed., *Confederate Memoirs: Early Life and Family History, William Frederic Pendleton, Mary Lawson Young Pendleton* (Bryn Athyn PA: N.p., 1958), 41.

7. Black, *Railroads of the Confederacy*, 185, 189; Longstreet, *From Manassas to Appomattox*, 436–37.

8. Freeman, *Lee's Lieutenants*, 3:223–24; Edward B. Williams, "Reinforcements by Rail at Chickamauga," *America's Civil War* 8 (January 1996): 48.

9. John B. Jones, *A Rebel War Clerk's Diary at the Confederate States Capital*, ed. Howard Swiggett, 2 vols. (New York: Old Hickory Bookshop, 1935), 2: 37; Entry for 11 September 1863, Thomas M. Mitchell Journal, CCNMP; Entries for 10–11 September 1863, W. R. Montgomery Diaries, South Caroliniana Library, University of South Carolina, Columbia; Silver, ed., *A Life for the Confederacy*, 164–65; Pendleton, ed., *Confederate Memoirs*, 41–42; Harold B. Simpson, *Hood's Texas Brigade: Lee's Grenadier Guard* (Waco TX: Texian Press, 1970), 299.

10. H. M. Drane to Sims, 13, 14, 15 September 1863, Telegrams to and from Sims.

11. S. S. Soloman to Sims, 12 September 1863, Telegrams to and from Sims; Black, *Railroads of the Confederacy*, 188–89; W. S. Shockley to Eliza, 18 September 1863, W. S. Shockley Papers, Special Collections Library, Duke University, Durham NC; Entry for 16 September 1863, Mitchell Journal; DuBose Egleston to "Miss Annie," 27 September 1863, DuBose Egleston Letters, Ruffin, Roulhac, and Hamilton Family Papers, SHC, UNC.

12. I. H. Bowen to Sims, 12 September (two telegrams), 14, 15 September (two telegrams), 16, 21 September 1863, Telegrams to and from Sims.

13. Silver, ed., *A Life for the Confederacy*, 164–67.

14. Entries for 26 August–20 September 1863, Montgomery Diaries.

15. Alexander, *Military Memoirs*, 449.

16. Entries for 10–21 September 1863, J. B. Clifton Diary, CCNMP.

17. G. Moxley Sorrel, *Recollections of a Confederate Staff Officer* (New York: Neale, 1905), 189; Natalie Jenkins Bond and Osmun Latrobe Coward, eds., *The South Carolinians: Colonel Asbury Coward's Memoirs* (New York: Vantage Press, 1968), 83; John Coxe, "Chickamauga," *Confederate Veteran* 30 (1922): 291–92.

18. D. Augustus Dickert, *History of Kershaw's Brigade, with a Complete Roll of Companies, Biographical Sketches, Incidents, Anecdotes, Etc.* (Newberry SC: Elbert H. Aull, 1899), 263; Mixon, *Reminiscences of a Private*, 42; Bond

and Coward, *South Carolinians*, 83; W. Mck. Evans, "The Artillery at Knoxville," *Confederate Veteran* 31 (1923): 424.

19. Mixon, *Reminiscences of a Private*, 43; Dickert, *Kershaw's Brigade*, 263.

20. Dickert, *Kershaw's Brigade*, 264; Joseph A. Graves, *The History of the Bedford Light Artillery* (Bedford City VA: Press of the Bedford Democrat, 1903), 33–34; Mixon, *Reminiscences of a Private*, 42.

21. John C. West, *A Texan in Search of a Fight: Being the Diary and Letters of a Private Soldier in Hood's Texas Brigade* (Waco TX: Press of J. S. Hill, 1901), III; Richard Lewis, *Camp Life of Confederate Boy, of Bratton's Brigade, Longstreet's Corps, C.S.A. Letters Written by Lieut. Richard Lewis, of Walker's Regiment, to His Mother, During the War, Facts and Inspirations of Camp Life, Marches, &c* (Charleston SC: News and Courier Book Presses, 1883), 56.

22. Lafayette McLaws to Wife, 19 September 1863, Lafayette McLaws Papers, SHC, UNC; Sorrel, *Recollections*, 191.

23. Longstreet, *From Manassas to Appomattox*, 437. See also Mixon, *Reminiscences of a Private*, 42–43.

24. Axalla John Hoole to Wife, 18 September 1863, Axalla John Hoole Letters, Darlington County Historical Society, Darlington SC.

25. John Daniel McDonnell, Recollections of the Civil War, Archives and Special Collections, Winthrop College, Rock Hill SC.

26. William R. Houghton and Mitchell B. Houghton, *Two Boys in the Civil War and After* (Montgomery AL: Paragon Press, 1912), 137–39.

27. Coxe, "Chickamauga," 291.

28. Simpson, *Hood's Texas Brigade*, 304.

29. OR, vol. 29, pt. 2, p. 710; vol. 51. pt. 2, pp. 763–64.

30. *Raleigh North Carolina Standard*, 2 October 1863.

31. OR, vol. 51, pt. 2, p. 765.

32. OR, vol. 51, pt. 2, pp. 768, 770–71.

33. OR, vol. 51, pt. 2, pp. 777–78; *Raleigh Spirit of the Age*, 26 October 1863.

34. OR, vol. 30, pt. 4, pp. 643, 649, 652; William C. Oates, *The War Between the Union and the Confederacy and Its Lost Opportunities with a History of the 15th Alabama Regiment and the Forty-eight Battles in Which It Was Engaged* (New York: Neale, 1905), 253.

35. Oates, *War Between the Union and the Confederacy*, 253; Joab Goodson to Niece, September 28, 1863, in W. Stanley Hoole, ed., "The Letters of Captain Joab Goodson, 1862–1864," *Alabama Review* 10 (1957): 149; Taylor, *History of the 48th Alabama*, 20; OR, vol. 30, pt. 4, p. 652.

36. Peter Cozzens, *This Terrible Sound: The Battle of Chickamauga* (Urbana: University of Illinois Press, 1992), 95, 110–11, 119, 202–25, 238–39.
37. Wert, *Longstreet*, 305–6; Cozzens, *This Terrible Sound*, 294, 368–76.

3. PLANS AND PERSONALITIES

1. Stanton to Dana, 24 September 1863, Stanton Papers.
2. OR, vol. 29, pt. 1, p. 146.
3. Stover, *History of the Baltimore and Ohio*, 79–80, 89, 93–94; Edward Hungerford, *The Story of the Baltimore & Ohio Railroad*, 2 vols. (New York: Knickerbocker Press, 1928), 1:316–32.
4. Quoted in Festus P. Summers, *The Baltimore and Ohio in the Civil War* (New York: G. P. Putnam's Sons, 1939), 46.
5. Summers, *Baltimore and Ohio*, 45–46; Stover, *History of the Baltimore and Ohio*, 101; Festus P. Summers, "The Baltimore and Ohio: First in War," *Civil War History* 7 (1961): 239–54.
6. Hungerford, *Story of the Baltimore & Ohio*, 2:27; Garrett to Stanton, 24 September 1863, Stanton Papers.
7. Samuel Richey Kamm, *The Civil War Career of Thomas A. Scott* (Philadelphia: University of Pennsylvania Press, 1940), 1–3.
8. Kamm, *Scott*, 19–130.
9. Kamm, *Scott*, 2.
10. Kamm, *Scott*, 21–22; Summers, *Baltimore and Ohio*, 53–56, 102–6; Turner, *Victory Rode the Rails*, 52–59.
11. Kamm, *Scott*, 24, 59–63.
12. Weber, *Northern Railroads*, 182–83.
13. OR, vol. 29, pt. 1, pp. 153, 183; Kamm, *Scott*, 166–67.
14. OR, vol. 29, pt. 1, pp. 147–48.
15. OR, vol. 29, pt. 1, p. 148; George A. Thayer, "A Railroad Feat of War," MOLLUS Ohio 3:221.
16. OR, vol. 29, pt. 1, pp. 149–50.
17. OR, vol. 29, pt. 1, pp. 149–50; Meade to Halleck, Stanton to Meade, 24 September 1863, Stanton Papers.
18. Garrett to Perkins (two telegrams), 25 September 1863, Garrett to Wilson, 25 September 1863, Garrett to Smith, 25 September 1863, Baltimore and Ohio Railroad Papers, MHS.
19. Garrett to Hooker, ca. 25–26 September 1863, Garrett to Ford, 26 September 1863, Baltimore and Ohio Railroad Papers; Summers, *Baltimore and Ohio*, 169; OR, vol. 29, pt. 1, p. 170.

20. Garrett to Jewett, 24 September 1863, Garrett to Ricketts, 24 September 1863, Garrett to Hubby, McCullough, L'Hommedieu, Clement, and Newman, 24 September 1863, Stanton Papers; Weber, *Northern Railroads*, 183–84.

21. OR, vol. 29, pt. 1, p. 153; Ser. 3, vol. 3, p. 1; Thomas C. Cochran, *Railroad Leaders, 1845–1890: The Business Mind in Action* (Cambridge MA: Harvard University Press, 1953), 310.

22. OR, vol. 29, pt. 1, pp. 151–52, 160.

23. Hebert, *Fighting Joe Hooker*, 1–35.

24. Hebert, *Fighting Joe Hooker*, 36–50.

25. Hebert, *Fighting Joe Hooker*, 55–167.

26. The Lincoln letter is quoted in full in Hebert, *Fighting Joe Hooker*, 8–9.

27. Hebert, *Fighting Joe Hooker*, 171–84.

28. The most recent accounts of the Battle of Chancellorsville are Ernest B. Furgurson, *Chancellorsville 1863: The Souls of the Brave* (New York: Knopf, 1992), and Stephen W. Sears, *Chancellorsville* (Boston: Houghton Mifflin, 1996); an account harshly critical of Hooker is Edward J. Stackpole, *Chancellorsville: Lee's Greatest Battle* (Harrisburg PA: Stackpole, 1958).

29. Hebert, *Fighting Joe Hooker*, 244–50.

30. Hooker to Brig. Gen. R. Allen, 25 September 1863, Stanton Papers.

31. John A. Carpenter, *Sword and Olive Branch: Oliver Otis Howard* (Pittsburgh: University of Pittsburgh Press, 1964), 12–41.

32. Carpenter, *Sword and Olive Branch*, 43–49; Bruce Catton, *Glory Road: The Bloody Route from Fredericksburg to Gettysburg* (Garden City NY: Doubleday, 1952), 156–211.

33. Charles Elihu Slocum, *The Life and Services of Major General Henry Warner Slocum* (Toledo: Slocum, 1913), 13–60.

34. Slocum, *Slocum*, 82–83; Furgurson, *Chancellorsville*, 226.

35. OR, vol. 29, pt. 1, p. 156.

36. Roy P. Basler, ed., *The Collected Works of Abraham Lincoln*, 8 vols. (New Brunswick NJ: Rutgers University Press, 1953–55), 6:486.

37. Slocum, *Slocum*, 140; Hebert, *Fighting Joe Hooker*, 251; Dennett, ed., *Lincoln and the Civil War*, 94, 106.

38. Oliver Otis Howard, *Autobiography of Oliver Otis Howard*, 2 vols. (New York: Baker & Taylor, 1908), 1:452–53.

39. Dennett, ed., *Lincoln and the Civil War*, 94; Hebert, *Fighting Joe Hooker*, 252.

4. WEST TO THE OHIO

1. Henry C. Morhous, *Reminiscences of the 123rd Regiment N.Y.S.V., Giving a Complete History of Its Three Years' Service in the War* (Greenwich NY: People's Journal Book and Job Office, 1879), 62; Charles Edward Benton, *As Seen from the Ranks: A Boy in the Civil War* (New York: Knickerbocker Press, 1902), 90–91.

2. OR, vol. 29, pt. 1, pp. 154–55.

3. OR, vol. 29, pt. 1, pp. 159, 161–62.

4. Entry for 28 September 1863, Lyman Daniel Ames Diaries, OHS; Rufus Mead to "Folks at Home," 25 October 1863, Rufus Mead Letters, LC; McCallum to Devereux, 24, 25 September 1863, United States Military Railroad Telegrams, RG 92, NA; Entry ca. 25 September 1863, Frederick Von Fritsch Diary, ed. Jessie Kaufman, LC; Horatio Dana Chapman, *Civil War Diary: Diary of a Forty-niner* (Hartford CT: Allis, 1929), 37; OR, vol. 29, pt. 1, pp. 158–59.

5. Twelfth Army Corps Records, RG 94, NA. Orders to Williams and Geary mentioned in the following paragraphs are in the same source.

6. Milo M. Quaife, ed., *From the Cannon's Mouth: The Civil War Letters of General Alpheus S. Williams* (Detroit: Wayne State University Press and the Detroit Historical Society, 1959), 3–8.

7. Harry Marlin Tinkcom, *John White Geary: Soldier-Statesman, 1819–1873* (Philadelphia: University of Pennsylvania Press, 1940), 1–103.

8. OR, vol. 29, pt. 1, pp. 162–64; Stanton to McCallum, 25 September 1863, Stanton Papers.

9. McCallum to Stanton, 28 September 1863, Stanton Papers; OR, vol. 29, pt. 1, p. 156; Edmund R. Brown, *The Twenty-seventh Indiana Volunteer Infantry in the War of the Rebellion, 1861 to 1865* (Monticello IN: N.p., 1899), 436.

10. Sebastian Duncan to Mother, 28 September 1863, Sebastian Duncan Letters, NJHS; OR, vol. 29, pt. 1, p. 172.

11. David Nichol to Father, 27 September 1863, quoted in James P. Brady, comp., *Hurrah for the Artillery! Knap's Independent Battery "E," Pennsylvania Light Artillery* (Gettysburg PA: Thomas Publications, 1992), 291–92.

12. Brown, *Twenty-seventh Indiana*, 436–38.

13. Howard, *Autobiography*, 1:455; George Metcalf, Reminiscences, 116, Harrisburg CWRT, Gregory Coco Collection, USAMHI.

14. Patricia L. Faust, "Baron Adolph Wilhelm August Friedrich von Steinwehr," in *Historical Times Illustrated Encyclopedia of the Civil War*, ed. Patricia L. Faust (New York: Harper & Row, 1986), 792; Hans L. Trefousse,

Carl Schurz: A Biography (Knoxville: University of Tennessee Press, 1982), 3–140.

15. John Richards Boyle, *Soldiers True: The Story of the One Hundred and Eleventh Regiment Pennsylvania Veteran Volunteers and of Its Campaigns in the War for the Union, 1861–1865* (New York: Eaton & Mains, 1903), 147; Luther Mesnard, Reminiscences, CWMC, USAMHI; Chapman, *Civil War Diary*, 36–37.

16. Hungerford, *Story of the Baltimore & Ohio*, 2:53; Entry for 27 September 1863, Mead Diary.

17. Entries for 28, 30 September 1863, Ezra Carman Journal, NJHS; George K. Collins, *Memoirs of the 149th Regiment N.Y. Vol. Inft.* (Syracuse NY: Author, 1891), 180–81; Howard, *Autobiography*, 1:453.

18. Summers, "Baltimore and Ohio," 249; Stover, *History of the Baltimore and Ohio*, 104–5.

19. Summers, *Baltimore and Ohio*, 93–96, 112–16, 119–22, 125–39; Stover, *History of the Baltimore and Ohio*, 106–10.

20. Baltimore and Ohio Railroad Company, *Thirty-seventh Annual Report of the President and Directors to the Stockholders of the Baltimore and Ohio R. R. Co. for the Year Ending September 30, 1863* (Baltimore: J. B. Rose, 1865), 4–5, 8, 23.

21. Theodore F. Lang, *Loyal West Virginia from 1861 to 1865* (Baltimore: Deustch, 1895), 320–22; Summers, *Baltimore and Ohio*, 104, 147–52.

22. Andrew J. Boies, *Record of the Thirty-third Massachusetts Volunteer Infantry from Aug. 1862 to Aug. 1865* (Fitchburg MA: Sentinel, 1880), 42.

23. OR, vol. 29, pt. 1, p. 161; Mead to "Folks at Home," 23 October 1863, Mead Letters; Boies, *Record of the Thirty-third Massachusetts*, 42.

24. OR, vol. 29, pt. 1, pp. 162, 167; Koontz to Stanton (three telegrams), 27 September 1863, Stanton Papers.

25. OR, vol. 29, pt. 1, pp. 167, 169–70, 172, 181–83; Thayer, "Railroad Feat of War," 428; Butterfield to Schurz, 27 September 1863, Joseph Hooker Orderbooks, RG 94, NA; Summers, *Baltimore and Ohio*, 172–74.

26. Hooker to Howard, 25 September 1863, Hooker Orderbooks.

27. Samuel Toombs, *Reminiscences of the War, Comprising a Detailed Account of the Experiences of the Thirteenth Regiment New Jersey Volunteers in Camp, on the March, and in Battle* (Orange NJ: Journal Office, 1878), 100; S. G. Cook and Charles E. Benton, *The "Dutchess County Regiment" (150th Regiment of New York State Volunteer Infantry) in the Civil War: Its Story as Told by Its Members, Based upon the Writings of Edward O. Bartlett* (Danbury CT: Danbury Medical Printing Company, 1907), 53; John M. Gould, *History of*

the First-Tenth-Twenty-ninth Maine Regiment, in the Services of the United States from May 3, 1861, to June 21, 1865 (Portland ME: Stephen Berry, 1871), 362.

28. *Zanesville Daily Courier*, 28, 29 September 1863; *Ohio State Journal* (Columbus), 29 September 1863; *Richmond Jeffersonian*, 1 October 1863; *Indianapolis Daily Evening Gazette*, 30 September 1863; Robert Hubbard to Wife, 29 September 1863, Robert Hubbard Letters, USAMHI.

29. Alonzo H. Quint, *The Potomac and the Rapidan: Army Notes from the Failure at Winchester to the Reenforcement of Rosecrans, 1861–63* (Boston: Crosby & Nichols, 1864), 358–59; Gould, *History of the First-Tenth-Twenty-ninth Maine*, 361; Mead to "Folks at Home," 25 October 1863, Mead Letters.

30. Stover, *History of the Baltimore and Ohio*, 54–57, 69–71; Mead to "Folks at Home," 25 October 1863, Mead Letters; Collins, *Memoirs of the 149th*, 181–82.

31. Stover, *History of the Baltimore and Ohio*, 70; Duncan to Mother, 28 September 1863, Duncan Letters; Benton, *As Seen from the Ranks*, 93–94; Collins, *Memoirs of the 149th*, 182.

32. Entry for 29 September 1863, Carman Journal; Quint, *The Potomac and the Rapidan*, 359.

33. A. Anderson to Garrett, 1 October 1863, Baltimore and Ohio Railroad Papers.

34. OR, vol. 29, pt. 1, pp. 167–72.

35. J. Cutler Andrews, *The North Reports the Civil War* (Pittsburgh: University of Pittsburgh Press, 1955), 466; Noah Brooks, *Washington, D.C., in Lincoln's Time*, ed. Herbert Mitgang (Chicago: Quadrangle Books, 1971), 64–65.

36. OR, vol. 29, pt. 2, pp. 753–54.

37. OR, vol. 29, pt. 2, pp. 756–58, 766.

38. Garrett to Stanton, 25 September 1863, Stanton Papers; OR, vol. 29, pt. 1, p. 167.

39. The itemized bill for the pontoon bridge can be found in the J. B. Ford Papers, West Virginia Collection, West Virginia University Library, Morgantown WV.

40. For details on the crossing times, see the Ford Papers; A. Anderson to Garrett, 1 October 1863, Baltimore and Ohio Railroad Papers.

41. Summers, *Baltimore and Ohio*, 174; OR, vol. 29, pt. 1, pp. 183–84.

5. "LIKE AN OASIS"

1. Eugene H. Roseboom, *The Civil War Era*, vol. 4 of *The History of the State*

of Ohio. ed. Carl Wittke, 6 vols. (Columbus: Ohio State Archaeological and Historical Society, 1944), 409–14.

2. Lawrence Wilson, ed., *Itinerary of the Seventh Ohio Volunteer Infantry, 1861–1864* (New York: Neale, 1907), 266.

3. John H. Sullivan, *Remarks on the Importance of the Central Ohio Railroad to the Interests of Baltimore* (Baltimore: Printing Office, 1852), 3–15; Stover, *History of the Baltimore and Ohio,* 82–84; Baltimore and Ohio Railroad Company, *Thirty-seventh Annual Report,* 9–10; Walter Rumsey Marvin, "Columbus and the Railroads of Central Ohio Before the Civil War" (Ph.D diss., Ohio State University, 1953), 230, 247–50, 253–58.

4. Roseboom, *Civil War Era,* 390; Marvin, "Columbus and the Railroads of Central Ohio," 262, 414–15; Garrett to Stanton, 25 September 1863, Stanton Papers.

5. Collins, *Memoirs of the 149th,* 183; Toombs, *Reminiscences of the War,* 101.

6. Brown, *Twenty-seventh Indiana,* 440; Richard Eddy, *History of the Sixtieth Regiment New York State Volunteers from the Commencement of Its Organization in July 1861, to Its Public Reception at Ogdensburgh as a Veteran Command, January 7th, 1864* (Philadelphia: Author, 1864), 288.

7. William H. H. Tallman, Memoirs, 78–80, Charles Rhodes III Collection, USAMHI.

8. Fanny B. Ward, Battery *"I," First Ohio Artillery* (N.p., n.d.), 57–58; Chapman, *Civil War Diary,* 38; *Zanesville Daily Courier,* 30 September 1863; cf. *Wheeling Daily Intelligencer,* 1 October 1863.

9. Captain Alex Caldwell to ?, ca. 2–5 October 1863, Caldwell Family Papers, 46th Pennsylvania Infantry Regimental Correspondence, CWTI Collection, USAMHI.

10. Eddy, *History of the Sixtieth Regiment,* 288; David Nichol to Annie Nichol [his sister], 10 October 1863, David Nichol Letters, Harrisburg CWRT Collection, USAMHI; Collins, *Memoirs of the 149th,* 184; David Mouat, Unpublished Reminiscences, Historical Society of Pennsylvania, Philadelphia.

11. Benton, *As Seen from the Ranks,* 94–95.

12. Mesnard, Reminiscences; Boyle, *Soldiers True,* 150.

13. Nichol to Annie Nichol, 10 October 1863, Nichol Letters; Toombs, *Reminiscences of the War,* 101–2; Chapman, *Civil War Diary,* 38.

14. Quint, *The Potomac and the Rapidan,* 361–62; Howard, *Autobiography,* 1: 453–54; Eddy, *History of the Sixtieth Regiment,* 288; Benton, *As Seen from the Ranks,* 95–96; Cook and Benton, eds., *"Dutchess County Regiment,"* 54; Toombs, *Reminiscences of the War,* 101.

15. Smith to Stanton, 28, 29 September 1863, Stanton Papers; OR, vol. 29, pt. 1, pp. 172–73, 178; Quint, *The Potomac and the Rapidan*, 361.

16. Garrett to Scott, 28 September 1863, Andrew Anderson to Garrett, 30 September, 1 October 1863, Baltimore and Ohio Railroad Papers.

17. Garrett to Smith, 28 September 1863, Baltimore and Ohio Railroad Papers.

18. Caldwell to ?, ca. 2–5 October 1863, Caldwell Letters; Collins, *Memoirs of the 149th*, 185.

19. Collins, *Memoirs of the 149th*, 185; Gould, *History of the First-Tenth-Twenty-ninth Maine Regiment*, 363; Ward, *Sketch of Battery "I,"* 58.

20. Marvin, "Columbus and the Railroads of Central Ohio," 120–23, 134, 137; Little Miami Railroad Company and Columbus & Xenia Railroad Company, *Eighth Joint Report of the Directors to the Stockholders for the Year 1863* (Cincinnati: N.p., 1864), 19, 24.

21. *Chicago Evening Journal*, 30 September 1863.

22. Adin B. Underwood, *The Three Years' Service of the Thirty-third Massachusetts Infantry Regiment, 1862–1865* (Boston: A. Williams, 1881), 149; Ward, *Sketch of Battery "I,"* 58; Toombs, *Reminiscences of the War*, 102; Collins, *Memoirs of the 149th*, 185.

23. *Indianapolis Daily Evening Gazette*, 29 September 1863.

24. Morhous, *Reminiscences of the 123rd Regiment*, 67; Wilson, *Itinerary of the Seventh Ohio*, 266.

25. Brown, *Twenty-seventh Indiana*, 440–42; Slocum, *Slocum*, 141–42.

26. Brown, *Twenty-seventh Indiana*, 442.

27. John M. Paver, *What I Saw from 1861 to 1864: Personal Recollections of John M. Paver, 1st Lieutenant, Company C, and R.Q.M., 5th Ohio Vol. Infantry* (Indianapolis: N.p., 1906), 43; Nichol to Annie Nichol, 10 October 1863, Nichol Letters.

28. Tallman, Memoirs.

29. Boyle, *Soldiers True*, 148.

30. Lewis C. Baird, *Baird's History of Clark County, Indiana* (Indianapolis: B. F. Bowen, 1909), 367; S. H. Church, *Corporate History of the Pennsylvania Lines West of Pittsburgh*, 13 vols. (Philadelphia: F. Chivis, 1899–1918), Ser. A, vol. 3, pp. 101–13.

31. Hubbard to Wife, 30 September 1863, Hubbard Letters; Mead to "Folks at Home," 25 October 1863, Mead Papers.

6. RETURN TO THE CONFEDERACY

1. OR, vol. 29, pt. 1, pp. 178–79.

2. OR, vol. 29, pt. 1, pp. 162, 166–67, 174–75, 181, 188–90; Kamm, *Scott*, 172–73.

3. Chapman, *Civil War Diary*, 39; John Love to Wife, 1, 3 October 1863, John Love Letters, NJHS.

4. Butterfield to Scott, 28 September 1863, Butterfield to "Lt. Oliver," 29 September 1863, Hooker Orderbooks, RG 94, NA; *Cincinnati Enquirer*, quoted in *Louisville Daily Journal*, 3 October 1863.

5. Henry Villard, *Memoirs of Henry Villard, Journalist and Financier, 1835–1900*, 2 vols. (Boston: Houghton Mifflin, 1904), 2:178.

6. Hubbard to Wife, 5 October 1863, Hubbard Letters; Love to Wife, 1 October 1863, Love Letters.

7. Entry for 4 October 1863, Carman Journal.

8. Maury Klein, *History of the Louisville & Nashville Railroad* (New York: Macmillan, 1972), 4–12.

9. Klein, *History of the Louisville & Nashville*, 12–13; John E. Tilford Jr., "The Delicate Track: The L&N's Role in the Civil War," *Filson Club Historical Quarterly* 36 (July 1962): 210–11.

10. Klein, *History of the Louisville & Nashville*, 27–28; Tilford, "Delicate Track," 211–13; R. S. Cotterill, "The Louisville and Nashville Railroad, 1861–1865," *American Historical Review* 29 (1924): 701–5.

11. Klein, *History of the Louisville & Nashville*, 28–29; Tilford, "Delicate Track," 213.

12. Cotterill, "Louisville and Nashville," 705–6.

13. Klein, *History of the Louisville & Nashville*, 27–37; Cotterill, "Louisville and Nashville," 706–11; Tilford, "Delicate Track," 214–17.

14. Louisville and Nashville Railroad Company, *Annual Report of the President and Directors of the Louisville and Nashville R.R. Company, Commencing on the First of July, 1862, and Ending on the Thirtieth of June, 1863* (Louisville: Hanna, 1863), 9, 28, 38–39, 54.

15. Mead to "Folks at Home," 25 October 1863, Mead Letters; Brown, *Twenty-seventh Indiana*, 443; Hubbard to Wife, 2 October 1863, Hubbard Letters; Entry for 5 October 1863, Ames Diary.

16. Howard, *Autobiography*, 1:456; James T. Miller to Robert E. Miller, 8 October 1863, Miller Family Papers, CL; Collins, *Memoirs of the 149th*, 186; Brown, *Twenty-seventh Indiana*, 443.

17. Hubbard to Wife, 2 October 1863, Hubbard Letters; Cook and Benton, "Dutchess County Regiment," 55; Collins, *Memoirs of the 149th*, 186–87; Chapman, *Civil War Diary*, 39.

18. Brown, *Twenty-seventh Indiana*, 443; Entry for 3 October 1863, Mead

Diaries; Collins, *Memoirs of the 149th*, 187; Mouat, Unpublished Reminiscences.

19. S. J. Folmsbee, "The Origins of the Nashville and Chattanooga Railroad," *East Tennessee Historical Society's Publications* 6 (1934): 81–94.

20. Jesse C. Burt Jr., "The Nashville and Chattanooga Railroad, 1854–1872: The Era of Transition," *East Tennessee Historical Society's Publications* 23 (1951): 58–62.

21. Burt, "Nashville and Chattanooga," 62–63; OR, Ser. 3, vol. 5, pp. 584, 936.

22. Julian Wisner Hinkley, Reminiscences in Hinkley Papers, State Historical Society of Wisconsin; Edwin E. Bryant, *History of the Third Regiment of Wisconsin Veteran Volunteer Infantry, 1861–1865* (Madison: N.p., 1891), 217; Entry for 3 October 1863, Carman Journal.

23. OR, vol. 29, pt. 1, pp. 180, 183–84.

24. OR, vol. 29, pt. 1, pp. 184, 187.

25. OR, vol. 29, pt. 1, pp. 194–95.

26. OR, vol. 29, pt. 1, pp. 171, 180, 185, 187; Smith to McCallum, 29, 30 September 1863, United States Military Railroads, Telegrams Received, RG 92, NA.

27. OR, vol. 29, pt. 1, p. 187.

28. Garrett to Jewett, 3 October 1863, Garrett to Ford, 4 October 1863, Garrett to Cole, 5, 6 October 1863, John Garrett Letterbooks, Letters Sent by the Baltimore and Ohio Railroad, MHS.

29. OR, vol. 29, pt. 1, p. 188.

30. Koontz to McCallum, 4, 5, 6 October 1863, United States Military Railroads, Telegrams Received.

31. OR, vol. 29, pt. 1, pp. 192–93.

32. Smith to McCallum, 9 October 1863, United States Military Railroads, Telegrams Received; Garrett to Jewett, 8 October 1863, Garrett to Smith, 9 October 1863, Letters Sent by the Baltimore and Ohio Railroad.

33. OR, vol. 29, pt. 1, pp. 183, 187–91.

34. Phillip Shaw Paludan, *"A People's Contest": The Union and Civil War, 1861–1865* (New York: Harper & Row, 1988), 141; Klein, *History of the Louisville & Nashville*, 38–39; Tilford, "Delicate Track," 218; Louisville and Nashville Railroad Company, *Annual Report*, 49.

35. Scott to Innes, 25 (two telegrams), 27, 28, 29 (two telegrams) September 1863, United States Military Railroads, Telegrams Received.

36. OR, vol. 30, pt. 4, pp. 32–33; Kamm, *Scott*, 177.

37. OR, vol. 30, pt. 4, pp. 167–68, 193, 207.

38. OR, vol. 30, pt. 4, pp. 150–75.

39. OR, vol. 30, pt. 4, pp. 208, 245, 333–34.

40. OR, vol. 30, pt. 4, pp. 334–35.

41. OR, vol. 30, pt. 4, p. 361.

42. OR, vol. 30, pt. 4, pp. 414, 416; Kamm, *Scott*, 182.

43. OR, vol. 30, pt. 4, p. 434.

44. OR, vol. 29, pt. 1, pp. 171–72, 179.

7. "WE ARE NEARLY OUT OF THE WORLD"

1. OR, vol. 30, pt. 2, pp. 684–85; vol. 30, pt. 3, p. 952.

2. OR, vol. 30, pt. 2, p. 723; vol. 30, pt. 4, pp. 37–38, 44–45; Peter Cozzens, *The Shipwreck of Their Hopes: The Battles for Chattanooga* (Urbana: University of Illinois Press, 1994), 25.

3. OR, vol. 30, pt. 3, p. 904; vol. 30, pt. 4, pp. 71–72.

4. OR, vol. 30, pt. 4, pp. 93–95.

5. Edwin E. Marvin, *The Fifth Regiment Connecticut Volunteers* (Hartford CT: Press of Wiley, Waterman, & Eaton, 1889), 287; Brown, *Twenty-seventh Indiana*, 445; John D. Hill to "Friends," 6 October 1863, John D. Hill Letters, CWMC, USAMHI.

6. William Sharp to ?, 14 October 1863, William T. Sharp Letters, CWMC, USAMHI.

7. Bryant, *History of the Third Regiment*, 218; Quint, *The Potomac and the Rapidan*, 365–67.

8. OR, vol. 30, pt. 2, pp. 713–14; vol. 30, pt. 4, pp. 134–36. For the explanations of Cols. John Coburn and John P. Baird, commanders at Garrison's Fork Bridge and Wartrace respectively, see OR, vol. 30, pt. 4, pp. 697–700, 717.

9. OR, vol. 30, pt. 2, pp. 715–16; vol. 30, pt. 4, pp. 136–37, 160–64.

10. OR, vol. 30, pt. 2, pp. 715–16; vol. 30, pt. 4, pp. 188, 209, 223.

11. OR, vol. 30, pt. 4, pp. 261, 266; Charles Howard to Mother, 11 October 1863, Charles H. Howard Papers, Bowdoin College, Freeport, Maine.

12. Alpheus S. Williams to Daughter, 12 October 1863, quoted in Quaife, *From the Cannon's Mouth*, 266.

13. Rice C. Bull, *Soldiering in the Civil War: The Diary of Rice C. Bull, 123rd New York Volunteer Infantry* (San Francisco: Presidio, 1977), 91–94.

14. Charles Howard to Mother, 7, 11 October 1863, Howard Papers.

15. Mouat, Unpublished Reminiscences.

16. Hubbard to Wife, 13 October 1863, Hubbard Letters; Quint, *The Potomac and the Rapidan*, 363; Love to Wife 13, 17 October 1863, Love Letters.

17. Love to Wife, 13 October 1863, Love Letters; Williams to Daughter, 12 October 1863, quoted in Quaife, *From the Cannon's Mouth*, 267.

18. John C. Griswold to Wife, 20 October 1863, John C. Griswold Letters, Michael Winey Collection, USAMHI; Love to Wife, 8 October 1863, Love Letters.

19. Love to Wife, 8 October 1863, Love Letters.

20. Entries for 4, 28 October 1863, Carman Journal; Hubbard to Wife, 5 October 1863, Hubbard Letters; Griswold to Wife, 2 October 1863, Griswold Letters; Carpenter, *The Sword and the Olive Branch*, 59.

21. Hubbard to Wife, 16 October 1863, Hubbard Letters; Williams to Daughter, 12 October 1863, quoted in Quaife, *From the Cannon's Mouth*, 267; Chapman, *Civil War Diary*, 41–42.

22. Morhous, *Reminiscences of the 123rd Regiment*, 73; Love to Wife, 11 October 1863, Love Letters; Hubbard to Wife, 16 October 1863, Hubbard Letters.

23. Morhous, *Reminiscences of the 123rd Regiment*, 73; Griswold to Wife, 20 October 1863, Griswold Letters.

24. Quint, *The Potomac and the Rapidan*, 370–71; Love to Wife, 8, 21 October 1863, Love Letters; Brown, *Twenty-seventh Indiana*, 448.

25. Hubbard to Wife, 11 October 1863, Hubbard Letters; Ario Pardee Jr. to Father, 11 October 1863, Ario Pardee Letters, Pardee-Robison Family Papers, USAMHI; Metcalf, Reminiscences.

26. Entry for 22 October 1863, Henry Henney Diary, CWTI Collection, USAMHI; Collins, *Memoirs of the 149th*, 185–86.

27. Pardee to Father, 11 October 1863, Pardee Letters; Alonzo H. Quint, *The Record of the Second Massachusetts Infantry, 1861–65* (Boston: James P. Walker, 1867), 196–97; Charles Fessendon Morse, *Letters Written During the Civil War, 1861–1865* (N.p., 1898), 148–49.

28. 1st Division, 12th Army Corps, General Orders 56, 21 October 1863, RG 94, NA.

29. Division Order, 3rd Division, 11th Army Corps, 15 October 1863, RG 94, NA; Special Orders, Headquarters, U.S. Forces, Murfreesboro, 19 October 1865, RG 94, NA; Collins, *Memoirs of the 149th*, 189.

30. OR, vol. 30, pt. 4, pp. 291, 322.

31. OR, vol. 30, pt. 4, p. 344; Twelfth Army Corps Papers, RG 393, NA.

32. OR, vol. 30, pt. 4, pp. 397–99.

33. George Edwards to Wife, 20 October 1863, George Edwards Papers, INHS; Hill to "Friends at Home," 18 October 1863, Hill to Sister, 30 October 1863, Hill Letters; Toombs, *Reminiscences of the War*, 103.

34. Charles H. Howard to Mother, 11 October 1863, Howard to Brother, 14 October 1863, Howard Papers.

35. Howard to Schurz, 5 October 1863, Eleventh Corps Papers, RG 393, NA; OR, vol. 30, pt. 4, pp. 165, 262, 426, 437, 445, 457, 467.
36. OR, vol. 30, pt. 4, pp. 191–92.
37. William G. Le Duc, "The Little Steamboat That Opened the 'Cracker Line,'" in Robert U. Johnson and Clarence C. Buel, eds., *Battles and Leaders of the Civil War*, 4 vols. (1887–88; rpt. New York: Thomas Yoseloff, 1956), 3:676–78; OR, vol. 30, pt. 4, pp. 323, 436, 467.
38. OR, vol. 30, pt. 4, p. 404.
39. OR, vol. 30, pt. 1, pp. 194, 202, 215, 218–19.
40. OR, vol. 30, pt. 4, pp. 57, 79, 306–7, 414.
41. T. Harry Williams, *Lincoln and His Generals* (New York: Knopf, 1952), 284–85.
42. Quint, *The Potomac and the Rapidan*, 368–69.
43. Brown, *Twenty-seventh Indiana*, 448.
44. Howard, *Autobiography*, 1:460; Oliver Otis Howard, "Chattanooga," *Atlantic Monthly* 38 (1876): 206; cf. James Harrison Wilson, *Under the Old Flag: Recollections of Military Operations in the War for the Union, the Spanish War, the Boxer Rebellion, Etc.*, 2 vols. (New York: D. Appleton, 1912), 1:264–65.
45. Howard, "Chattanooga," 206; Hubbard to Wife, 23 October 1863, Hubbard Letters.

8. "YOU HAVE OPENED UP OUR BREAD LINE"

1. William S. McFeely, *Grant: A Biography* (New York: Norton, 1981), 145; OR, vol. 31, pt. 1, p. 70.
2. Catton, *Never Call Retreat*, 259; Horace Porter, *Campaigning with Grant*, ed. Wayne C. Temple (Bloomington: Indiana University Press, 1961), 1–2, 5, 8.
3. Ulysses S. Grant, *Personal Memoirs of U. S. Grant*, 2 vols. (New York: Charles L. Webster, 1885–86), 2:28.
4. Grant, *Personal Memoirs*, 2:31–32; Cozzens, *Shipwreck of Their Hopes*, 39–42, 51.
5. OR, vol. 31, pt. 1, pp. 43, 77–78, 841.
6. Cozzens, *Shipwreck of Their Hopes*, 53–64; Wiley Sword, *Mountains Touched with Fire: Chattanooga Besieged, 1863* (New York: St. Martin's Press, 1995), 114–21.
7. OR, vol. 31, pt. 1, pp. 43–44.

8. Howard, *Autobiography*, 1:458–59.

9. OR, vol. 31, pt. 1, p. 44.

10. OR, vol. 31, pt. 1, p. 112; Albert R. Greene, "From Bridgeport to Ringgold by Way of Lookout Mountain," in *Personal Narratives of Events in the War of the Rebellion, Being Papers Read Before the Rhode Island Soldiers and Sailors Historical Society*, 4, no. 6 (Providence: The Society, 1890), 15–16.

11. Douglas R. Cubbison, "Midnight Engagement: John Geary's White Star Division at Wauhatchie, Tennessee, October 28–29, 1863," *Civil War Regiments* 3, no. 2 (1993): 78; Geary to Wife, 25 October 1863, quoted in William Alan Blair, ed., *A Politician Goes to War: The Civil War Letters of John White Geary*, selected and intro. by Bell Irvin Wiley (University Park: Pennsylvania University Press, 1995), 129.

12. OR, vol. 31, pt. 1, pp. 45–46.

13. Eleventh Corps Records, CL; OR, vol. 31, pt. 1, p. 112; Howard, *Autobiography*, 1:461.

14. Hubbard to Wife, 28 October 1863, Hubbard Letters.

15. Howard, *Autobiography*, 1:461; Underwood, *Three Years' Service of the Thirty-third Massachusetts*, 154; Boies, *Record of the Thirty-Third Massachusetts*, 46; Collins, *Memoirs of the 149th*, 195; Cubbison, "Midnight Engagement," 79; Entry for 26 October 1863, Henney Diary.

16. OR, vol. 31, pt. 1, pp. 55, 97, 113.

17. OR, vol. 31, pt. 1, pp. 97, 101; Cozzens, *Shipwreck of Their Hopes*, 72.

18. Wert, *Longstreet*, 325–26; OR, vol. 30, pt. 4, pp. 705–6.

19. Wert, *Longstreet*, 327–29. For an account supportive of Bragg, see Steven E. Woodworth, *Jefferson Davis and His Generals: The Failure of Confederate Command in the West* (Lawrence: University Press of Kansas, 1990), 238–43.

20. Thomas Lawrence Connelly, *Autumn of Glory: The Army of Tennessee, 1862–1865* (Baton Rouge: Louisiana State University Press, 1971), 255–59; Cozzens, *Shipwreck of Their Hopes*, 57–58, 66–71.

21. Metcalf, Reminiscences; OR, vol. 31, pt. 1, pp. 97, 105; Howard, *Autobiography*, 1:464; Hubbard to Wife, 28 October 1863, Hubbard Letters.

22. Howard, *Autobiography*, 1:464–65; Samuel H. Hurst, *Journal-History of the Seventy-third Ohio Volunteer Infantry* (Chillicothe OH: N.p., 1866), 85–86; "Frank," anonymous member of the 136th New York, to "William," 4 November 1863, 136th New York Regimental File, CCNMP.

23. OR, vol. 31, pt. 1, pp. 56–60, 113; Cubbison, "Midnight Engagement," 78, 80.

24. OR, vol. 31, pt. 1, pp. 53–54, 72, 112, 125, 127, 133.

25. OR, vol. 31, pt. 1, p. 113.

9. WAUHATCHIE

1. Cubbison, "Midnight Engagement," 100.

2. Connelly, *Autumn of Glory*, 259–60.

3. Guy R. Swanson and Timothy D. Johnson, "Conflict in East Tennessee: Generals Law, Jenkins, and Longstreet," *Civil War History* 31 (June 1985): 102–5.

4. Connelly, *Autumn of Glory*, 260.

5. J. L. Coker, "Battle of Lookout Valley or Wauhatchie," *Confederate Veteran* 28 (1910): 473.

6. OR, vol. 31, pt. 1, pp. 113–23.

7. OR, vol. 31, pt. 1, p. 123; Cubbison, "Midnight Engagement," 80–81.

8. OR, vol. 31, pt. 1, p. 113; Cubbison, "Midnight Engagement," 82–83.

9. OR, vol. 31, pt. 1, p. 231; James Lide Coker, *History of Company G, Ninth S.C. Regiment, Infantry, S.C. Army and of Company E, Sixth S.C. Regiment, Infantry, S.C. Army* (1899; rpt. Greenwood SC: Attic Press, 1979), 131.

10. Mouat, Unpublished Reminiscences.

11. OR, vol. 31, pt. 1, pp. 113, 125–26.

12. Although some sources note that clouds occasionally obscured the moon, most of the participants described the night as brightly moonlit.

13. James R. Hagood, Memoirs, 122, South Caroliniana Library, University of South Carolina, Columbia, South Carolina.

14. Hagood, Memoirs, 113, 128, 132–33.

15. Boyle, *Soldiers True*, 162.

16. OR, vol. 31, pt. 1, pp. 127, 129; Greene, "From Bridgeport to Ringgold," 23–24.

17. OR, vol. 31, pt. 1, p. 126; Boyle, *Soldiers True*, 164; Miller to Father, 2 November 1863, Miller Family Papers, CL.

18. Hagood, Memoirs; Letter of an unidentified soldier, 5th South Carolina, *Columbia Daily Southern Guardian*, 11 November 1863; OR, vol. 31, pt. 1, pp. 231, 233.

19. OR, vol. 31, pt. 1, pp. 114, 135, 231.

20. OR, vol. 31, pt. 1, p. 122; Boyle, *Soldiers True*, 163; Miller to Father, 2 November 1863, Miller Family Papers.

21. OR, vol. 31, pt. 1, pp. 231–32; Elijah J. Tollison, Memoirs, CWTI Collection, USAMHI.

22. OR, vol. 31, pt. 1, pp. 128, 132; Tollison, Memoirs.

23. OR, vol. 31, pt. 1, p. 231; Mouat, Reminiscences.

24. OR, vol. 31, pt. 1, pp. 115, 117, 124, 135; Greene, "Bridgeport to Ringgold," 23; Lewis to Mother, 30 October 1863, in Lewis, *Camp Life of a Confederate*

Boy, 65; Nichol to Sister, 11 November 1863, in Brady, comp., *Hurrah for the Artillery!*, 316; Mouat, Unpublished Reminiscences.

25. OR, vol. 31, pt. 1, pp. 115, 133.

26. OR, vol. 31, pt. 1, p. 124; Mouat, Unpublished Reminiscences.

27. OR, vol. 31, pt. 1, pp. 115, 129, 231.

28. Howard, "Chattanooga," 208.

29. Howard, "Chattanooga," 208; OR, vol. 31, pt. 1, p. 94.

30. OR, vol. 31, pt. 1, pp. 98, 149, 160, 163.

31. OR, vol. 31, pt. 1, pp. 101, 110.

32. OR, vol. 31, pt. 1, pp. 227, 229.

33. OR, vol. 31, pt. 1, pp. 227, 229; Jeffrey D. Stocker, ed., *From Huntsville to Appomattox: R. T. Coles's History of 4th Regiment, Alabama Volunteer Infantry, C.S.A., Army of Northern Virginia* (Knoxville: University of Tennessee Press, 1996), 146.

34. OR, vol. 31, pt. 1, pp. 227, 229; Stocker, *From Huntsville to Appomattox*, 146.

35. OR, vol. 31, pt. 1, pp. 101–2; Underwood, *Three Years' Service of the Thirty-third Massachusetts*, 157.

36. OR, vol. 31, pt. 1, pp. 103, 108; Hurst, *Journal-History of the Seventy-third Ohio*, 87.

37. OR, vol. 31, pt. 1, p. 104.

38. Underwood, *Three Years' Service of the Thirty-third Massachusetts*, 160.

39. Underwood, *Three Years' Service of the Thirty-third Massachusetts*, 160; John R. Ryder, *Reminiscences of Three Years' Service in the Civil War by a Cape Cod Boy* (New Bedford MA: Reynolds, 1928), 42–43; OR, vol. 31, pt. 1, p. 104.

40. OR, vol. 31, pt. 1, pp. 108–9; Hurst, *Journal-History of the Seventy-third Ohio*, 88.

41. Ryder, *Reminiscences*, 43.

42. OR, vol. 31, pt. 1, p. 106; Metcalf, Reminiscences, 126.

43. OR, vol. 31, pt. 1, pp. 230, 234.

44. Ryder, *Reminiscences*; OR, vol. 31, pt. 1, pp. 104, 109.

45. Metcalf, Reminiscences, 127–28; "Frank," anonymous member of the 136th New York, to "William," 4 November 1863, New York Regimental File, CCNMP.

46. Miles Vance Smith, Memoirs, CWMC, USAMHI.

47. "Captain Waddell," 1876 letter to Ezra Carman, quoted in Underwood, *Three Years' Service of the Thirty-third Massachusetts*, 167–68.

48. OR, vol. 31, pt. 1, p. 228.

49. OR, vol. 31, pt. 1, pp. 110, 207; vol. 52, pt. 1, p. 90.

50. This account is taken from the testimony of various witnesses at the court of inquiry, OR, vol. 31, pt. 1, pp. 143, 147, 152–53, 155, 171.

51. OR, vol. 31, pt. 1, pp. 149, 160, 187, 207–11.

52. OR, vol. 31, pt. 1, pp. 165, 167, 175, 177.

53. OR, vol. 31, pt. 1, p. 208.

54. Howard, "Chattanooga," 209; Howard, *Autobiography*, 1:468–69; for corroboration of Howard's exploits in capturing the Confederate soldiers, see Hubbard to Wife, 31 October 1863, Hubbard Letters.

EPILOGUE: AFTERMATH OF BATTLE

1. Mouat, Unpublished Reminiscences.

2. OR, vol. 31, pt. 1, pp. 68, 774.

3. Slocum to Geary, 17 November 1863, William C. Armor Papers, Pennsylvania History and Museum Commission, Harrisburg, Pennsylvania.

4. Wilson, *Under the Old Flag*, 1:278–79.

5. OR, vol. 31, pt. 1, pp. 73, 740.

6. John Bratton to Wife, 29 October 1863, John Bratton Letters, Special Collections, Emory University.

7. OR, vol. 31, pt. 1, p. 233; see Cubbison, "Midnight Engagement," 96–97.

8. OR, vol. 31, pt. 1, p. 120.

9. OR, vol. 31, pt. 1, pp. 74–75.

10. OR, vol. 31, pt. 1, pp. 230, 235.

11. D. G. Brinton Thompson, ed., "Dr. Daniel Garrison Brinton with the Army of the Cumberland," *Pennsylvania Magazine of History and Biography* 90 (1966): 466, 477; OR, vol. 31, pt. 1, pp. 100–101.

12. OR, vol. 31, pt. 1, pp. 100–101; Hubbard to Wife, 31 October 1863, Hubbard Letters.

13. Entry for 30 October 1863, Ames Diary; Miller to Joseph H. Miller, 7 November 1863, Miller Family Papers.

14. Metcalf, Reminiscences; "Frank," anonymous member of the 136th New York to "William," 4 November 1863, 136th New York Regimental File, CCNMP; OR, vol. 31, pt. 1, p. 104; Boies, *Record of the Thirty-third Massachusetts*, 49.

15. Collins, *Memoirs of the 149th*, 199; Boyle, *Soldiers True*, 166; OR, vol. 31, pt. 1, p. 63.

16. Collins, *Memoirs of the 149th*, 199–200.

17. Geary to Wife, 2, 6, 8, 17 November 1863, quoted in Blair, *A Politician Goes to War*, 131–36, 139–40.

The starting point for this work, as for so many others on the Civil War, was U.S. War Department, *The War of the Rebellion: A Compilation of the Official Records of the Union and Confederate Armies*, 128 vols. (Washington DC: U.S. Government Printing Office, 1880–1901). It not only provides valuable correspondence on the transfer but also much on the activities of the XI and XII Corps once they arrived in Tennessee and Alabama.

The holdings of the National Archives include orders and correspondence not found in the *Official Records*. Especially useful were Record Group 92, which includes telegrams of the U.S. Military Railroads; Record Group 94, including the Joseph Hooker order books and records of various units involved; and Record Group 393, which also has records of several units.

A variety of manuscript collections were consulted. Among the most important were the Baltimore and Ohio Railroad Papers at the Maryland Historical Society. Particularly useful were the John W. Garrett letterbooks, which contain the B&O president's detailed instructions to his subordinates before and during the transfer.

The Edwin M. Stanton Papers at the Library of Congress contain a great deal of correspondence on the transfer. Much of it, however, can also be found in the *Official Records*.

Two collections at the U.S. Military History Institute at Carlisle Barracks, Pennsylvania, provided extensive information. The Robert Hubbard Letters offer details of life in General Howard's camp and penetrating—if cynical—observations of Tennessee and its residents. The George Metcalf Reminiscences were also valuable.

Other particularly useful manuscript collections for the Union were the David Mouat Reminiscences, Historical Society of Pennsylvania; the Rufus Mead Jr. Papers, Library of Congress; and three collections at the New Jersey Historical Society, the Ezra Carman

Journal, the Sebastian Duncan Letters, and the John Love Letters. Many other manuscript collections supplied worthwhile information, but in smaller quantities. For those, readers are referred to the notes.

On the Confederate side, the telegrams to and from Frederick W. Sims, Confederate Railroad Bureau, located at the Valentine Museum in Richmond, are an important source. They include virtually the only reports available of the transfer of Longstreet's corps while that transfer was in progress.

Other important Confederate manuscript sources are the J. B. Clifton Diaries, Chickamauga-Chattanooga National Military Park; the W. R. Montgomery Diaries and the James R. Hagood Memoirs, University of South Carolina; and the Elijah J. Tollison Memoirs, U.S. Army Military History Institute.

Although no previously published book deals exclusively with the transfer of the XI and XII Corps, several secondary works touch upon one or more aspects of the movement. For the background of American railroads in the 1850s, the works of Alfred D. Chandler Jr. are valuable. Especially useful for this work were *The Visible Hand: The Managerial Revolution in American Business* (Cambridge MA: Belknap Press of Harvard University Press, 1977) and *The Railroads: The Nation's First Big Business, Sources and Readings* (New York: Harcourt, Brace and World, 1965). John F. Stover's *Iron Road to the West: American Railroads in the 1850s* (New York: Columbia University Press, 1978) is a solid, readable survey.

The role of railroads in the Civil War is covered by George Edgar Turner's *Victory Rode the Rails: The Strategic Place of Railroads in the Civil War* (Indianapolis: Bobbs-Merrill, 1953). Representing the two regions are Robert C. Black III, *The Railroads of the Confederacy* (Chapel Hill: University of North Carolina Press, 1952) and Thomas Weber, *The Northern Railroads in the Civil War* (New York: Columbia University Press, 1952). Particularly useful for this work was Festus P. Summers, *The Baltimore and Ohio in the Civil War* (New York: G. P. Putnam's Sons, 1934).

While Black includes a useful account of the transfer of Longstreet and his corps, memoirs by two of Longstreet's officers add helpful details. They are E. Porter Alexander's *Military Memoirs of a Confederate* (Bloomington: Indiana University Press, 1962) and G. Moxley Sorrel's *Recollections of a Confederate Staff Officer* (New York: Neale, 1905).

Summers's work on the Baltimore and Ohio provides vital background information on that strategically important line. Many of the small connecting lines are discussed by Walter Rumsey Marvin in "Columbus and the Railroads of Central Ohio Before the Civil War" (Ph.D. diss., Ohio State University, 1953). Maury Klein's *History of the Louisville & Nashville Railroad* (New York: Macmillan, 1972) is the standard history of that railroad. Also useful for the L&N are R. S. Cotterill's "The Louisville and Nashville Railroad, 1861–1865," *American Historical Review* 29 (1924): 700–715 and John E. Tilford's "The Delicate Track: The L&N's Role in the Civil War," *Filson Club Historical Quarterly* 36 (July 1962): 209–21. For the Nashville & Chattanooga, see Jesse C. Burt's "The Nashville and Chattanooga Railroad, 1854–1872: The Era of Transition," *East Tennessee Historical Society's Publications* 23 (1951): 58–76, and S. J. Folmsbee's "The Origins of the Nashville and Chattanooga Railroad," *East Tennessee Historical Society's Publications* 6 (1934): 81–95.

Published unit histories and personal memoirs vary widely in the amount of attention devoted to the transfer. Two of the most extensive and detailed are Edmund R. Brown's *The Twenty-seventh Indiana Volunteer Infantry in the War of the Rebellion, 1861 to 1865* (Monticello IN: N.p., 1899) and George K. Collins's *Memoirs of the 149th [New York Volunteer Infantry]* (Syracuse: Author, 1891). Other useful works include John R. Boyle's *Soldiers True: The Story of the One Hundred and Eleventh Regiment Pennsylvania Veteran Volunteers and of Its Campaigns in the War for the Union, 1861–1865* (New York: Eaton & Mains, 1903); Horatio Dana Chapman's *Civil War Diary: Diary of a Forty-niner* (Hartford CT: Allis, 1929); Henry C. Morhous's *Reminiscences of the 123d Regiment N.Y.S.V*

Giving a Complete History of Its Three Years' Service in the War (Greenwich NY: People's Journal Book and Job Office, 1879); and Samuel Toombs's *Reminiscences of the War, Comprising a Detailed Account of the Experiences of the Thirteenth Regiment New Jersey Volunteers in Camp, on the March, and in Battle* (Orange NJ: Journal Office, 1878). Two works by Chaplain Alonzo H. Quint, *The Potomac and the Rapidan: Army Notes, from the Failure at Winchester to the Reeinforcement of Rosecrans* (Boston: Crosky and Nichols, 1864), and *The Record of the Second Massachusetts Infantry, 1861–1865* (Boston: James P. Walker, 1867), add both details and humor.

Biographies of the chief military figures vary greatly in quality. Walter H. Hebert's *Fighting Joe Hooker* (Indianapolis: Bobbs-Merrill, 1944) remains the standard study. Although it is a solid work, this important general is deserving of a capable modern biographer.

John A. Carpenter's *The Sword and the Olive Branch: Oliver Otis Howard* (Pittsburgh: University of Pittsburgh Press, 1964) is of little value for the transfer of the two Union corps, covering the movement in two paragraphs. More valuable is Howard's own *Autobiography of Oliver Otis Howard*, 2 vols. (New York: Baker and Taylor, 1908), written largely from the general's letters. Charles Elihu Slocum's *The Life and Services of Major-General Henry Warner Slocum* (Toledo: Slocum, 1913) is, not surprisingly, laudatory of the author's ancestor.

Hans L. Trefousse's *Carl Schurz: A Biography* (Knoxville: University of Tennessee Press, 1982) is an excellent work and was very useful in the preparation of this book. Less helpful was Harry Marlin Tinckom's *John White Geary: Soldier-Statesman, 1819–1873* (Philadelphia: University of Pennsylvania Press, 1940). Like Hooker, Geary's story is worthy of telling, and a biography based on recent scholarship would be a great addition to the literature of the Civil War era.

Samuel Richey Kamm's *The Civil War Career of Thomas A. Scott* (Philadelphia: University of Pennsylvania Press, 1940) was the most useful biography I consulted. It provided a wealth of background information and invaluable details concerning Scott's role in the transfer.

Several fine works on the Chattanooga Campaign, including the engagement at Wauhatchie, have appeared in recent years. They include Peter Cozzens's *The Shipwreck of Their Hopes: The Battles for Chattanooga* (Urbana: University of Illinois Press, 1994); James Lee McDonough's *Chattanooga: A Death Grip on the Confederacy* (Knoxville: University of Tennessee Press, 1984); and Wiley Sword's *Mountains Touched with Fire: Chattanooga Besieged, 1863* (New York: St. Martin's Press, 1995). An excellent, detailed work on Geary's division at Wauhatchie is Douglas R. Cubbison's "Midnight Engagement: Geary's White Star Division at Wauhatchie, Tennessee, October 28–29, 1863," *Civil War Regiments* 3, no. 2 (1993): 70–101.

The Mouat Reminiscences, Hagood Memoirs, and Tollison Memoirs all contain detailed accounts of the fighting at Wauhatchie. Three published works recount the Battle of Smith's Hill from the Union perspective: Samuel H. Hurst's *Journal-History of the Seventy-third Ohio Volunteer Infantry* (Chillicothe OH: N.p., 1866); John J. Ryder's *Reminiscences of Three Years' Service in the Civil War* (New Bedford MA: Reynolds, 1928); and Adin B. Underwood's *The Three Years' Service of the Thirty-third Mass. Infantry Regiment, 1862–1865* (Boston: A. Williams, 1881).

A valuable firsthand account of the Confederate failure in Lookout Valley is found in William C. Oates's *The War Between the Union and the Confederacy and Its Lost Opportunities with a History of the 15th Alabama Regiment and the Forty-eight Battles in Which It Was Engaged* (New York: Neale, 1905). The best secondary source is Thomas Lawrence Connelly's *Autumn of Glory: The Army of Tennessee, 1862–1865* (Baton Rouge: Louisiana State University Press, 1971).

INDEX

Military units below the level of army corps are listed under the state name (e.g., Alabama troops).

Index

Index

Index

Richmond VA, 19, 27, 28; Longstreet's
Corps passes, 29–30, 31, 32, 33
Rickards, Col. William, Jr., 155, 178, 187
Ricketts, Dillard, 56
Rider, Lt. Col. Godfrey, 190, 191, 192
Ringgold GA, 31, 33, 34, 42
Robertson, Gen. Jerome, 29, 30, 39, 42,
43, 178; at Smith's Hill, 189, 192, 202
Roddey, Gen. Philip A., 145
Rosecrans, Gen. William Starke, 2–4, 27,
45, 54, 69–70, 111, 135–36, 138–39, 141–42,
163; at Chickamauga, 1, 43; removed
from command, 159–60
Rowden cabin (Wauhatchie), 178–79, 182,
183, 203
Ruger, Gen. T. H., 154, 155

Savannah GA, 30, 34
Schurz, Gen. Carl, 80, 152, 157, 171;
reprimanded for delaying trains, 89–92;
at Smith's Hill, 188–89, 195–97
Scott, Col. Thomas A., 45, 47–48, 147; and
Garrett, 48–51; and W. P. Innes, 134–39;
and Stanton, 48, 117; and transfer of
soldiers, 109, 117–18, 130
Scott, Gen. Winfield, 58, 59
Seaboard & Roanoke Railroad, 22
Seddon, James, 27, 97, 172
Sedgwick, Gen. John, 57, 66
Seibert, Col. J. J., 156
Sequatchie Valley (TN), 141
Seward, William Henry, 4–5
Seymour IN, 114
Sharp, William, 143
Sheffield, Col. James, 42, 43; at Smith's
Hill, 178, 189, 191, 202
Shelbyville TN, 144, 155
Shellmound TN, 170, 175
Sherman, Gen. William T., 4, 123
Sigel, Gen. Franz, 66, 80
Sims, Capt. Frederick W., 25–26, 28–30
Slocum, Gen. Henry Warner, 53, 57,
200–201; background of, 67–69; and
Hooker, 69–70, 119–20, 142, 153, 201; in
Tennessee, 144, 145, 154; and transfer of
troops, 74, 77, 112–13

Smith, Miles Vance, 194
Smith, Myron, 184
Smith, Col. Orland, at Smith's Hill, 188,
190, 191–92, 195
Smith, Gen. William Farrar, 164
Smith, William P., 45, 51, 53, 55, 86, 109;
and transfer of equipment, 131, 132, 134;
and transfer of troops, 55–56, 73, 75–77,
88–89, 98, 108
Smith's Hill, engagement of, 189–97,
199–200, 201–2, 203, 204
Soloman, S. S., 30
Sorrel, Moxley, 34, 35, 37
South Carolina, Longstreet's Corps in,
36–38
South Carolina Railroad, 29
South Carolina troops: 1st Infantry, 35,
36, 179, 180–82, 183, 201; 2nd Rifles, 29,
179, 183, 184; 5th Infantry, 34, 37, 179,
183, 201; 6th Infantry, 178, 179, 184; 8th
Infantry, 37; Hampton's Legion, 184;
Palmetto Sharpshooters, 36, 179, 185
Stanton, Edwin M., 1, 3, 9, 21, 43, 52,
64, 85, 135, 136, 153, 199, 205; proposes
transfer, 4–6; and Rosecrans, 159–60;
and Schurz, 89–92; and Scott, 48, 117,
137; and transfer of equipment, 131–34;
and transfer of troops, 45, 54, 77, 88,
95–96, 97, 130
Steinwehr, Gen. Adolph von, 79, 168, 171;
at Smith's Hill, 188, 190, 192
Steubenville OH, 47
Stevenson AL, 130, 142, 147, 149, 161
Stevenson, Vernon K., 129
Stones River, 1, 2, 144, 156
Strang, Joseph, 180
strap rail, 34, 130
Sullivan, John H., 102
Sumter SC, 36

Tantalon TN, 142, 153, 156
Taylor, John Dykes, 42
Tennessee, 1–2, 27; Union soldiers'
opinions of, 148–50
Tennessee & Alabama Railroad, 56–57

Index